Dominatrix

Dominatrix

Gender, Eroticism, and Control in the Dungeon

DANIELLE J. LINDEMANN

The University of Chicago Press
Chicago and London

Danielle Lindemann is a postdoctoral research scholar at Vanderbilt University. She received her PhD in sociology from Columbia University in 2010.

The University of Chicago Press, Chicago 60637
The University of Chicago Press, Ltd., London
© 2012 by The University of Chicago
All rights reserved. Published 2012.
Printed in the United States of America

21 20 19 18 17 16 15 14 13 12   1 2 3 4 5

ISBN-13: 978-0-226-48256-9 (cloth)
ISBN-13: 978-0-226-48258-3 (paper)
ISBN-13: 978-0-226-48259-0 (e-book)
ISBN-10: 0-226-48256-1 (cloth)
ISBN-10: 0-226-48258-8 (paper)
ISBN-10: 0-226-48259-6 (e-book)

Library of Congress Cataloging-in-Publication Data

Lindemann, Danielle J.
     Dominatrix : gender, eroticism, and control in the dungeon / Danielle J. Lindemann.
          pages. cm.
     Includes bibliographical references and index.
     ISBN 978-0-226-48256-9 (cloth : alkaline paper)
     ISBN 0-226-48256-1 (cloth : alkaline paper)
     ISBN 978-0-226-48258-3 (paperback : alkaline paper)
     ISBN 0-226-48258-8 (paperback : alkaline paper)
     ISBN 978-0-226-48259-0 (e-book) (print)
     ISBN 0-226-48259-6 (e-book) (print)
     1. Sexual dominance and submission.   2. Sex customs.   I. Title.
     HQ79.L554 2012
     306.77′5 — dc23

                                                        2011050363

♾ This paper meets the requirements of ANSI/NISO Z39.48-1992 (Permanence of Paper).

This book is dedicated to Jessica Porter Hickok.

Contents

Acknowledgments

Many people have supported me, both personally and professionally, throughout the course of this project. First and foremost, this book would not have been possible without the generosity of the women and men who agreed to sit for interviews and who allowed me to tag along with them to their dungeons, parties, meetings, video shoots, and discussion panels. I would also like to thank Priscilla Ferguson, Peter Bearman, Shamus Khan, Lynn Chancer, and Elizabeth Bernstein, whose diverse viewpoints and areas of expertise served to make this a much stronger project. It is crucial that I acknowledge Paul DiMaggio, for giving me the idea that Bourdieu may have had something to say about pro-dommes' claims to artistic purity, as well as for inspiring my interest in sociology by giving me a research job when I was a lowly undergraduate at Princeton.

It goes without saying that this project would not have come to fruition without the enthusiasm and dedication of the people at the University of Chicago Press. In particular, I would like to thank Doug Mitchell (for his guidance on this manuscript and his perspective on jazz versus rock drumming), Tim McGovern, and Carlisle Rex-Waller.

The following people were also influential in the successful completion of this project and cannot go unmentioned: the proprietors of the Dallas BBQ restaurant chain (for concocting giant, cheap margaritas); Virginia Kao and Danielle Nunez (my D-BBQ buddies); Natacha Stevanovic and Jen Kondo (my partners in crime); Shaina Steinberg (for her occupational empathy); and Ilana Keane (for her unyielding support and unparalleled Ms. Pac-Man abilities). I owe a great deal to my mother, Louise Lindemann, who now chats about dominatrices with her neighbors and her ophthalmologist, and who couldn't possibly be a better Sunday crossword buddy. I'd also like to thank my late father, Bruce Lindemann. I'm grateful that he was able to read an early version of this book.

Portions of this book have been previously published in other venues and have been reprinted with the publishers' permission. An alternate version of chapter 3 appears in *Sociological Forum* ("Will the Real Dominatrix Please Stand Up: Artistic Purity and Professionalism in the S&M Dungeon," 25, 2 [2010]: 588-606), and an alternate version of chapter 5 appears in the journal *Sexualities* ("BDSM as Therapy?," 14, 2 [2011]: 151-72). Additionally, material from chapter 6 has been included in Christina Bobel and Samantha S. Kwan's edited collection *Embodied Resistance: Challenging the Norms, Breaking the Rules*, published by Vanderbilt Press in 2011.

Last, but not at all least, I need to thank Hunter Murdock, whose love, support, feedback, hugs, informal legal advice, and general sanity have seen me through this project. YMB.

Introduction

In an office building in Midtown Manhattan, a woman in her early twenties is describing the last time she flogged someone in this room. She's clutching the flogger she used, which consists of a wooden handle, wrapped in straps of leather, from which hang a series of other flat straps. It's like a stubby mop, but it's designed to administer pain. Clutching the handle, she begins to move her hand from side to side in circular motions, making figure eights with her fist. "I did the heaviest corporal I have ever done on him," she explains, "Lot of flogging." Her hand begins to speed up, and she flicks the device at one of the posts of a large metal suspension frame for emphasis. "I used the tack whip on him while he was bound to the cross, and then I took him off the cross and tied him to one of the posts of the suspension frame, and I did a lot of, like, kicking him and punching him in the chest and some ball and cock slapping and a lot of nipple torture." I begin to understand how she inspires fear in her clients, though she is young and small.

It's an unseasonably warm afternoon in early March of 2008, toward the end of my fieldwork for this project. I had arrived here early, pressed the buzzer and waited to be let inside, then waited again in the elevator for the receptionist upstairs to view me on the elevator's closed-circuit television and send me up to their floor. When I got out of the elevator, I was in a dimly lit entryway with one wooden door, flanked by two vases holding decorative twigs. On the wall to my left was a mirror in an ornate frame. I knocked. The receptionist let me in, led me to the waiting room, and asked if I'd like something to drink. I opted for water, and she returned with a chilled bottle, along with a glass and a paper napkin, which she placed on the table in front of me. Then she left, drawing the purple curtain that separated the waiting room from the rest of the space. I was alone in the room.

I took out my notebook and recorder. To my right was a small end table on which were arrayed a jar of peppermints, a box of tissues, a cup filled with pens, and a pad of paper. The coffee table in front of me was stocked with a variety of reading material ranging from issues of *New York* magazine to erotic photography books to *The Encyclopedia of Wine*. Next to the table was a green padded bench with five thick black straps stretching over the seat, in parallel. The floor was hardwood, and the room was windowless but somehow airy. The ceiling was high.

I'd been waiting for about five minutes when my informant arrived. A well-spoken woman, apologizing for being late in a soft voice, at first glance she seemed too shy to command much fear, but then I wasn't one of her clients. Looking at her in her tank top and lounge pants, at the glasses stuck on her nose, at the blond hair pulled back into a bun, my immediate impression was that she could easily be one of my undergraduate students. She offered to give me a tour of the space and took me out of the waiting room, to the right, past the receptionist's area, to a door marked "1."

This is where she demonstrates the flogger. The main feature of room 1 is the suspension frame, a metal apparatus with an industrial feel that towers over our heads. Cables run down from each of the four supporting posts and attach to the corners of a floating table. To the right of the frame is the cross that the woman describes having used in her last session and a closet filled with a variety of items in plastic bins with computer-printed labels: platform heels, cleaning supplies, shackles, mummification wrap, straitjackets, medical implements, twine, mitts, canes, floggers. Several body bags hang on the closet door. On the way out of the room, she gestures at the iPod player on the table by the door and indicates that she and the other "girls" make playlists to keep track of time in their sessions.

We leave the room and walk past the receptionist again, down a long hallway, past the girls' dressing room on the left, and then back through the waiting area. I remark about the bench with the straps, and she explains that sometimes she does sessions in the waiting room, but it's generally used for consulting with clients beforehand. The straps are "primarily decorative." We move further down the hallway, past a kitchenette and then an art deco bathroom with a shower, past a door marked "3," to the end of the hallway and a door marked "2."

Room 2 is about half the size of room 1, and its main feature is a large four-poster bed. It, too, has a St. Andrew's cross, in addition to a "spanking horse" (which resembles a padded sawhorse), a wooden throne ("for foot worship"), and a chest of drawers stocked with items for clients who enjoy cross-dressing—jewelry, hats, and lingerie. There is also a closet with a mirrored door. It contains a variety of items, including more shoes, gags, a latex maid's outfit, and about a dozen wigs arranged on a line of foam heads.

Room 3, which is used primarily for cross-dressing and foot worship, is the smallest of the session rooms. It also includes a throne, as well as a padded table edged with eyebolts: a "bondage bed." There is a chest of drawers containing cleaning supplies, puppy toys, condoms, and vibrators. There is a mirror over the bondage bed and mirrors on all the walls. I remark about the multiple mirrors in all of the session rooms. "For the clients, it's all about the visuals," I am told. We make our way back to the waiting room, where she tucks her legs under her as she settles on the couch. I perch on the edge of the couch again, and we begin the interview.

This book is about women like the one I interviewed on that warm March day: professional dominatrices—hereafter, "pro-dommes."[1] Male clients (also referred to as "submissives," "subs," or "slaves") pay them money for the experience of being physically and verbally humiliated, flogged, spanked, whipped, caned, slapped, kicked in the groin, urinated on, "forcibly" cross-dressed, tied up, treated like pets, and to play out a variety of other sadomasochistic and fetishistic "scenes." Pro-dommes refer to their work spaces as "dungeons," "houses of pain" (or simply "Houses"), or "play spaces." Few have intercourse with their clients, but their work is erotic in nature and more often than not involves sexual release on the parts of the clients—either through vibrator stimulation, spontaneous orgasm without touch, or most commonly, the clients masturbating to climax.

The puzzle that this book presents is the following: What can pro-dommes' narratives about their encounters in the dungeon, seemingly on the periphery of society, teach us about the set of tensions that undergird our daily lives in the "real" world? To work through this puzzle, I develop a main argument with two prongs that operate in tandem. First, although this industry is structured around interactions that are organized as inversions of the male/female power hierarchy, the industry is also normatively patterned, in the sense that social expectations from everyday life work themselves into the dungeon. Pro-dommes' stories about their interactions with their submissives thus contribute to our understanding of gender and control by allowing us to understand what an inversion of our gender power arrangement can look like, while at the same time speaking to the persistence of this arrangement. In short, although their activities are subversive in many ways, pro-dommes also reproduce relationships of hierarchy and illuminate them.

Second, the people who inhabit this social world highlight a set of social relations that we suppress in daily life. These include hidden facets of gender, control, hierarchy, and eroticism—for instance, relationships of control within professional exchanges and elements of male gender display that are subordinated to compulsory expressions of hegemonic, or "complicit," masculinity.[2] In this sense, observing this set of relations within daily life is akin to looking through a foggy window. We know that things are happening. We can make out the vague movement of shapes, the play of light, the green blur of the grass, and the mushroom tops of the trees. Being given access to a world that is structured around these supressed social elements is like sliding a hand across that window and looking again. Now, in the clear patch of glass, we can see the blades of grass. Now we can see the leaves on the trees.

Professional dominatrices' narratives about their labor thus "defog" a series of classic binaries that structure everyday experience—male/female, normal/abnormal, dominator/dominated, provider/consumer, researcher/subject, and purist/commercialist—bringing them into crisp focus. In doing so, they also call these binaries into question. One of the salient arguments of this text, for instance, is that pro-dommes' characterizations of their work elucidate the fact that neither these women nor their clients maintain total control over the BDSM (bondage, discipline, sadism, masochism) encounter.[3] Generally, the participants jockey for control, both within the dungeon and during their "scripting" sessions beforehand. This struggle may be viewed as deeply transcendent of the dominant/submissive binary, at the same time that the very essence of pro-dommes' work relies upon this duality.

It is important not only to seek out corners of social life that have not been fully limned by social scientists but also to assess the basic social processes at work in daily life. By setting out to do both, I embrace a framework that is inherently queer in nature. Steven Epstein points out that queer theory "analyzes putatively marginal experience, but in order to expose the deeper contours of the whole society and the mechanisms of its functioning," describing the "assertion of the centrality of marginality" as "the pivotal queer move" (1994, 197). By considering the world of commercial BDSM not only interesting in its own right but also revealing of larger social processes and conventions, we can make this move. Though not explicitly about LGBTQIA (lesbian, gay, bisexual, transgender, questioning, intersex, asexual) issues, this text represents a "queering" of everyday life. It applies a queer theoretical framework to a particular set of liminal activities, shedding light on the binaries (for instance, normal/abnormal and kinky/conventional) that perpetuate the marginalization of such practices.

By focusing on pro-dommes, this book thus identifies the principles of erotic exchange at work in a largely unexplored subculture, but it also limns the depths of everyday practices, contributing to our understanding of such major elements of social life as gender relations, power, dominance and submission, and the exchange of money for erotic labor. Ultimately, I argue that professional erotic dominance is interesting not for its exoticism but for its mundaneness—for the "normal" social dramas that play out on its stage.

Goodbye, Omaha: Some Background on the Project

The germ of the idea for this book emerged in 2005, when I was a second-year graduate student taking a sociological methods course at Columbia University. I was writing a paper about catcalling on the streets of New York, and another student in my class mentioned that some of the women where she worked often discussed their experiences with catcalling and might be eager informants for my project. It turned out she worked at a dungeon.

After speaking with several of the dominatrices at this particular House, I had many rich catcalling narratives on my tape recorder and many more questions. Who were these women, and what did they do behind those closed doors? Did they really have control over their male clients? How did gender and power "work" in these interactions? Certain that this topic would be supersaturated, I pored through the usual academic resources and was surprised to find no studies that focused on professional dominatrices and few answers to my questions. The professor who taught my methods class was concerned for my professional future as an academic were I to pursue such an unconventional and potentially prurient topic. "You'll never get a job as a professor in Omaha if you do this," he cautioned. Shortly thereafter, however, my intellectual masochism got the better of me. I bid Omaha farewell and began conceptualizing this project.

A couple of years later, during an early stage of my research on this topic, I attended a "fetish party" at a club on the Lower East Side of Manhattan. When I was introduced as a researcher who was working on a project about pro-dommes, one of the partygoers, a thirty-something man in lederhosen, smiled and said, "So *you're* the one this month." The attitude that research in this subject area has become redundant was prevalent not only among people at these parties and my interviewees but also among academics with whom I discussed the study. On one level, this attitude is surprising, considering how often I encountered the seemingly contradictory position that it was a frivolous or useless topic of study. On another level, however, it was expected. After all, I had also been one of those people who had not anticipated the dearth of published research about professional erotic dominance.

To date, there has not been a systematic study of professional dominatrices. Research on erotic labor has focused primarily on prostitutes, and studies of sadomasochism absorb dominatrix/client relationships into the category of all sadomasochistic (SM) relationships, without exploring what makes these paid encounters unique. The most extensive of these latter studies is the work of Martin Weinberg, Colin Williams, and Charles Moser (1984) on gay and straight sadomasochistic communities in New York City and San Francisco from 1976 to 1983, which included but was not limited to dominatrices (see also Kamel and T. Weinberg 1983, Lee 1983, and Patrias 1978; T. Weinberg 1983 provides an excellent summary of the relevant literature). The one study (Scott 1983) that deals with pro-dommes in their own right does so from the participant-observation standpoint of a researcher who had become a novice domme—an analysis that has been criticized as "not scientifically sound" (Moser 1984, 418).

To be clear, I am not asserting that this topic calls out to be studied because it fills a void in the literature. Depending upon which social scientist you ask, either all elements of our social worlds or no elements of our social worlds are worthy of study simply by virtue of existing. This topic is noteworthy not because it has never been examined sociologically before, but because, as I will argue throughout this text, by presenting in a clear way pervasive social elements such as microlevel control and gender display, dominatrices allow us to understand these elements in new and unexpected ways.

Looking at this corner of social life also sheds light on the erotic hierarchy that organizes our social world. Sadomasochism is a sexual practice that is at once complexly stigmatized, shrugged off as frivolous, and embraced within postmodern culture. In discussing the public response to this practice, it is useful to draw upon the work of feminist theorist Gayle Rubin, who argues that "sexual stratification" is one of the major systems of organization that underlie our experiences as human beings. She makes the claim that SM is just one form of eroticism that exists in a hierarchy of socially evaluated sexual activities. "Modern Western societies appraise sex acts according to a hierarchical system of sexual value," Rubin explains. "Marital, reproductive heterosexuals are alone at the top of the erotic pyramid," while sadomasochists are one of the "most despised" categories, towards the bottom (1992, 279).

To describe sadomasochism as a non-normative, socially stigmatized erotic practice, however, is to tell only part of the story. Certainly, individuals who engage in BDSM have historically been subject to reproach, particularly stemming from the psychiatric community. Nineteenth-century sex researcher Richard Krafft-Ebing, who is credited with coining the term "sadomasochism," for instance, described the practice as both a "perversion" and an "affliction" (1965, 53). This pathologizing attitude has continued to be evident in media accounts of BDSM practices, particularly when injuries resulting from these practices have come under public scrutiny. One 1976

Time magazine cover story, "The Porno Plague," warns its readers about the burgeoning representations of SM in popular culture. More recently, in a 2008 ABC News article, "Love Hurts: Sadomasochism's Dangers," published online on Valentine's Day, a Columbia University psychology professor characterizes interest in sadomasochistic practices as incompatible with a healthy psyche (Goldman 2008, quoting Judy Kuriansky).

At the same time that the psychiatric community has historically characterized dominatrices and their clients as maladjusted, however, such practices have not been subject to the same public scrutiny as other sexual activities at the bottom of Rubin's erotic pyramid. "Somehow," Chris Gosselin and Glenn Wilson explain, "most of the general public seem to have treated these excesses with some irreverence: although they have reacted strongly against those who would legalize sex with children, and even now have a considerable ambivalence towards homosexuality, they have made sadomasochism the subject of jokes, accepted it with a casual shrug, treated those who enjoy its practices with the sort of tolerant bemusedness reserved for the slightly mad or simply ignored it" (1980, 11).

We see this bemused acceptance manifest itself in the fashion industry, whose catwalks have featured models brandishing whips and wrapped in leather; Gianni Versace's bondage collection of the early 1990s is one example. Dolce and Gabbana put out a similarly themed collection in 2007, causing one newspaper headline to exclaim, "Dominatrix & Gabbana!" (Menkes 2007). The 1950s pinup girl Bettie Page made a career out of modeling in fetish clothing. And sadomasochistic themes in popular culture are not limited to the area of clothing design. A recent advertisement for Sunsilk hair products depicts a stiletto boot encircled by a whip and the tagline, "My frizz is so wild even a dominatrix couldn't tame it." In another advertisement—a commercial for Wonderful pistachios—a male voice intones, "Dominatrixes do it," and a domme in gleaming boots is seen cracking open a pistachio with her whip.

The cartoon characters on the television show *Family Guy* regularly dress in SM regalia for comedic effect. The movie *Secretary* introduced one overtly sadomasochistic relationship to mainstream audiences. The popular television show *CSI* has included a dominatrix as a recurring character. On a 2005 episode of the television show *House*, a patient was brought to the hospital for injuries inflicted by a pro-domme. On a 2008 episode of the prime-time drama *Private Practice*, one of the characters dressed up as a dominatrix, brandishing a flogger at her lover. On a 2009 episode of the reality series *Real Housewives of Atlanta*, one of the housewives greeted a friend dressed for an elegant party with, "Oooh, you look like a dominatrix—I love it!"

In 1982, American singer-songwriter John Mellencamp went to number 2 on the Billboard charts singing, "Sometimes love don't feel like it should / You make it hurt so good." In her 2004 song "La La," pop princess Ashlee Simpson crooned, "You can throw me like a lineman / I like it better when it hurts"—although censors required her to change the lyric to "I like it better when we flirt" for her halftime performance at the 2005 Orange Bowl. In 2011, a trip to the gym leaves the strains of Rihanna's "S&M" pounding in my ears: "Sticks and stones may break my bones / but whips and chains excite me." And who could forget Madonna's role in perpetuating the mainstreaming of kink? In the 1990s, the pop superstar inextricably linked her name to BDSM imagery—specifically, in the 1992 video for the song "Erotica," in which she donned a black bodice and mask and seductively handled a riding crop, and 1995's "Human Nature," in which dancers wrapped in shiny, form-fitting black fabric contorted amid whips, chains, riding crops, and suspension ropes, to the refrain "Express yourself, don't repress yourself."

The Facebook application SuperPoke includes a "dominate" option, illustrated by a whip-wielding cartoon avatar in a corset and fishnets. One issue of *Time Out New York* featured a dominatrix's dungeon in its "Apartments" section, among the other real estate items; the piece described the space as appearing "as if it sprang from the pages of *Martha Stewart Living* rather than the stories of the Marquis de Sade" (Yun 2007). And a search of the Amazon book list yields 3,835 hits for the keyword "dominatrix," ranging from tell-alls (*The Domestic Domina: My Life as a Suburban Mother and Celebrity Dominatrix*) to works of erotica (*She's on Top: Erotic Stories of Female Dominance and Male Submission*) to the sexual how-to (*The Mistress Manual: The Good Girl's Guide to Female Dominance*; *Sex Tips from a Dominatrix*) to books that, like this one, draw parallels between principles of erotic dominance and daily experiences (*The Corporate Dominatrix: Six Roles to Play to Get Your Way at Work*; *Whip Your Life into Shape! The Dominatrix Principle*).

SM practices, then, and the figure of the powerful dominatrix in particular, while they continue to be characterized as subversive, are also to some extent normalized and maintain a relatively high level of cultural visibility. One night in March of 2008, I watch a rerun of *Frasier*. Frasier's producer, Roz, is attending a costume party dressed in a bondage costume. Waiting for her doctor to call with the results of a pregnancy test, she worries aloud that she will make a bad mother. "Well, I don't think discipline will be a problem," Frasier quips. A few days later, the British tabloid *News of the World* comes out with the story that Max Mosley, head of Formula One's governing body, has been caught in a Nazi-themed sadomasochistic orgy.[4] That same week, I walk past (the now-defunct) Kim's Video in the Morningside Heights area of Manhattan, and a large, glossy book propped in the window catches my eye. Its cover features a photograph of a dominatrix in leather regalia, posing seductively on a flight of stairs. The cultural symbol of the Dominatrix, like that book, is both taboo and regularly on display. She is perceived with an unsteady mixture of repulsion, disinterest, concern, amusement, and fascination.

Unfogging the Window

Not only is sadomasochism a prevalent theme in popular culture, but prior studies have indicated that the predilection for sadomasochistic sexuality is prevalent enough to call into question the classification of SM as an "alternative" sexual practice. Pro-dommes and their clients are less than exotic, in the sense that sadomasochistic arousal is not unique to niche groups. In putting forth the argument that sadomasochistic practices illuminate a basic series of oppositions in the "real world," I stand on the shoulders of those theorists who have argued the inverse, conceptualizing sadistic and masochistic impulses as essential components of human life.[5]

Sadomasochism's practitioners include not only those "hardcore" individuals who go to BDSM clubs or pay to be flogged by women in leather. The sadistic and masochistic impulses have implications beyond the sexual sphere and have been theorized as phenomena that pervade daily life. Sociologist Lynn Chancer, for instance, argues that a variety of relationships are "sadomasochistically oriented," regardless of whether "the pattern appears in the well-publicized realm of sexuality, or in other instances of everyday life, whether between a particular teacher and student, or a worker and boss, or in other highly charged encounters between partners caught in symbiotic enmeshments of power and powerlessness" (2000b, 1). Anthropologist and sexologist Paul Gebhard concurs, noting that sadomasochism "is embedded in our culture since our culture operates on the basis of dominance-submission relationships, and aggression is socially valued" (1969, 77). For the same reason, historian and sexologist Vern Bullough makes the claim that "to ignore sadomasochism . . . is to ignore life itself" (1983, 11).

Give and take, aggression and submission, love of pain and love of giving pain, are not features of social life unique to a visit to the dungeon. Rather, we can use the dominatrix's workplace as a laboratory for looking at a particular way that these basic principles manifest themselves. While pro-dommes are both organizationally and conceptually embedded in a multitiered system of social relations—for instance, the SM "Scene" in New York City—the dungeon provides a relatively circumscribed arena in which to explore broader social mechanisms.

In considering the prospect that sadomasochism has implications beyond the sexual sphere, it is useful to draw a parallel with Judith Butler's work on the practice of drag. Drag is a kind of theater in which gender display becomes both exaggerated and denaturalized. Butler contends that drag "reveals the distinctness of those aspects of gendered experience which are falsely naturalized as a unity through the regulatory fiction of heterosexual coherence. *In imitating gender, drag implicitly reveals the imitative structure of gender itself—as well as its contingency*" (1999, 175; emphasis in original). She goes on to argue, "Although the gender meanings taken up in these parodic styles are clearly part of hegemonic, misogynist culture, they are nevertheless denaturalized and mobilized through their parodic recontextualization" (176). In essence, drag contributes to our understanding of gender by exposing femininity as a performed role. Similarly, practices of sadomasochism that are naturalized in everyday life—for instance, a boss reprimanding his underling—are recontextualized in the dominatrix's dungeon. The sadomasochistic theater, by caricaturing them, increases their visibility and contributes to our understanding of them. Sadomasochistic interactions are stylized representations of dominance and submission, but they are able to both lay bare and destabilize the taken-for-granted assumptions underlying such practices. Further—and here is where the queer theoretical frame comes in—in their putative reversal of gendered erotic roles, they actually provide an amplification of those roles as they exist in the "real world."

Why Pro-Dommes?

If sadomasochistic practices are a window into a set of relationships within postmodern society, why focus only on women who are *paid* for these practices? While a commercial dungeon happened to be the particular rabbit hole I fell into during that semester in 2005, there are several other reasons why I chose to pursue research focusing on pro-domme / client relationships, rather than on other types of sadomasochistically charged interactions. First, there is evidence that the results of studies of BDSM clubs and SM organizations are not representative of heterosexual sadomasochistic practices (Spengler 1977). However, some sociological explorations of sadomasochism, notably Weinberg, Williams, and Moser's 1984 work, have sampled via sadomasochistic organizations. Thinking about sadomasochistic encounters among individuals with network connections to these organizations as representative of all heterosexual SM dyads is problematic, and it has potentially skewed our understanding of heterosexual sadomasochistic practices.

Professional dominatrices differ from other individuals who go to BDSM clubs in that their livelihood is bound up in the performance of socially proscribed eroticism. In these senses, the research presented here contributes to the literature about "secret deviation" (Patrias 1978) in a way that studies that have sampled via sadomasochistic organizations have not.[6] While both dominatrices and their clients maintain varying levels of secrecy about their participation in these socially proscribed erotic and wage-earning practices—from complete openness to selective openness to extreme closeting—it is clear that their negotiation of this secrecy is, in a practical sense, different from that engaged in by people who are not involved in the commercial end of sadomasochism. Pro-dommes and their clients are not representative of all people who engage in SM, just as those who go to BDSM clubs or join sadomasochistic organizations are not representative of that population, but this study helps to complete the picture begun by those authors who focused on the latter.[7]

Another key reason to focus on professional erotic dominance is that, as noted, prior studies have turned their attention to erotic commodification and to sadomasochism but seldom to the intersection of the two.[8] Studying, in particular, women who receive compensation for BDSM practices adds a layer of broader implications to this project. Ultimately, these women's stories teach us not only about the worlds of SM and erotic labor but also, more generally, about interactions within commercial exchanges and the transformative power of money over intimate relationships. As Viviana Zelizer compellingly argues in *The Purchase of Intimacy*, "Routine social life makes us all experts in the purchase of intimacy," in the sense that individuals "often mingle economic activity with intimacy. The two often sustain each other" (2005, 1). Like dominance and submission, the role of capital in personal relationships is not unique to sex work but permeates everyday life. This examination of pro-dommes as a particular subset of SM participants, in sum, contributes new insights to several interlocking academic discourses: about sadomasochism, about secret deviation, about sex work, and about the larger connection between intimate relationships and economic exchange.

Finally, although clients are the individuals whose desires drive this industry, and although I do include client data and discuss the ways in which this social sphere sheds light on the repressed elements of masculinity within daily life, the voices we hear in this text are primarily female. My interest, from the first day I sat in a dungeon interviewing a group of women about catcalling, was in this social sphere that appeared to represent an inversion of the gender/power hierarchy and, particularly, in the dominant end of this exchange. At its core, this book is about the narratives told by a group of women who share the same job—a job that is, as they are acutely aware and as they often articulate, organized as a reaction to the relationships of gender and power that pervade everyday life.

The Sample, Veracity, and the Power of Narrative

Between September of 2007 and April of 2008 I conducted in-depth, semistructured interviews with fifty-two female professional dominatrices in the New York City metropolitan area and fourteen in the San Francisco Bay Area. I primarily located informants through their Internet advertisements and then through snowball sampling, although I found nine directly through my own personal connections—colleagues, friends, and friends of friends in the BDSM "Scene."

Although there are male doms, they are much less socially visible and much less prevalent in the industry of professional dominance than females who do sessions with male clients. For this reason, this project focuses on female pro-dommes. However, I conducted interviews with three male prodoms, whose paying clients are almost exclusively male. I also did observational fieldwork at a dungeon and a BDSM club, as well as both formal and informal interviews with participants in the New York "Scene." In addition, I conducted ten in-depth interviews with male clients—men who had paid for erotic dominance at least once—whom I found through my connections in "the Scene." In addition, I was given access to 305 preference forms filled out by clients at a New York City dungeon (see the table in chapter 1). I have confined most of the methodological details of this project—including sample selection and demographics, the interview process, representativeness, and some methodological hurdles I encountered—to appendix A.

Although I observed sadomasochistic and fetishistic interactions at BDSM clubs and parties, I never observed encounters between pro-dommes and their clients in dungeon settings for a variety of reasons. For one thing, I felt that my presence as a researcher would irrevocably alter the content of the exchange in a one-on-one, private setting, whereas in a more populated locale I could observe these activities less obtrusively—though, of course, the element of performativity was also present in these more public interactions. It is important to make clear, then, that this is a book about the things prodommes have to say about their encounters with clients. Ultimately, it is about *narratives* about interactions, not the interactions themselves.

The data presented here thus involve statements about activities mediated through the perceptions of human beings who have their own particular agendas. The sample is skewed, for instance, toward those who are "lifestyle" dommes (that is, who participate in BDSM activities in their personal as well as professional lives) and who have the most to gain from legitimating these practices in the eyes of the public. For instance, several informants indicated that they had accepted the interview invitation because they felt they had some duty to rectify misconceptions about this lifestyle.

Accordingly, I do not adopt pro-dommes' descriptions of their activities wholesale. However, for the purposes of this project, it does not necessarily matter if the informants' statements are completely unbiased—as though such a thing were ever possible in a research study. This book's central concern is what professional dominatrices' discursive constitutions of their work can teach us about the worlds inside and outside of the dungeon. The informants' narratives offer a window into a world in which gender and power can work in both typical and atypical ways, whether or not the informants are interpreting their labor in particular ways to accomplish particular goals— for instance, the project of normalization. I do not treat their words as objective truth; rather, I argue that their ways of talking about their work open up alternative modes for thinking about some of the main social categories that structure human experiences, both within and outside of the walls of the dungeon.[9]

In short, the stories told by professional dominatrices allow us to understand how these women generate meaning in this sphere of social life. We can then use these meanings to recontextualize and further understand the meanings of gender, power, and sexuality in the world outside the dungeon. Pro-dommes offer up alternative ways of thinking about both realms.

The Research as Sociological Object

During the third interview I undertook for this project, I found myself drinking bottled water off a Bugs Bunny coaster in the living room of a professional male dominant who is married to a female dominatrix. When I accidentally spilled the bottle on the floor, he exclaimed, "Good thing my wife isn't here or she'd have you up on the rack for that!" Another time, while confirming an interview over the phone, I mentioned to my interviewee that she would be able to recognize me by my red hat at the diner where we had arranged to meet. "Little Red Riding Hood coming to see the Big Bad Wolf," she purred into the phone, in her thick Eastern European accent. In these instances, and many others like them, informants drew me into their world, implicating me in the object of study. Of course, they were also having a little bit of fun with me. I became not a researcher, in these moments, but another participant in the theater of professional erotic dominance. The interview room became a generative space in which data was produced, not simply collected.

Partly for this reason, from the opening sentence of this text I draw upon my own experiences conducting this research as central pieces of data in this book. Throughout, I characterize both the observational fieldwork and interview components of this study as "ethnography." I do this not only because I was trained as a sociologist in an environment in which the interview method fell under the rubric of ethnography. I also characterize this work as ethnographic because I draw from the interactions between myself and the informants during the interview process, in the same way that other ethnographers draw from participant-observational research. Further, I make metaethnographic observations about public reactions to the research itself. Finally, ethnography is, fundamentally, the immersive study of culture. Thus, this book is ethnographic in the sense that it is an attempt to explore not only the particular culture of the dungeon but its reflection in the culture of the "mainstream" world that erroneously exoticizes its practices.

In interpreting my own interactions with informants as sociological objects, I am wary of coming across as the subject of an objectifying and voyeuristic gaze. I am inspired by Elizabeth Bernstein, who addresses this issue in her ethnography of sex workers, noting that she maintains her "situatedness" in the text in order to "best avoid the exoticizing and 'othering' stance which has characterized much of the existing sociological literature on prostitution" (2007, 15). Similarly, I continually position myself within the context of interactions with my informants.

During my fieldwork, I attended many Scene events, visited about a dozen dungeons, and made connections with informants whom I still consider my friends today; thus, in many ways, I became integrated into this community. During moments in this text in which I position myself as an outsider, it is usually because that is how the informants in those scenarios reacted to my presence—developments that were sociologically significant in their own right. Finally, the content of one of my main arguments—that this world is interesting not for its exoticism but rather for the light it sheds on more mundane processes—separates me from those scholars who have viewed marginalized erotic communities through an exoticizing lens.

Another reason why my own experiences as a researcher become central to this text is that in the eyes of the academic community, scholars who pursue qualitative analyses of sexuality are uniquely "contaminated" by their work in ways that other qualitative researchers are not. Chancer makes this argument, asserting that researchers who undertake studies of sex work often feel that they need to make a sharp distinction between I and them, subject and object, in order for their work to carry weight in the academe. This is one of the reasons why, for instance, there are few studies of sex work in which social scientists "go native" as sex workers.[10] Chancer argues that this threat of contamination stems from the "good woman / bad woman" dichotomy, in which the researcher, ostensibly a "good woman," runs the risk of being labeled a bad girl, and thus the risk of academic delegitimation, if she engages in the same behavior as her "deviant" informants (1998, 188).

Two basic tenets of feminist ethnography are the notions of continued reflexivity and vigilance about gender as a basic organizing principle of social life (Reinharz 1991, 46). The latter includes an awareness of how gender relationships structure the practices involved in doing research.[11] Certainly, sexuality is not the only field in which the audience for a particular work has conflated researcher and subject. However, ethnographers who research sexually charged topics are unique in that this conflation has the potential to lead to delegitimation within the academic community. At the same time, there is a masculinist bent to traditional ethnography, wherein male ethnographers are professionally rewarded for immersing themselves in other "deviant" populations, such as street gangs. Bernstein addresses this issue:

> Although some (most frequently, male) ethnographers have put themselves at physical risk in the name of social science, the bravery and heroism that are associated with such efforts continue to enhance their sense of identity as men as well as their status as academics. By contrast the female ethnographer of prostitution must make herself vulnerable in profound and potentially intimate ways, both within any performance of sex work and within its later reportage. The "whore stigma" is capable of producing very real social and professional dangers, ones which cannot be found in the mirror image of masculinist social science. (2007, 201)

Bernstein indicates that she was repeatedly asked the same question that plagued Chancer—"often hinted at or insinuated, rather than spoken directly"—whether or not she had worked as a prostitute (201). Academics and other individuals who heard about my project often wanted to know the extent of my own involvement in BDSM, and—predictably, it seems—whether or not I had ever been a pro-domme.

Further, whether seriously or derisively, many people conflated researcher and researched in their reactions to the topic. Colleagues chuckled and made comments about "participant-observation." During a dinner party, a retired sociologist laughed out loud when I explained this project. "Academia sure has gone downhill since I left," he said. Later in the meal he leaned over and asked, "So, does this project require any take-home work?" A colleague I had never met before, who was seated next to me at a conference dinner and had heard me speak earlier in the day, initiated conversation with me with the line, "So where's your whip?" An older woman at a party, upon hearing about my topic, told me earnestly that she had some tights from her days as a nurse that I could borrow if I'd like. In this text, I exploit this subject/object conflation, mining attitudes about the research as potentially illuminating sources of data. Reactions to this project shed light on public attitudes toward pro-dommes as well as toward the study of sexuality in general.

To answer that lingering question, though I became implicated in the world of professional erotic dominance in the ways described above, I never made participation in BDSM activities a part of my research. There were interviews I did not obtain because of this decision. One male client, for instance, offered to let me interview him if I would let him "hold and rub" my feet in return. Similarly, a pro-domme indicated that both she and a client would be willing to speak with me, but only if I would be a "voyeur" during one of their sessions. I made the decision not to "go native" as a researcher *not* for either ethical or methodological reasons, but rather for instrumental ones. Although working as a pro-domme, hiring one, or becoming a participant at the BDSM club would have undoubtedly provided additional insights into the world of erotic dominance, the cost to my professional reputation would not have been worth the benefits of that knowledge. From an ethical standpoint, however, I cannot see a fundamental difference between compensating an interview subject with coffee and compensating him with a foot. From a methodological standpoint, would participating in a flogging at a BDSM club have rendered me a better or worse ethnographer? That seems to me a question that is only important in the context of the insider/outsider problem—not in regard to the particular content of the act in question.

Is This Sex Work?

Thus far, I have referred to professional erotic dominance in the context of sex work without interrogating that classification. Again, very few pro-dommes are what is known in the industry as "full service"—that is, women who have intercourse with their clients.[12] A larger number will provide oral sex or hand jobs, or allow clients to perform "full-body worship" (cunnilingus) on them,[13] but these were not widespread practices among the women interviewed for this study. This is partially because these acts are more common among women who work at the larger dungeons[14]—spaces owned by House managers who provide the location and equipment, hire women specifically to work at those locations, set guidelines for those women, and take a cut of the money they earn—than among independent (indie) dommes who rent or own space and work for themselves. "Dungeon dommes" are underrepresented in this study because they tend to have relatively short career tenures *as* dungeon dommes. After less than a year of dungeon work, most either leave the industry or "go indie."

Some of the women I interviewed for this study would be affronted by the characterization of their jobs as "sex work." Others self-define as sex workers. My intention here is not to pin labels on people who do not identify with those labels or to engage in a semantic discussion about sex. Whether or not anally penetrating a client with a dildo constitutes a "sex act," or whether slapping a client's genitals until he spontaneously ejaculates is more or less "sexual" than a hand job, for instance, are not questions that are substantively important to this text. However, it is useful to theorize professional erotic dominance in the context of sex work, and I will continue to do that throughout this text, because it is like sex work from an analytical perspective in that it involves financial compensation for sexually charged, socially taboo erotic practices. In terms of the actual acts involved, professional dominance is best characterized not as "sex work" but as "erotic labor"—to borrow Wendy Chapkis's term (1997), which encompasses a variety of practices, from exotic dancing to prostitution.

A Note about Terminology

Throughout this text, "the Scene," capitalized, denotes the parties, workshops, meetings, and other events that constitute the public worlds of BDSM in New York City and San Francisco. The term "lifestyle" indicates participation in BDSM activities outside of paid sessions. Many, but not all, lifestyle pro-dommes are also "in the Scene"; that is, they attend public events and parties, and/or go to local BDSM clubs.[15] A domme may be "lifestyle" but not "in the Scene" if she engages in dominance and submission with her romantic partners but does not attend public events. A Venn diagram illustrates the breakdown of the pro-dommes in the interview sample into these categories. The shaded area denotes eligibility for the study. Fifty-nine of the sixty-six informants self-identified as "lifestyle." Forty-eight were "in the Scene."

Interactions between pro-dommes and clients are referred to either as

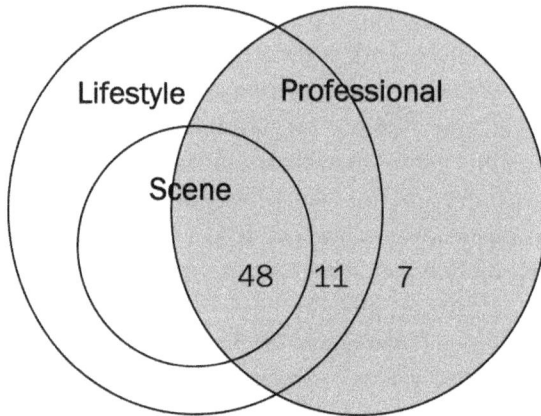

Pro-dommes, interview sample (N = 66; not to scale)

"scenes" or as "sessions." Pro-dommes and other BDSM participants use "play," both as a noun and a verb, as an umbrella term for BDSM-related activities: "We did some hot wax play" or "I was playing with my sub."

Though I have contextualized this project within a literature on sado-masochism, I generally refer to its subject matter as "professional erotic dominance," not as "professional sadomasochism," because SM is just one facet of what pro-dommes do. "Sadomasochism," as noted, is a term coined by Krafft-Ebing. It derives from the surnames of the Marquis de Sade and nineteenth-century Austrian writer Leopold von Sacher-Masoch, whose 1870 novel *Venus in Furs* describes the experiences of a man who willingly submits to a female lover. Sadomasochism refers to the giving and receiving of physical or psychological pain for erotic pleasure, and its practices include "corporal punishment" activities such as spanking, caning, paddling, flog-ging, and whipping, as well as other acts in which pro-dommes engage, like "electric play" (using shocks) and genital piercing. However, not all activities in which pro-dommes and clients engage are about pain. Most, on the other hand, are about dominance and submission (D/S)—a term that refers to one partner assuming control while the other ostensibly relinquishes his or her power. Examples of dominant practices that are not pain related include, for instance, imprisoning the client in a cage, "golden showers" (urinating on the client), and "foot worship" ("forcing" the client to hold, kiss, and massage one's feet). I use the term "professional *erotic* dominance" to distinguish be-tween what pro-dommes do and dominance within other professions. How-ever, throughout this text, I also use the terms D/S, BDSM, and SM inter-changeably, because they are all aspects of professional erotic dominance. For a comprehensive list of vocabulary and definitions, see appendix D.

A Note about Names

I seldom knew informants' real names—only the names by which they went as pro-dommes, their "Scene names." No interview subjects are mentioned by any name in this text, and none are given pseudonyms. Where necessary, proper names are elided in interview responses.[16] Unless I had chosen distractingly unique names, any pseudonyms I could have attached to them would likely have been the Scene names of other women currently working as pro-dommes.

Organization of the Book

This book begins with an exploration of the ways in which aspects of social class from the real world filter into the fantasy realm of professional dominance and fundamentally shape, and are illuminated by, its practices. I explore the topics of authenticity and power exchange in the dungeon, making the argument that notions of purity and relationships of control between dominatrix and client shed light on the nuances of professional interactions and other microlevel exchanges. I then turn to a discussion of what dungeon interactions can teach us about eroticism, intimacy, and both the production and reproduction of gender. While the thematic flow of the book generally moves in this direction, power, intimacy, fantasy, eroticism, authenticity, and the production of gender in this subversive space are all discursive threads that run throughout the text.

Chapter 1 looks at pro-dommes' discussions of power exchange through the lens of dramaturgy, interrogating the role of control in the process by which dungeon encounters are "scripted" and subsequently enacted. Although the domme/client interaction is superficially organized as a unidirectional power relationship, it can, in fact, tell us about the nuances of control within professional interactions more generally, as both domme and sub strive to "get over" on each other during the scripting process. In particular, it "unfogs" one facet of the ethnographic interview process, bringing into focus the ways in which the researcher/informant relationship mirrors that struggle for power.

In chapter 2, I examine professional erotic dominance as a career, looking at three archetypal dominatrix career trajectories. I argue that this profession is uniquely structured around the concepts of knowledge and training, which tie into pro-dommes' conceptions of their own authenticity as pro-dommes. While commercial BDSM is interesting in that it represents an industry organized around the production of subversive sexuality, what is more interesting is the light it sheds on claims to professional authenticity in larger society.

Chapter 3 picks up the thread of authenticity and ties it to this discussion about the struggle for control within the domme/sub exchange. Here, I use one of Pierre Bourdieu's theories of art as a structural analogy for thinking about the discourse whereby pro-dommes legitimate themselves as "artists." What does it mean to be a "real" dominatrix and a "real" submissive, what is the relationship between those concepts and the struggle for control over the interaction, and what can this purity regime within the dungeon tell us about the exchange of power within other service industries that are considered "artistic" by their practitioners?

Chapter 4 illustrates how pro-dommes can enhance our knowledge about the social importance of make-believe and adult "play," as well as problematizing issues of boundary crossing in erotic labor. What is it about the erotic sphere that allows us to "play" in a way that we cannot within everyday life? I argue that part of the appeal of the dungeon is that it allows participants to be who they are *not* in larger society; it brings out the repressed facets of their gendered sexualities, thus illuminating them. I conclude by exploring the permeability of the boundary between professionalism and intimacy in these fantasy-sustained interactions.

In chapter 5, I look at informants' rhetoric about BDSM as a therapeutic practice. Pro-dommes put forth folk theories of desire, whereby they take a disease paradigm and kick it on its head. They reconceptualize pathologized activities as a treatment. The main question I seek to answer in this chapter is not whether they are "correct" that their work is therapeutic for their clients, but what is significant about the fact that they *say* it is therapeutic. In this way, chapter 5 both adds to and problematizes the assertion in chapter 4 that the dungeon provides a unique fantasy space for the distortion of gendered paradigms. In one sense, powerful men explore alternative modes of masculine expression (dependence, emotional openness) inside this social space. In another sense, in positing themselves as therapists, pro-dommes engage in a nurturing femininity that has traditionally characterized female labor forms, erotic labor in particular.

Chapter 6 explores the production of gender during dominatrix sessions, asking how pro-dommes and their clients "do" their gender on the dungeon floor, and in what ways their gender displays reproduce and subvert norms from the "real" world. By taking on the role of the powerful female in the erotic dyad, dommes destabilize the gender hierarchy, challenging normative conceptions of female passivity in erotic encounters as well as in everyday life. At the same time, they play upon conventional tropes of femininity in order to sustain this dominance. It is in this section of the book that I most explicitly deal with how gender roles are played out in this erotic space, as dommes and subs both transgress and duplicate normative gendered behaviors. The chapter serves as the anchor for the discursive thread running through the text concerning femininity and masculinity in the dungeon and their relationship to broader society: this social world illuminates both what we are not and what we are.

The conclusion reviews the importance of professional erotic dominance as a tool for looking at interactions in other spheres of social life. There has been a long tradition within my discipline of sociology to pay attention to how people in marginalized and stigmatized communities negotiate the "secret deviation" of their practices, and I do explore the ways in which pro-dommes navigate the dual worlds of stigma and normalcy. Ultimately, however, this is not just a book about deviation, or about making the invisible visible. It is a book about many of the underlying qualities of our everyday lives, highlighted in an unexpected social space.

But What Are They *Like*?

Now that my fieldwork is complete, I sometimes play a game with myself that I call "Which One's the Dominatrix?" While waiting in line at the post office or at a coffee shop or on the subway platform I wonder, "If one of these people surrounding me were a pro-domme, who would it be?" The impulse comes from months of waiting in cafés to interview possible informants, scanning the faces of strangers and attempting to connect one to a photo from the Internet—or, perhaps, to identify the woman with no photo to guide me at all—despite the sometimes extreme disjuncture between dommes' session personas and their everyday self-presentations. Because pro-dommes tend to be indistinguishable from the other faces in the crowd, unless they are wearing subtly coded markers of the trade (leather pants, a necklace in the shape of tiny handcuffs), I began telling prospective interviewees that I would be wearing a red knit cap, so that they could approach me.

A question I get asked a lot is, "What sort of woman is a dominatrix?" Recently, while teaching an undergraduate course in sociology, I was discussing my research and a student raised her hand and wanted to know the answer. I gave her my usual spiel about age and demographic trends: "They tend to be in their thirties. They're mostly white. A high proportion are bisexual."

Another student raised her hand: "But, you know, what are they *like*?" The fact that I am so often asked that question—both by academics and other people with whom I discuss the topic—is revealing of larger social attitudes toward these erotic laborers. The implication that rests like skin on the surface of this question is that there is some exotic quality to these women.

Similarly, "Weren't you afraid?"—another question repeatedly posed to me by students—presupposes that within this exoticism lies something potentially threatening.

My own conceptualization of informants as nonthreatening crystallized during an incident that occurred when I was interviewing a pro-domme out in Oakland, and she offered to give me a ride back to San Francisco. After I got into the passenger's seat of her car, I noticed that the inside door handle had been broken off. "Didn't I tell you? This is the kidnapping car!" she exclaimed, sticking her key in the ignition. We both laughed and proceeded to have a pleasant (if traffic-filled) ride back to the city, during which we talked about her girlfriend, martial arts, and Eliot Spitzer. In this instance, my "captor" made an ironic joke about public perception of the industry and I, keyed into her frame, happily played along.

In answer to both questions posed by my students, professional dominatrices, for the most part, are not people that a stranger would be scared to get into a car alone with. However, unlike many interviewees, who explicitly stated that this was their goal in being interviewed, I did not make it the project of this book to "prove" how benign or normal these women really are. Nor have I produced an earnest tale about a social scientist's shattered perception of a deviant population she had previously viewed as reprehensible. Such normative projects are not really the purpose of sociology, and frankly, whether pro-dommes are dull or eccentric, or morally corrupt or saintly, are not questions that interest me. As someone who has acquaintances in the industry, I did not expect pro-dommes to be any "weirder" than, say, the average sociologist.

However, I do think pro-dommes' relative normalcy is important in the context of public perceptions of them, as exemplified by other people's concern about my personal safety when interviewing. To be clear, then, the vast majority of the women I interviewed were socially high-functioning individuals who regularly navigated between the dual worlds of social "normalcy" and secret (or not-so-secret) deviation. Ultimately, not only are pro-dommes "like everybody else," but looking at the social world they inhabit can fundamentally tell us something about everybody else.

It is my hope that this text will prove illuminating, and not only for people who have an intellectual curiosity about this area of social life or about the unexamined patches of our social tapestry in general. I have also written it for people who may have no interest in this topic but who do care about some of the basic elements that shape our everyday experiences as members of society, including gender, power, sexuality, and hierarchy. Finally, for those readers who have some experience with this social world, including pro-dommes themselves, it is my intention that they will be able to get a sense of their individual experiences within the context of something larger. Their corner of society has everything you might expect from a good soap opera: money, power, erotic intrigue. But, as I argue on the pages that follow, its normalcy is what makes it truly exciting.

Scripting Pain:
Power Exchange and the Theatrical Frame

One night, I realize I've accidentally stepped on a man rolled up in a carpet. We're at a Scene party in the basement of a restaurant in New York's East Village. I approach the bar and put my foot on what I assume is a step, when I hear a faint "Oof!" The man is laid out in front of the bar, fully submerged in the rug, his face peering out of a roughly cut hole. I step off and apologize, but I am immediately "corrected" by a nearby domme.

"That's okay, sweetie—he likes it!" She proceeds to kick the carpet repeatedly and with great force in her platform boots, while the other people at the bar look on with a mixture of nonchalance and delight. The man in the rug beams the whole time. I return to the table where I've been sitting.

"I just accidentally stepped on a guy rolled in a rug," I tell the group of people who've brought me to the party.

"Carpet Guy's here?" one responds.

Looking at BDSM interactions in contexts such as this one, in which dommes and subs perform these actions publicly, in front of members of the local Scene who are familiar with some of the key players and their attributes, it is easy to see that there is an element of theatricality to such practices. However, it is useful to conceptualize BDSM even in the commercial dungeon, where there are typically no "audiences" for such exchanges, as dramatic because such interactions also represent stylized enactment of relationships of power. In this chapter, inspired by prior work that has examined SM through a dramaturgical frame, as well as my interviewees' own conceptions of their work as "theatrical," I interrogate the role of control in the process by which dungeon encounters are "scripted" and subsequently enacted. Doing this illuminates the professional nuances of these relationships. Although the domme/client interaction is superficially organized as a unidirectional power relationship, it can actually tell us about the nuances of control within other service-industry interactions.

From the outset, rather than viewing control as a 0/1 proposition (one partner has it all and one has none), I reject the common contention among BDSM participants that the sub is the one with "the control" in a D/S exchange. I argue instead that the dominant/submissive interaction actually represents a heavily nuanced struggle for control, in which each party has some role in determining process and outcome. During the interaction prior to the session, in which they determine the parameters for the encounter, dommes and clients strive to "get over" on each other—a form of power exchange, I contend, that is belied both by the image of the all-powerful dominant and by the concept of the submissive who "really" directs the exchange. Looking at the process by which both domme and sub negotiate the encounter is useful in that it unfogs the dynamics of other professional relationships as well as the dynamics of the ethnographic interview process, bringing into focus the manner in which the researcher/informant relationship mirrors that struggle for power.

BDSM and the Theatrical Frame

When I conceptualize BDSM relationships as "scripted" performances, I am standing on the shoulders of other scholars who have applied a dramaturgical frame to these interactions, and I am also echoing BDSM participants' own descriptions of their practices. Thomas Weinberg has theorized that sadomasochism can best be analyzed through what Erving Goffman (1974) terms the "theatrical frame," crucial components of which are performance and make-believe. Weinberg explains that, within the theatrical frame, "various sorts of keyings are used by the participants," including "those which transform what might appear to an outsider to be violence into make-believe or a kind of play-like behavior" (1983, 106).[1] When it comes to sadomasochism, what the uninitiated onlooker may view as brutal is perfectly reasonable to the participants themselves. SM, of course, involves pain, but it is an agreed-upon level of pain that has been pre-scripted and with which both parties are comfortable (Lee 1983, 185–86).

Using a theatrical frame to examine BDSM helps clarify why safe words are used; the dominant may interpret the submissive's expressions of agony within the context of his role in the scene. A staple of BDSM, a safe word can be any term (like "pineapple") that, when called out by the submissive during a scene, indicates that he does not wish to continue. Verbal protests, such as "Stop," "That hurts," or "Let me go," may be misinterpreted by the dominant as part of a particular role-playing scenario, while a safe word unambiguously ensures termination of the session. One client explained,

> You can define your safe words to be whatever you want, but most people just use "yellow" and "red." "Yellow" basically means "I'm approaching the point of 'I can't take it anymore.'" "Yellow" is supposed to mean, like, "Don't go any harder." Because then you're going to break my headspace, basically. Red basically means "That's it. Scene done." If you call out red, that's it.[2]

As one pro-domme told me, "I usually will continue what I'm doing, and I don't stop unless they safe word. I basically tell them at the beginning of the session that if they say, like, 'No, stop' or 'It hurts' then I won't stop if they're not using the safe word."

It makes sense to think about BDSM as theatrical, not only because dramaturgy is such an apt conceptual tool for considering these exchanges, but also because the participants themselves often view their actions as performative. About half the pro-dommes I interviewed agreed with the statement that professional dominance is "theater" or a "performance." I spoke with a Bay Area woman, for instance, who described "setting the stage" for sessions with props, lighting, a sound system, and even a fog machine. She added, "Essentially it is always performance art between you and the person you're playing with." A New York domme explained, similarly, "It's a theater with an audience of one. You put makeup on. The nails, the hair. There's a performance. It just happens to be for an audience of one. And there's audience participation [laughs]." Even those interviewees who rejected the characterization of their work as theatrical generally added that there are aspects of theater, performance, or illusion to the exchange. Further, they used dramaturgical lingo to characterize the interactions; most referred to BDSM interactions as "scenes," and some explicitly referred to the pre-session negotiation as a "scripting" process.[3]

Negotiating a Scene

When I discuss the "scripting" of a dungeon encounter, I am defining a "script" as the plan for interaction that is developed by one or both parties before the interaction itself occurs. The submissive has a certain degree of control over this process, even within noncommercial (lifestyle) BDSM.

However, which participant really controls a dominatrix/client interaction is not a useful question here, since the argument being made is that that these exchanges are mutually constituted. It is apparent, however, that the submissive has more control over the scene than an onlooker not keyed into the exchange might assume. The negotiation process prior to a session is directed toward, among other things, discerning a client's interests and fantasies, so that these may be played out on the dungeon floor. In this sense, the client has control over the general course the scene will take. One Manhattan-based pro-domme told me that she begins this negotiation over the phone: "Usually when I talk to them, I get an idea of what their interests are—pre-screen people. Then they come in, and we chat for ten to fifteen minutes. I have a set list of questions that I ask that have kind of worked for me before." Though some dungeons ask clients to fill out a form, she indicated that she does not:

> I mean, I was just trained to interact with people. It's much easier for me to see their reactions and to better understand where they are, and see how they react when they describe—you know, first I ask, "What are your interests? Let's go over your interests." They talk about that, and, you know, you look at where they linger and how they look when they're talking about something. . . . Then I ask them about—it's a very, very important question and not a lot of people ask this—"What's the worst session you ever had?" And so then I know, all right, this is what's important to him. And I'll ask him what's the best session he ever had. And in between the two of those things, and how he says it, I'm like, okay, now I understand.

Most informants told me that this negotiation process was geared toward determining a sub's preferred activities and "triggers" (which words, props, or sensations especially excite him), as well as his physical and emotional "limits."

In the Dungeon

Client tastes vary widely. Consequently, professional dominance is an extremely multifaceted industry. It would be a herculean task to construct a typology of all the requests pro-dommes get, but they may be generally organized into three ideal types: pain-producing dominant,[4] non-pain-producing dominant, and fetishistic. These categories overlap; sessions commonly involve some combination of pain, dominance without physical pain, and fetish.

Scenarios in which the domme inflicts physical pain are often "corporal" sessions, in which she strikes the client's body—for instance, by spanking, paddling, flogging, caning, whipping, or punching. Other popular types of pain-producing sessions that are not classified as "corporal" include electric stimulation, hair pulling, genital piercing, nipple clamping, and smothering—which, along with choking, falls under the rubric of "breath play." A

common session request from clients who prefer pain is "cock-and-ball torture" (CBT), which some use interchangeably with "ball bondage" (tying-up
of the testes), and some apply as a general term for inflicting genital pain.
Sessions involving dominance without pain infliction include practices
such as body bondage, urinating on the client (golden showers), and verbal
humiliation.

Another key aspect of pro-domme/client interactions is fetish. The
women I interviewed had encountered clients with fetishes for shoes, articles
of clothing, particular fabrics, body hair, and sweat, in addition to body parts
and various scents. One client wrote "I love smelly feet!!!" all over his request
form. Informants told me that "foot worship"—in which the client rubs,
kisses, compliments, and/or washes the dominatrix's feet—was by far the
most common manifestation of a body part fetish, though dommes who specialized in wrestling also commonly added that they get requests for "muscle
worship." For those pro-dommes who are willing to do nudity, "ass worship"
and "breast worship" are common. Other typical fetishistic scenarios include
cross-dressing, "adult babies" (infantilism), medical scenes (in which the
domme plays the role of doctor or nurse, sometimes performing an enema),
and "transformation" scenarios in which the client wishes to be treated as an
animal—most commonly, "pony play" and "puppy play."

While many pro-dommes emphasized that there is no "typical" session,
it is instructive to look at the sample of 305 client preference forms from a
New York dungeon, to get a sense of some general trends in session requests.
The table below tallies the items checked by clients on their preference forms,
organized into the categories "like," "love," and "dislike." The activity categories most "loved" by clients were submission to multiple mistresses (136 clients), foot slavery (117 clients), genital chastisement (105 clients), dildo service (105 clients), and mild to moderate bondage (101 clients). Slightly more
people liked or loved being urinated on (126 clients) than disliked it (115 clients). These trends line up with reports from the women I interviewed; one
dungeon domme, for instance, told me, "You couldn't be a mistress without
doing golden and dildo."

Some of the patterns here we might expect from the media image of the
professional dominatrix, especially as relates to her attire. Of 237 clients, for
example, 159 indicated that they loved high-heel shoes; this was the category
most "loved" by clients. And 102 out of 232 loved "exotic boots." Some clients emphasized this point by writing in requests for stereotypical dominatrix
gear—for instance, "HIGH HEELED THIGH HIGH LEATHER BOOTS (black)."

The corporal categories, however, tell a story that complicates the stereotype: most clients do not come to this dungeon to receive extreme pain. Some

Interests, as expressed in client preference forms ($N = 305$)*

	Like	Love	Dislike	Total
Leather	150	93	12	255
Patent leather	132	66	11	209
Latex	141	75	9	225
Vinyl / PVC	111	87	45	243
Exotic lingerie	105	126	15	246
Garter belts, stockings, etc	83	138	29	250
High-heel shoes	72	159	6	237
Exotic boots	92	102	38	232
Gloves	90	60	69	219
Bondage (mild to moderate)	101	101	36	238
Bondage (moderate to severe	69	66	93	228
Spanking (mild to moderate)	120	69	63	252
Spanking (moderate to severe)	48	9	133	190
Flagellation (mild to moderate)	75	20	75	170
Flagellation (moderate to severe)	55	5	132	192
Discipline (mild to moderate)	134	66	33	233
Discipline (moderate to severe)	69	15	108	192
Verbal humiliation	126	79	63	268
Public humiliation	78	57	105	240
Suspension	109	34	90	233
Cage imprisonment	69	18	129	216
Nipple play / torment	112	97	37	246
Genital chastisement, bondage, etc.	108	105	38	251
Equestrian training	9	52	151	212
Puppy training	12	33	162	207
Infantilism	3	34	183	220
Cross-dressing	54	52	144	250
French maid servitude	21	48	152	221
Candle wax	79	9	117	205
Butt plugs	75	95	71	241
Dildo service	66	105	69	240
Submission to multiple mistresses	82	136	15	233
Overnight / weekend slavery	73	54	79	206
Wrestling	51	14	144	209
Foot slavery / worship	60	117	66	243
Bare feet	85	96	57	238
Feet in shoes and stockings	88	81	48	217
Toilet service	45	36	132	213
Golden showers	63	63	115	241
Enemas	60	34	137	231
Teacher/student fantasies	99	47	80	226
Nurse/patient fantasies	81	57	72	210
Mommy/son fantasies	7	36	150	193
Boss/employee fantasies	90	54	78	222
Prisoner/interrogation fantasies	69	60	50	179
Secret agent / hostage fantasies	63	45	85	193

*Clients typically left items blank.

types of pain infliction, such as nipple torture and genital chastisement, were common, but when it came to acts such as spanking and flagellation, few clients requested "moderate to severe" pain. Only five clients loved moderate to severe flagellation, and only nine loved moderate to severe spanking. At least in part, this avoidance of "severely" masochistic acts may be a function not of taste but of the unwillingness to have evidence of the session left on one's body. Informants told me that avoiding telltale marks was a common client concern, particularly for married men, and some clients specified "no marks" on their request forms. At the same time, this tally of client preferences indicates the extent to which sessions are a mixed bag and by no means always about physical pain, thus complicating the image of the brutal, whip-wielding dominatrix. It is telling, for instance, that one client specified on the "comments" section of his form, "No Discipline. No Pain. No Meanness."

It would be misleading to flatten out this area of social life by limiting the analysis to only the most commonly requested practices, or to those that exist on a set form, in the same way that it would be misleading to focus on only the most outlandish stories. A good way to describe the world of professional erotic dominance is that outliers are commonplace. One dominatrix may encounter only a single client with a particular outlier request, but she will encounter many clients with outlier requests. A line I heard repeatedly from pro-dommes as well as from people in the Scene was, "There's someone with a fetish for *everything*." The following four dommes' descriptions of the last session they had done before being interviewed underscore the great variation that exists in this industry:

> I forced him to drink a lot of champagne. . . . It's not an explicit thing, but a lot of our session revolves around this kind of playful humiliation, where he says—he'll be like, "I love you." [I say,] "Of course you do." [He says,] "Do you love me?" [I say,] "Of course I do." [He says,] "You're lying!" [I say,] "Of course I am." . . . You know, this whole banter where he's like, "Oh! I *loooove* you!" and it's just kind of very playful [*laughs*]. . . . It's really a fun, silly—it's just basically me making fun of him like that. Not in a really mean way.

> The last session was with a pantyhose fetishist. I like those fetishists because they're really easy to work with. I mean, he loves anything as long as it involves pantyhose [*laughs*]. So of course I have him wear them. I make a straightjacket out of them. I do bondage with them. I do cock-and-ball bondage with them. And then I'll incorporate other kinds of SM play. So I'll like tie the cock and balls up and then do other types of CBT or whatever, but it's the combination of the fetish object with the other activities that he really enjoys.

This was a rare case where this guy had never even seen a mistress before, and he's asking me to shit in his mouth. I'm like, "Are you *sure*, honey?" He's that kind of fetishist that's probably been thinking of it for fifteen years and just never did it. And he was into, like, ingesting some of it and having some of it on him.

It was a CBT session for two hours with a lot of ballbusting. He just wanted me to hit him in the balls over and over again.

Finally, there are sessions in which the dominatrix, paradoxically, plays the role of the submissive partner in the interaction. The most common example of a session in which the dominatrix is not dominant is a "switch" session, which can refer to a scene in which the dominatrix is the submissive participant (also called a "sub session") or in which the two people arrange to "switch" in the middle of the session, so that the dominated becomes dominant. Switching was not commonplace among informants, though many of the independent dommes had previously done switch sessions when they worked in larger dungeons. Switch sessions are more common in the dungeons than among indies. There are also a handful of female "pro-subs" working independently in both New York and San Francisco.

Clients, Scripts, and "Getting Over"

The extent to which a client controls the content of a scene can vary widely. The pro-dommes with whom I spoke indicated that, during the scripting process, clients put forth requests ranging from general areas of interest to highly specific scenarios. The responses from the "Other Specific Interests" and "Special Requests" sections of the client forms from the New York dungeon illustrate the varied levels of detail clients used when framing these interactions. While all clients at this House were given the space to express their desires, some scripted their scenes more heavily than others. Their comments range from general requests to descriptions of more highly developed fetishes—down to the specific age of the child role to be played, the kind and color of the clothing and shoes to be worn, and the plot of the scene as well as suggested dialogue. At one end of the scripting spectrum, we find clients who ask dominatrices to do "whatever you want." At the other extreme, clients bring in written scripts for the interactions.

Clients' requests for specific dialogue also emerged as a recurrent topic in my interviews. Most women recalled at least one client who had brought in a script for them to review and enact. An interviewee who worked out of a

House in San Francisco, for instance, explained that one tourist couple regularly requested complex, heavily scripted scenes on their visits: "They're both subs, and so they come and they do this four-hour-long incredibly scripted scene with multiple dommes. The first time they were here, we were an animal shelter and they were a French poodle and a Labrador retriever. Branded and neutered and sold and various things [*laughs*]." That particular scene ran the couple over a thousand dollars.

As a practical matter, unless a domme has a photographic memory, it is impossible for her to read and memorize a multipage dramatic scene in the short time she typically has to prepare for a scene. Most women who do these scenes thus rely on key words or activities that they find to be pervasive themes in a given script. These triggers are akin to Goffman's "keys," in that they function to transmit shared meanings; they are signposts that cue in a client to the current location within the narrative, and they are designed to elicit a particular response from him. One woman who works out of a House in Manhattan, discussing a regular client who supplied her with typed scenes every time he came in—"I don't know how he finds the time to write them!"—explained that, over time, she had learned it was not necessary to reproduce a script verbatim, as long as she remembered triggers and the general order of events. "You don't have to get every single word," she told me, "but you know, in this context, what he wants to happen."

Some pro-dommes indicated that they would not currently accept these kinds of scripts, either because they did not consider themselves skilled at recitation or because they felt such scripts eliminated their own influence over the interaction. As an indie in her late thirties explained:

> Scripts, you know, they can be kind of boring because it gives the client the control. And there's nothing worse than having some guy all tied up and he's like, "You didn't say the word 'snap' before you hit me!" And I'm like, "Are you in this or not?" I mean, I understand if people have certain buzzwords. Like there was this one guy that really liked the word "torture." And it was great because I'd drop it every so often and he'd just be like, "Whooaa. Yes! You're going to torture me!" And I'm like, "Oh yes. I am *torturing* you right now." It's one thing if people will, like, work with me on it, but it's another thing if they expect me to be an automaton. . . . Like, "Okay, you are visiting McDonald's and I am now going to say the same script that you have used with every other dominatrix you've met."

It is not uncommon for pro-dommes to indicate on their websites, "I will not recite dialogue." Some women—particularly the "Old Guard," the old-school dommes who had been in the industry for decades—stood against reciting dialogue on principle. The above dominatrix's assertion that she does "what he wants [me] to do" would be an anathema to those women, for whom the female's control over the encounter is central to the experience of professional D/S. As one woman put it: "*I* am dominant. *You* are submissive. You serve *me.*"

Interestingly, most informants, including women in the Old Guard who refused to take sessions requiring memorization, spoke about this loss of their control in the context of the client's pleasure. That is, they argued that giving the client a high degree of control over process would ultimately limit his own enjoyment of the exchange. As one Brooklyn-based domme explained, in the context of being asked to recite dialogue, "You *think* you want *this*, but you *really* want *this*." An interviewee who worked at a House added, "I feel like it doesn't give them the full potential of the session since you have to work with those barriers." Another woman, who had been in the industry for decades, when asked if she ever recited dialogue in session, exclaimed, "This is the thing that *so* pisses me off!" She went on to explain:

> The work of a professional dominant is to *train* the people to be dominated, *not* to serve them their fucking pizza with any topping on it they ask. That is not the work of a professional dominant. That is the work of a kinky sex worker. And they can have it! God, that pisses me off! . . . If someone would say, "I have this fantasy. First you do this, and then you do that, and blam blam blah," I would say, "I'm sorry. This is not a pizza ordering service." . . . I would say, "In your fantasy, *you're* the top. *And* the bottom. You're running it, in your mind. You created the whole thing, the scenario. . . . How satisfying is that going to be? I'm gonna fail to top, and you're gonna fail to bottom." And then they go, "Oh, huh, I didn't think about that." And *then* I start negotiating with them.

Her narrative here typifies the dominatrix's claim to professional expertise. She contends that clients ultimately enjoyed the sessions more than they would have had they been given more control over the content of the exchanges.

Her "pizza topping" analogy is in line with a cartoon published in the *New Yorker* in November 1999. In the image, a woman outfitted in thigh-high stockings and clutching a whip stands next to a man tucked into bed, gazing up at her. The caption at the bottom reads: "Please listen carefully, as my menu options have changed" (Duffy 1999, 66). Here, intentionally or not, the artist humorously encapsulates one of the fundamental paradoxes of commercial BDSM: that the dominatrix, while ostensibly in control in the context of a session, is, like any other service-sector employee, catering to her clients' requests. The extent to which this is true varies widely from woman to woman, but most pro-dommes discuss scenes with clients beforehand, ascertaining their particular fantasies and playing them out in the dungeon.

The preference forms that some Houses provide are not unlike menus, on which clients check off their desired session activities.

The industry of professional erotic dominance is thus contradictory, in that some clients identify as "submissive" but desire sessions that are cooked to order; this particular complaint pervaded many of the women's narratives. One interviewee, who worked out of a larger dungeon in San Francisco, for instance, asserted, "I'm not just an instant domme, just add water, plug me into your fantasies. You have to *think* a little bit and be mindful of what I'm requiring of you." She added, however, "You have to be a bit of a service top to do this work happily,[5] because you really are fulfilling other people's fantasies. You need to get some enjoyment out of the fact that you're fulfilling their fantasies. Otherwise it's just not going to work." Tellingly, one Bay Area House is called Fantasy Makers.

For many informants, when a client gives his dominatrix dialogue to recite, it is a classic example of what is known in the BDSM world as "topping from the bottom." In *SM101*, Wiseman defines this phenomenon (also known as "topping from below"): "Attempting to control the session while ostensibly in the submissive (non-controlling) role. A type of behavior generally frowned upon" (1996, 375). The struggle for control between domme and sub is thus more nuanced than the superficial image of a powerful female and powerless male would suggest. In the push-and-pull social space of a dyadic D/S exchange, the client may attempt to set the parameters for an interaction in which he is not, ostensibly, the dominant party. The dominatrix, in turn, can decide whether to assert her professional claim and deny the client that particular interaction or, if she chooses to proceed, how much of his input to use.

At the same time that some dommes rejected fully written scripts from clients, others declared that they particularly enjoyed heavily scripted scenes. They argued that such sessions required less of them; as the informant above explained, "[It] makes it really easy for me." They also asserted that there was less guesswork as to what the clients wanted. Still others found the element of dramaturgy entertaining. "Common scenes might be, we're both competing for the position of CEO and one of us blackmails the other," a Bay Area woman explained. "Like, he blackmails me and forces me to submit to him, but then I turn around with some piece of information and blackmail him. . . . Or he's like, "What? You fucked my wife?! How *dare* you!" So I guess it's like this soap opera kind of dialogue. But it's fun. I mean, *I* enjoy it." Another interviewee giggled with delight as she recounted one session she had done at an upscale Manhattan hotel:

He wanted a scenario that he's the boss and I'm the secretary, seducing him. I wasn't sure what he really wanted. . . . We started the scene, and I was saying, "No! No! I'm innocent! I'm innocent, I tell you!" But he says, "No, no, no, you don't understand. You're supposed to seduce me and take over the company and tell me how evil you are that you're seducing the boss. Let's start over." [I said], "Okay, so we'll start from the beginning." It's like, "Take two!" [*laughs*].

This particular dominatrix continued to make an interesting mental move, arguing that, because this session particularly amused her, she was not bothered by the sub's desire to direct the exchange. This is one variation of a common contention: that if a pro-domme derives enjoyment or entertainment from a scene, the client's topping from the bottom is not as egregious. The essence of this claim is: "I *like* reciting dialogue, so I have control over the encounter in the sense that I am doing what I enjoy." What results is an equation in which enjoyment = power. The cost-benefit analysis of a client's topping from the bottom may work out in the domme's favor, in her view, if she obtains a certain unspecified level of pleasure (usually not erotic) from the exchange. Within this particular formulation, the client, in not "making" the domme do anything she finds distasteful, has not taken the upper hand within the dyad. In fact, the domme feels she is "getting over" on him by receiving money to engage in an enjoyable activity.

I borrow the term "getting over" from *Sidewalk*, Mitchell Duneier's ethnography of the men and women who sell reading materials on New York's Sixth Avenue. Sidewalk vendors use the term to describe a kind of "hustle"— the jostling for control, between themselves and their customers, over these commercial interactions (Duneier 1999, 68).

This process by which workers and consumers vie for control over the transactional relationship is not limited to booksellers and professional dominatrices but has reverberations within a variety of commercial exchanges. Recently, while watching a reality show about up-and-coming fashion designers, I witnessed one of the contestants, when confronted by a client who had elaborately sketched her own wedding gown, roll her eyes and comment, "I'm not a *dressmaker*." The distinction she made between being a "designer," who takes into account the customer's predilections but whose creativity influences the final product, and a "dressmaker," who reproduces a client's sketch in cloth, is indicative of the same basic tension being discussed here. SM argot is useful for thinking about why being a "dressmaker" in this scenario was so anathema to the contestant: her client (a woman with "disgusting taste") was "topping from the bottom."

Nor is this dynamic limited to industries we would typically think of as creative. A litigator I know recently made a similar complaint about his clients liking to "emphasize hypertechnical and losing arguments in briefs."

"Do you do what they say?" I asked him.

"You try to convince them otherwise, but yes," he shrugged.

Interactions in the dungeon are particularly revealing of this dynamic because pro-dommes are women who engage in dramatized representations of power exchange for a living, and they are, for the most part, hyperaware of the microdynamics of these relationships. Further, by their own accounts, many are women with "naturally" dominant personalities, in addition to being situated in the dominant role within the context of their relationships with clients; thus the friction in those relationships becomes particularly noticeable when dommes "push back." "Topping from the bottom" can be used to characterize the microdynamics of negotiations within a variety of other relational contexts, but BDSM participants, who regularly engage in displays of dominance and submission, lay it bare and give voice to it.

Pushing Back

Pro-dommes "push back" against their clients' attempts at control in a number of ways. Some of these ways are preemptive, such as rejecting certain clients entirely and publishing on their Internet profiles lists of activities in which they will not engage. The most common of these activities, among pro-dommes in this sample, were "brown showers" (defecating on clients), bloodletting, sexual "extras," nudity, switch, and wrestling sessions.[6]

In accordance with the "enjoyment = control" formulation, many women indicated that they refused to pursue activities that they, personally, found disagreeable. Consider these statements from three informants, all independent pro-dommes based in New York:

> Like I said, there are certain aspects of BDSM that I don't like, so if people ask for it, I just say, "No." So I really do what I like and get paid for it. . . . I have this kind of concept that I won't sell myself, no matter what. And [I] probably will have less clients than some other dommes, but that's my principle.

> I'm not going to do things I don't enjoy. If it's not up my alley, I'm not doing it. Doesn't amuse me? It's not gonna happen.

> If it's something that revolts me, I won't do it. I'll be like, "Oh, I'm not the mistress to play with you. Try——." If I like the person I would recommend them, or I would say, "Go to domina.ms and search for that."

While the client actively participates in the scripting process, the dominatrix organizes the interaction to her own specifications, in the sense that she determines the universe of erotic possibilities that will structure the scene. Returning for a moment to the *New Yorker* cartoon, the domme provides the "menu": the parameters for the exchange. At the same time, there are still fiscal realities to the life of a professional dominatrix.

Dommes vary in the extent to which they are able to stick to session activities that interest them personally. The more one requires the income from professional dominance, the higher the incentive to engage in a wide spectrum of session types, even those one does not find particularly "amusing." A Queens-based indie, discussing her process of client selection, told me, "I'm actually quite choosey because I don't need [the clients]." A former dungeon manager, on the other hand, explained that though she did not fire women for refusing to perform specific acts, they could not feasibly earn a living under certain self-imposed limitations: "There were girls who would try to refuse to do golden showers and then realize that this wasn't the business for them. . . . [Golden showers were] *very* common requests. . . . I had one girl who refused to do dildo, and she didn't last long either."

There was a difference, generally speaking, in the extent to which dungeon dommes and indies had control over aspects of their occupation such as client selection and session activities. While some Houses were more lax in their operation, many current or former dungeon dommes said that they had experienced pressure from management to do sessions with certain men or cater to certain interests. One Manhattan-based dominatrix, who had recently gone indie, mused, "I think that's another reason people leave [the larger dungeons]—you don't have any control over your sessions."

You have zero control?

Yeah. If someone wants a strap-on session, you do a strap-on session. If they wanna be tied up, you tie them up. Like, at the House, it was very dictated by the clients.

My interaction with this dominatrix serves as a compelling illustration of Michael Agar's contention (1996), contrary to many textbooks on the ethnographic method, that at times it is fruitful, and even preferable, to challenge one's informants. In this instance, my interviewee began with a sweeping generalization: dungeon dommes have "zero control" over their interactions with clients. I nudged her on this point—"You have zero control?"—and she stood firm in her assertion. Later in the interview, however, when discussing certain acts she "absolutely would never" perform with clients when she worked at the larger dungeon, this informant spontaneously referenced our early dialogue, adding, "so I shouldn't say 'no control.'" This dialectical process whereby my challenging of an informant resulted in a modification of her response is one example of how the interview exchange can represent an instantiation of the same control dynamics that pervade the dungeon. Rather than being "dommed" by this woman's initial generalization, I gently pushed back, ultimately to have her slightly reevaluate her response.

In reality, pro-dommes had some power to push back, not only against their clients but against the individuals who ran the Houses. If they pushed too hard, however, this could mean losing their jobs, or failing to be hired in the first place. One pro-domme from New York, a woman in her early twenties, described a moment in her career that had set the stage for her experiences at larger Houses:

> I interviewed for one of the big commercial Houses and the woman—I did a phone interview, and she gave me this long, like, list of activities that they do there, and she asked me if I would do them as a domme or as a sub, or if they were things I would *try*, and I had too many things—I wasn't really interested in subbing and I wasn't—there were a lot of things I wasn't really interested in doing as a domme, either. Like, I didn't want to do anal play. I didn't really wanna do showers. And so she said, "You're a really closed-minded person" [*laughs*]. And, "You can't work here, if you're not willing to try these things." And she was really, like, pressuring me. "Just, okay, just say that you will try these things that you haven't tried. You can just come in and work for a while. Just try this stuff in your sessions and you can see how you feel about it." [I was] like, "Uhh, I'm really sure I don't wanna shit on people. Even though I've never done it" [*laughs*].

Like the dungeon domme discussed earlier, who asserted that the work of a pro-domme is "fulfilling other people's fantasies," other pro-dommes also made the claim that working at a House required one to be a "service top," putting the client in a de facto position of dominance by catering to his desires, even as he tops from the bottom.

As indicated, many indies asserted that one of the reasons they had gone independent was to avoid this kind of service topping. They wanted to maintain more control over aspects of their sessions such as wardrobe, client selection, and their range of activities. A Manhattan-based indie, who had previously worked in a House, for instance, told me:

> I turn down more than half of the people who contact me. When I was at the commercial House . . . you didn't have any choice about who you saw. I remember once this guy came in, and he was really drunk. He was slurring

his words. And I remember I went to the Head Mistress and was like, "I really don't want to see this guy. He's really drunk. He makes me nervous." And she was like, "No, no, I'll watch on the camera from my office. If anything happens, I'll come in. It'll be fine." So she made me do the session. You didn't have that choice. That was one of the reasons I wanted to leave, because I didn't have any control over who I saw. . . . So now, it's very important to me to *not* be able to take people on.

Such commentary about the advantages of being able to reject clients was a crucial piece of the "going indie" narrative for many of the women with whom I spoke. All of the independents I interviewed said that they had turned away at least one potential client, and some, like this woman, regularly turned away half or more of the men who contacted them. Dommes typically rejected potential clients who had session interests that were on their "will not do" lists, but it was also common practice to reject men who seemed as though they could be dangerous or who had medical issues.

A final reason pro-dommes gave for refusing to take on particular clients was because these men had failed to engage in acceptable negotiation etiquette prior to a session. One San Francisco–based indie told me that she turns away people who say "stupid shit" on the phone. When asked to go into greater detail, she replied, "I think the biggest example would just be, like, [someone who is] really disrespectful, and kind of talking to you like you're just some broad. You know? Just, like, some chick." Another Bay Area domme made a similar point about her filtering process. "I am very controlling in the manner in which I screen my clients," she explained. "I don't really allow people to ask me questions, so if somebody calls me and they're like, 'How much do you charge?' I'll be like, 'Whoa, whoa, whoa. Let's see if we have some manners here first. Who are you calling?' [*laughs*]. And I'll just take it over from there. . . . If somebody can't jump through my hoops then they can't be a client."

Those dommes who were "protocol-oriented" tended to make their clients jump through more hoops in the early stages of negotiation. Some women spoke more informally with their clients during these discussions or, by their own accounts, behaved as service tops, sussing out their clients' desires. Others, however, preferred more stylized modes of interaction, down to the specific language they required clients to use. An independent domme based in Manhattan, for example, explained that she took issue with clients who use the words "I want":

Somebody who says, "Well, mistress, I *like* . . . ," maybe I can hear you. "Mistress, I want to serve you. My enjoyments are . . . ," I can hear you, because you took the time to learn etiquette, protocols, and how to speak to me. . . . I don't like the fact that they say, "I want." That should never come out of your mouth when you're talking to me, if you're a submissive. You can say, "Mistress, may I . . . ?" You can say, "I enjoy . . ." You can say, "I'm into . . . ," but you never say, "Well, I want a session where . . ." That pisses me off. I hang up right away.

Here, she makes a mental move in which she "gets over" on the clients by symbolically denying them their "wants" and causing them to take a subservient position from their initial verbal approach: "Mistress, I want to serve you."

This particular type of "getting over," whereby the dominatrix does emotion work that allows her to perceive herself as the victor, is akin to Duneier's sidewalk vendors' haggling with their customers. Duneier explains the process by which two of his informants do this "hustle":

> Central to the ethos of the hustle Ron taught Marvin is "getting over," which, Marvin explains, means "getting a good transaction out of what you pursued." From that perspective, in every transaction Ron and Marvin either "get over" on the customer or the customer "gets over" on them. When Ron accepts a customer's offer of three dollars by saying "Give me three," he is saying, "You think you got over, but you really didn't." His self-worth is at stake as he haggles over the price. (1999, 68)

Pro-dommes make mental moves similar to those of Duneier's booksellers in order to maintain the feeling of dominance even though they generally must take the clients' desires into account. The pro-domme described above, like Ron, indicates that she needs to be the one directing the exchange. Though she will still listen to a particular client's session requests, she makes certain that he frames them as requests, rather than orders, thus creating a rupture between herself and service tops, such as the menu-toting *New Yorker* domme. Her dominance within the particular theater of commercial BDSM, in her view, remains intact, despite the fact that she ultimately determines the clients' interests and will play them out in the dungeon—but only, she insists, "if they amuse me."

One lens that is useful for looking at the dynamic at work here is a symbolic interactionist framework. That is, human beings react toward each other on the basis of the meanings we interpret in regard to each other's words and deeds, and these ascribed meanings arise from the interactions we have with each other and with our society (Blumer 1969). The client in this particular example sends out a signal to the pro-domme—"Mistress, I want"—and she receives and interprets it as an attempt to get over, within the context of the rules of BDSM etiquette into which she has been socialized. She then responds by sending out a signal of her own. By hanging up on him, she transmits the meaning, "No, you will not get over on me."

Of course, dommes and subs can have different conceptions about the power relationships that structure an encounter. A dominatrix and her client may have divergent ideas about who is getting over on whom at any particular moment. I do not mean to treat my informants' narratives about the power exchange that happens in the dungeon as unadulterated truth, but even if these descriptions are skewed based upon individual perception (as what narratives are not?), they nonetheless reveal a salient fact: that the operation of control in the dungeon is complex and nuanced, rather than unidirectional.

In addition to the symbolic value to be gained by saving face within the interaction, there are also practical reasons why a domme would reject a potential client for his failure to conform to acceptable phone etiquette. Within the symbolic interactionist framework, this is where the meanings that pro-dommes derive from interactions with other clients come into play. Many pro-dommes told me that the men who behaved rudely on the phone tended to be the ones who turned out to be difficult, or even potentially dangerous, once they were inside the dungeon. Boorish phone behavior activated the "feeling" or "little voice" that let a dominatrix know a man was a potential threat when she was vetting him. "If they're being really rude, I won't see them because I know they're going to be trouble in a session," one woman summarized. "Like, if they're being disrespectful right from the beginning, then I just—I don't care. I won't even deal with them."

The dominatrix is not completely "dominant" within the set of interactions that constitute the dungeon exchange, but nor does the common contention among BDSM participants that the submissive "really" controls the interaction hold true for professional erotic dominance. To characterize the client as "in control" over any commercial transaction is to ignore the agency that most service providers have to begin and terminate the professional relationship, to push back against topping from the bottom, and to design the parameters within which the interaction takes place by offering and withholding certain services.

Of course, at the same time that pro-dommes can accept or reject potential clients, clients can select which pro-dommes they will contact and visit, as well as which ones they will contact but never come in to see. They can thus get over on a domme by taking up her time with no financial investment on their parts. One prevalent form of this type of behavior—known in the business as "wanking," "spanking," or "stroking"—is when a man calls, sometimes ostensibly to schedule an appointment, and gets erotic pleasure from the phone conversation itself, ultimately never coming in to do a session.

Screening and the Internet

The primary medium through which dominatrices attract their clients is through Internet advertisements. The Internet is also replete with message boards and listserves, on which clients promote and critique pro-dommes they have visited. Many pro-dommes also maintain a presence on the Internet through blogs, profiles on social networking sites such as MySpace, and posts on the message boards of various BDSM groups. Informants who had been in the Scene prior to the popularization of the Internet told me that they used to take out advertisements in BDSM magazines, or in the back of general-interest publications, but relatively few use these media today. Advertising online is less expensive than paying for print ads and has the potential to reach a much larger audience. As one woman put it, "I used to [advertise in magazines], but print is dead. Nobody who can afford to see me doesn't have a computer."

Interestingly, some women indicated that they advertised via the Internet instead of print media in order to limit the number of "wanker" calls that they received. Promotional websites can contain much more lengthy and specific descriptions than print ads and thus potentially limit the number of calls from clients with questions. A thirty-three-year-old domme who had been in the industry for a decade explained that she had advertised in *New York* magazine just once, "And I just got horrible calls. Like, you'd get people and they'd be like, 'You charge what?' and, 'Does that include sex?' Ugh, *no!*" Another interviewee suggested that there is something about the type of man who reads specialty publications that is linked to wanking behavior: "I used to advertise in papers and magazines, like the *Vault* magazine or something like that, and it turns out that the only people left reading those are spankers. They look at the pictures and then they call me and wanna wank off. For one ad [the cost] is astronomical and I get nothing out of it except my phone bill going up because these wankers wanna call me instead of paying money for a 1–900 line." However, wanker calls were a common complaint of independent dommes in general,[7] regardless of the medium through which they had advertised.

Wankers may be different from those men who have every intention of doing a session but simply get cold feet, but the consequences are the same in the sense that the dominatrix (or receptionist, in the case of a House) spends time on the potential client, with no payoff. Many women told me that they store wankers' phone numbers, and some alerted their local friends who were dommes to avoid these men's calls as well. At least one House has first-time clients call from a nearby pay phone, so that the women can avoid wasting time preparing for sessions that will never occur. A number of women also charge for phone sessions, to accommodate clients who for various reasons may not be willing to do sessions in person.

Enslaving the Dominant: Problem Clients

When pro-dommes spoke about "problem clients," this was typically code for men who were trying to get over on them either inside or outside of the session room. Aside from the types of clients who were dangerous or who attempted to top from the bottom during the session itself, there were several categories of men whom my informants indicated that they found difficult. First were the demanding clients who engaged in extensive unpaid phone consultations between sessions. One twenty-six-year-old woman in the New York BDSM Scene explained to me, early in my fieldwork for this project, that she would never want to work as a pro-domme: "[It is] a high-maintenance job. You're on call to your high-end clients. They'll call you at fucking 3 a.m., stressing out about their wife. And I've heard from my friend [who is a pro-domme] that you've just gotta take it. You're on call, like, because they're your major client."

Her assertions about this aspect of the industry were supported by the behavior of informants during my field research. Dommes regularly took calls from clients during our meetings, and several women texted furiously throughout our discussions. One woman, after answering her cell phone for the second time during her interview, apologized, laughing, "I am sorry I have to answer my phone. You *have* to answer the phone, because if you don't answer, they won't leave messages. You can't call them back. So if you don't get them back when they call you, you miss business. You have to be a slave to your phone." Feeling tethered to one's phone was a common complaint among the indies I met. However, they could choose to what extent they were willing to let clients "enslave" them this way. Another informant, at one point during our interview, looked at her phone and sighed, "This idiot. He's done a few sessions with me, and now he thinks he can take up my time. He's just constantly bugging me." She did not take the call.

Like wankers, high-maintenance clients can get over on dommes by using up their time outside of sessions, thus maximizing what they pursue out of the transaction while minimizing their financial responsibility. Other problem clients more explicitly attempt to get something for nothing by haggling over session fees or attempting to barter for sessions instead of paying the tribute.[8] According to my informants, for instance, clients regularly request to do the dommes' housework in exchange for sessions.[9] One indie described another example of a problem client who had repeatedly attempted to schedule a session during a time of day she does not typically see clients. When she finally agreed to see him during that hour, he topped from the bottom throughout the session and, at the end, asked for a discount on his golden shower because it "wasn't torrential enough." The informant told me that she had felt "very defeated" by the exchange. In her mind, she lost the struggle for control that framed this encounter. In this way, problem clients expose the disjuncture between the ultimate power the domme enjoys in the theater of the dungeon and the "hustle" that often happens behind the scenes.

Reciprocity, Emotion Work, and the Scripting Process

It should be emphasized that there is a spectrum when it comes to the dominatrix's level of control over the fulfillment of a script. As we have seen, some pro-dommes claim not to heed clients' requests unless they find them particularly amusing, while at the other end of the continuum, there are pro-dommes who follow their subs' scripts to the letter. However, script negotiation is a process that typically requires some give-and-take from both parties. Even according to the narratives of self-identified service tops, there is almost always some disjuncture between a client's initial script and the scene the two parties execute on the floor of the dungeon.

The fact that professional dominatrices regularly pick and choose which of the clients' requests for a particular session they will honor, even if the requests are all activities that are on their "menus," distinguishes them from some other service-sector employees. In the culinary scenario, for instance, a customer who has ordered a multiple-course meal would find it unacceptable for the waiter to serve him only the salad and dessert courses. The professional dominatrix, however, can have that freedom. As a Queens-based indie explained, although she focuses on fulfilling clients' particular erotic fantasies, she often cannot accommodate all of their session interests on a single day:

> I wanna know their limits and their interests, and then I play based on that. If they try to script the session, I don't allow that. I tell them that the way that I do it is based on your limits and interests. I'm not going to go off a script and I'm not going to, you know, try to fit four things into an hour. I don't do that. You might get—you know, if you give me a list [of activities], you might get three of them. But it's not a good session for me or for them if I'm running from one thing to another, just trying to fit it all in.

Here, she indicates that she must negotiate sessions with clients because it is "not a good session for me *or for them*" if they receive exactly what they, as nonprofessionals, *think* they want. She also symbolically positions herself as dominant, and as the boundary setter, in the encounter ("I don't allow that"). Interestingly, however, while she negotiates sessions based on clients' particular interests, she does not consider the men's roles in that process to constitute scripting.

A dominatrix's attempt to influence a script prior to a session can also be necessary if a request is impractical or potentially dangerous. A Bay Area woman described a client "who wanted [her] to kill him and eat him." She recalled, "I renegotiated that to a role play where he'll be tied up, and I'll put his hand in a slow cooker. And I'll turn the heat up, so it feels nice and warm. And then I'll chop up vegetables and make soup, and we'll eat it together. . . . That guy scares me. He's gonna find somebody who's gonna off him one of these days."

Finally, my interviewees indicated that, even when they fulfilled all of their clients' session requests, they generally still felt they had maintained control over other facets of these scenes. "There's a lot of room to move in," a retired pro-domme from San Francisco told me, explaining that although she would take "little notes" on a client before going into a session, she, ultimately, was at the helm of the scene, giving and denying erotic gratification at will. A multitude of components go into a scene: the order in which the events unfold, the outfit worn, the particular implements used, the music played, the words uttered. Even in a "service topping" scenario, then, the domme exercises choice under constraint.

Still, the submissive has a degree of control over a commercial BDSM transaction that is belied by the word "dominatrix." Pro-dommes employ several cognitive strategies for dealing with this disjuncture between their total dominance in the theater of the dungeon and the underlying reality of the power exchange. Many perform a kind of emotion work in which they define topping from the bottom on their own particular terms. For instance, most reject fully formed scripts but are willing to recite words, phrases, or even bits of dialogue.

Most informants also drew a line between "negotiation" and "topping from the bottom"—a line that was defined on a subjective, individualistic basis. Discussing safe words, for instance, one woman described the process by which she allowed clients to provide feedback about the amount of pain they were receiving in session:

Yellow: "Slow down; I need to talk to you." Red: "We're stopping for good. We're not continuing. Period." . . . If someone reds out to me—because they have the option of yellow, except if it's a medical emergency. So, if someone has weird medical shit, I give them yellow, red, and medical. If it's anything—they can't breathe, they have asthma—then medical. But if they call red because they forgot to call yellow . . . I would stop the scene and not play again. Because red takes the power back. The client takes the power back when they call red, so why bother?

They don't take the power back when they call yellow?

No. They negotiate. You know, it's a negotiation safe word. Yellow is "I need to speak with you. I'm hitting my limit. Something's not working." Red is "Stop!"

For this particular pro-domme, the distinction between communicating about an activity and terminating the activity is crucial. On the other hand, some pro-dommes told me that a client who overuses "yellow" in session may be viewed as topping from the bottom. Still others did not view "redding out" (apparently a rare occurrence) as irreparable to the power hierarchy. One woman, for example, recalled a situation in which a client had "safe worded" because of an asthma attack. After he had used his inhaler, and after a short break, they continued the scene.

Acceptance was an additional cognitive strategy that pro-dommes used for mediating the disjuncture between the dramatization of their complete power and the reality of the arrangement. That is to say, they exposed their clients' complete powerlessness as a charade, only to shrug it off. "I don't mind if a person tops from the bottom as long as it's negotiated up front," one woman told me. "Someone who doesn't really want me to *be* dominant, they just want me to *play* at being dominant—fine, as long as I know that up front. I don't mind that. Sometimes it's easier, because then at least I can give them a good session instead of having to guess." A New York–based pro-domme in her mid-forties concurred that some clients do try to top from the bottom: "I don't mind that. I think that . . . it's an illusion of control, and they're paying for it. They need to be enjoying it. As long as they're not asking me to do things that are outside of my limits and that I'm uncomfortable with, I don't have a problem. They're not my [lifestyle] submissives. I don't require that they submit to me."

Power, Theater, and the Financial Component of the Exchange

It was common for pro-dommes who were in the lifestyle to draw a distinction between the level of topping from the bottom they would accept, and even expect, from a client, versus a man who was not paying for a session. While even lifestyle players contend that the submissive partner is really in control, in encounters where money changes hands the sub's agency is crystallized via his role as a scriptwriter. "Clients are a lot of work," one man who is both a pro and lifestyle dominant explained. "They're paying you for a service. They have basically a list of what they want done and don't want done, versus people you're just playing with. You always do what they say." The addition of money, informants who are also lifestylers indicate, can fundamentally alter the structure of the BDSM exchange. The transactional nature of these relationships, and the fact that clients have more leeway than personal subs to push back, serves to highlight aspects of the tension between dominant and submissive—as well as between professional and client in other social realms.

This distinction between interactions with clients and noncommercial exchanges with submissives, however, is not only the result of the financial component of the exchange. "Personal subs" are also more likely than clients to have had long-term relationships with their dommes and thus to have had greater opportunity to gain intimacy while testing out interests and limits. Further, as discussed, most clients do not prefer extreme forms of play, while experienced lifestyle subs and their dommes tend to play within fewer boundaries. One woman, a professional and lifestyle dominatrix in her late thirties, explained:

> In a paid session, even if they do that thing where they're like, "Oh, I just wanna please *you*," I stick to their interests. I'm not really gonna push their buttons, you know? . . . [Playing with my personal submissive] is a situation where I truly feel like, yeah, I *can* do whatever I want to do. It's not the sort of thing where they're like, "Oh yeah, I want *that*." Or, "No, I don't like needles." I just feel more comfortable in a wider range of activities, because I know this person, and I know that they truly want to please me, and I know more of their limits, if they even have any.

Sticking to a client's interests, ultimately, has a lot to do with the fact that he is paying for a service. "Client interactions are much more about trying to facilitate what the client is trying to experience, and so they're much more negotiated in that sense," a New York indie in her forties explained. "I see it as maintaining an illusion of control."

By drawing this particular boundary around erotic dominance in the commercial sphere, many informants cast its artifice in stark opposition to the "real" power dynamics involved in lifestyle play. As women who perform roles in dramatized relationships of power on a regular basis, pro-dommes often indicate that they are hyperaware of the control that they are giving up when they accede to their paying submissives' demands. Recall, for instance, the woman cited earlier in this chapter who told me that clients' enjoyment was the most important aspect of the exchange, adding, "They're not my [lifestyle] submissives. I don't require that they submit to me."

However, the spectrum between reality and performance and the spectrum between demanding client and fully "submissive" partner were not necessarily orthogonal dimensions in the minds of pro-dommes. In making this claim, I draw upon the words of the indie quoted earlier who would hang up on clients when they did not request session activities using the proper protocols ("Mistress, it would please me"). Within her narrative, commercial D/S *is* the real exchange; it is nonperformative, even in the context of a transactional relationship. Other informants, however, were more ambivalent about whether true power exchange was taking place on the dungeon floor. "While we're dommes, we're really there to satisfy *their* fantasies," one woman explained, in regard to commercial BDSM. "So I usually ask [what clients want]. Even if a person says, 'Anything you want, Miss!' I say, 'Be specific.'" However, when asked what she likes most about being a professional dominatrix, she replied that it is "being in power," adding, "It's really the power over another person. It's intoxicating."

Then she said, "I want you to extend your hand and almost touch my palm." We were sitting at a table in a diner, facing each other. I put up my hand so that our palms were about a centimeter apart.

"You feel that?" she asked me. "That's power. Yes. I have power. I have energy in my hand."

Although she maintained the feeling of being in power even as she pointed out that she was in the business of fulfilling other people's fantasies, clients told me that they came to the dominatrix to experience a *loss* of control—even as they paid to have their particular fantasies fulfilled. There is some evidence that this represents an inversion of the power-related illusion that takes place in prostitution. In a 1992 interview, one of Wendy Chapkis's informants, a sex worker named Lupe, characterized one of the differences between prostitution and professional erotic dominance in the following way: "With prostitution, I get to top from the bottom. I mean he may be fucking me, but I am absolutely running the fuck. It's an intricate dance, but I think it's one I play very well. I let the guy think he's in control. But I am" (Chapkis 1997, 193). In professional erotic dominance, conversely, there can be the illusion that the domme is fully in control, even as the client tops from the bottom.

The Ethnographer's Hustle

This jockeying for control that takes place between dominatrix and client, both inside and outside of the dungeon, is not only revealing of the micro-dynamics of other service interactions but also in many ways mirrors the struggle to get over that sometimes occurred during my interviews for this project. Here, I draw upon Sudhir Venkatesh's observation that both the ethnographer and his research subjects do a kind of "hustle," and that the "interaction of fieldworker and informant is itself potentially revealing of the local properties of social structure and may also be mined to illuminate chosen research questions" (2002, 92). Considering this particular researcher/informant relationship in terms of a D/S exchange lays bare a basic power dynamic underlying the ethnographic process, while at the same time informing our knowledge of the dungeon interaction.

Much has been made of the researcher's control over her research subject in a scientific context, and with good reason, considering the sordid history of human subjects abuse extending back to the Tuskegee syphilis study.[10] Discussing the "symbolic violence" the interviewer exerts over the interviewee, for instance, Pierre Bourdieu writes, "It is the investigator who starts the game and sets up its rules, and is usually the one who, unilaterally and without any preliminary negotiations, assigns the interview its objectives and uses. . . . This asymmetry is reinforced by a social asymmetry every time the investigator occupies a higher place in the social hierarchy of different types of capital, cultural capital in particular" (1999, 609). Fewer authors have considered the control that informants exert over the interview process, especially in cases, such as this study, in which the two parties are of relatively equal socioeconomic and educational status. At the time of this study, I was a graduate student in my late twenties, scraping by in New York City on roughly $20,000 a year. Ninety-eight percent of the pro-dommes interviewed for this project had gone to college, 72 percent were college graduates, and 39 percent had received graduate training. Though I had previously been unfamiliar with the BDSM Scene, I often moved in similar social circles as my informants.

Certainly, the researcher sets the rules of the game, but oftentimes, especially in cases of relative social symmetry, the informant can choose to ignore them or to set additional rules with which the investigator may or may not comply. "If you wish to speak with Me, you must abide by the following conditions," one pro-domme replied to the introductory e-mail for this study. She went on to ask to see the interview questions beforehand, and to have a copy of the interview tape as well as a written transcript. Several other pro-dommes made these same requests, and each time I complied with all except the first, explaining that they could choose not to answer any questions during the interview itself. One potential interviewee indicated that she had declined to speak with me because I had not complied with her request for a question list.

Furthermore, while I offered coffee or a snack as compensation for the interview, some potential interviewees wrote back and asked me to buy them a meal instead—which I always did. In addition, five of them initially agreed to my offer of coffee and then asked for food when I showed up. I had agreed, for instance, to purchase a beverage for one interviewee, whom I met at a Bay Area bookshop that also sold coffee and food.

"What would you like me to get you?" I asked her, gesturing to the drink list over the counter, and she replied that she would like a turkey sandwich and a large glass of milk. I looked at her.

"It's not expensive," she told me.

Whether this was an assertion of control on her part or whether she was just hungry at the time—or both—the fact remains that she negotiated these new terms and I complied. In my mind, she got over on me, maximizing her reward from the exchange. On the other hand, there were also plenty of informants who refused to take me up on my offer of coffee or even insisted upon buying me coffee or food—which itself may be seen (cynically) as a kind of power play, or (less cynically) as a friendly gesture, or even as a demonstration of empathy from former graduate students who had engaged in research themselves. Interestingly, the woman who requested the turkey sandwich also came to the interview bearing a gift for me: a silky black t-shirt.

Another interviewee agreed to my offer of coffee and then e-mailed me her very specific Starbucks order in advance of the interview. She requested that I be waiting at a table with the drink in advance of her arrival—mirroring the circumstance in which dommes ask that their clients bring coffee, candy, or cigarettes to their sessions. I did it.

While human subjects may be exposed to exploitation, they can also push back. Informants may want their stories to be told, and like many of these women who aspired to normalize or demystify BDSM, they may have a stake in the way these stories unfurl, but it is the researcher who truly needs the informants; ethnography cannot exist without them. While a client can generally move on to a different domme and dommes regularly reject clients for being "problems," as social scientists we cannot reject all potential interviewees who make us jump through hoops, or we fail to capture an important segment of our population. Thus, at the same time that I established inviolable limits for my behavior—no interview questions given beforehand, no expensive meals, no letting a male client "touch and rub" my feet in exchange for an interview—when necessary, I adopted the submissive role in order to "get a good transaction out of what [I] pursued."

One might argue that it is not clear who the domme is and who the sub is in the research exchange, but this is precisely the point: the exchange holds the potential to mirror the D/S relationship. While in the theater of the dungeon, it is very clear who is dominant and who is submissive, when it comes to the set of interactions that frame the dungeon relationship, as I have argued, these roles can become murky. Even Bourdieu, who characterizes the interview process as the investigator's "game," acknowledges that resistance is possible, arguing that interviewees can "impose their definition of the situation and turn to their advantage an exchange in which one of the stakes is the image they have of themselves, the image that they wish to give both to others and to themselves" (1999, 615). In contrast to my argument here, however, Bourdieu makes a claim about the information that the informant allows the social scientist to extract, rather than the control over the terms by which the interview takes place. In the case of this study, the power game took place within a context in which the interviewees' social, cultural, and intellectual capital arguably offered them increased possibilities for resistance.

Of course, it is probable that pro-dommes—women who regularly engaged in power games for a living—were more likely than other interviewees to attempt to get over on the researcher. In fact, one of the main arguments in this book is that they are adept at unfogging these relationships of power and control that may go unnoticed in daily life. Also, many of these women, by their own accounts, were particularly susceptible to feeling ill-used by interviewers, and thus their resistance to the interviewer's control may have been more pronounced. However, their uniqueness, in these respects, is precisely why their hustle with the ethnographer is so useful to observe. Not all research subjects attempt to get over on the researcher in the way that some dommes attempted to get over on me, but looking at interviews with women who are adept at getting over, because it is intimately involved in what they do as a job, highlights the struggle for dominance that can potentially take place during the ethnographic process.

Some of my informants clearly "dommed" me. But I let them, and I walked away with an extremely rich data set and the necessary tools to create what I believe is an accurate portrait of this corner of social life. By being particularly assertive about their demands for our interactions, these pro-dommes unlocked the potential for dominance that informants can possess in this kind of a qualitative study. Ethical governing bodies such as the Institutional Review Board have been created based on the premise that, as researchers, we have an inherent level of control over our informants that we could exercise with deleterious consequences if not checked. This is not a faulty premise, particularly in cases in which there is social asymmetry between researcher and informant. However, there is more happening in the space of the interview room than this premise would suggest. My informants' and my struggle to get over on each other was indicative of this fact that the control exercised during the ethnographic process can be dynamic, not unidirectional. In turn, this insight sheds light on the main topic of this chapter: the processes by which dominatrices and their submissives construct, negotiate, and set limits for their encounters.

Commercial D/S encounters are about dominance and submission in a different, and more nuanced, way than one might suspect. Because clients are paying for particular experiences, interactions with professionals are in general more heavily scripted than those in lifestyle play. To return to the culinary metaphor one final time, a client, selecting from the (literal or figurative) menu of activities, has an active role in determining the course of a scene. On the other hand, the dominatrix chooses which clients to take on and, according to the women with whom I spoke, she almost always negotiates the terms of a session, rather than serving up exactly what a client has ordered. The theatricalized nature of commercial D/S thus obfuscates the real underlying power dynamics at work in these exchanges.

At the same time, the major theoretical claim I have made in this chapter is that looking at commercial D/S as a performance can actually help us to zero in on these dynamics. Specifically, within the scripting process—the negotiation that occurs before the interaction itself—a great deal of the "action" of the domme/client struggle for control takes place. In making this argument, I have dismantled the one-dimensional image of the dominatrix "in control" of her submissive. However, I have also challenged the common conception among BDSM participants that the sub "really" directs the encounter. Pro-dommes' discourse about their work sheds light on a heavily nuanced dynamic—one that we can use as a lens through which to look at other types of interactions in new ways. It suggests that dommes and subs struggle to get over on each other, just like lawyers and their clients, fashion designers and their customers, and social scientists and their subjects. In the next chapter, I continue looking at the particularities of dominance as a professional exchange. By examining erotic dominance as a career, and dissecting pro-dommes' claims to professionalism, I shed light on the nature and importance of claims to professional authenticity within other occupational spheres.

All I Really Need to Know I Learned in BDSM Kindergarten: Dominatrix Careers

It's perfect sweatshirt-and-jeans weather in the Mission District of San Francisco, where a flame-haired woman in a black zip-up hoodie is telling me her story at an outdoor café. In her late thirties now, she entered the field of professional BDSM a decade ago for purely financial reasons. "I was working two jobs and wanted to make more money and work less time, and for some reason the page was open to, like, the sex pages of the local—like, the *SF Guardian* or something," she recalls, "and I saw an ad for a House that used to be in Oakland. . . . So at that point I interviewed at the House and the person did kind of a trial session with me. And then I started out as a pro-sub, and I did pro-subbing for years and learned the art of domination through the other women that were involved in the House."

"Were you at all involved in BDSM before that?" I ask.

"No," she says. "Not at all."

She takes a sip of her drink—a big beer that looks tempting on a sunny afternoon like this one. I'm devouring a salad, which she later insists on buying for me.

"Could you tell me about the first session you did?"

She tells me about the trial sub session with the man who owned the House. "There was bondage," she recounts, "and he was very psychological, so there was a lot of psychological stuff and then a little bit of pain. But I don't remember what he hit me with or whatever, at all." After pro-subbing at the House for a few years, she began working as a pro-domme and ultimately went independent.

Her narrative exemplifies one pathway by which women enter into the industry of professional erotic dominance. While my research interest, and subsequently my interviews, focused on pro-dommes' experiences in the dungeon, I did glean some information about these women's "pre-domme" work lives. Like the pro-domme described above, thirteen of the women I interviewed (about 20 percent of the sample), chose to begin working in a dungeon without either prior BDSM experience or experience performing erotic labor. Twenty-two others (roughly 33 percent of the sample) came to professional BDSM via another form of erotic labor. This percentage includes those who had both engaged in paid work of an erotic nature and had lifestyle backgrounds in BDSM. The largest percentage (thirty-one women, or about 47 percent of the sample) had lifestyle backgrounds but had not participated in other forms of erotic labor prior to entering a dungeon.

This chapter examines professional erotic dominance as a career, beginning with the occupational histories of three women who represent these archetypes and proceeding to a discussion of how the "career" aspects of commercial D/S shed light on the nuances of control within other, non-erotically-oriented, service industries. Pro-dommes put forth the narrative that success as a dominatrix requires a particular type of cultural capital. In a related vein, the profession is uniquely structured around the concepts of knowledge and training, which are intimately connected to pro-dommes' conceptions of their own authenticity as dominatrices. Thinking about erotic dominance in terms of training, skill, and professionalism allows us to use this area of social life to look into claims to professionalism within service-sector interactions more generally. Although pro-dominance is not a "profession" in the strict sociological sense, it can be used to unfog the microdynamics of dyadic interactions in which one party possesses the professional expertise and the other possesses both the demand and the economic means that have set the interaction into motion.

While the informant quoted above is an example of someone who came into the industry without a background in either BDSM or erotic labor, women like her represented a minority in this sample. A larger percentage of pro-dommes had experience with at least one other form of compensated eroticism, which in some way led them to pursue professional BDSM. I spoke with one of these women at her dungeon in New York City, where she told me she had originally been "horrified" by the prospect of professional dominance. In her twenties now, she'd initially read about a dominatrix in the *New Yorker* during her early teens. "I remember being quite disturbed by the article, actually," she recalled, "particularly because the woman was talking about crush fetishists, and she talked about a client bringing in a mouse and she talked about crushing the mouse with her shoe, and I was really horrified by that." She first met a pro-domme when she was sixteen, through a leftist feminist organization unrelated to BDSM. "Some of them were sex workers, and it did shape my view of sex work, in that the first sex workers that I really got to know were these, you know, feminist, educated, empowered, not-exploited women. So it definitely gave me the idea that I could do sex work and it didn't—that sex work didn't have to be, you know, a twelve-year-old trafficked girl in Thailand." Around the same time, she was also beginning to experiment with BDSM, playing with a lover she had met through the organization. Then when she was nineteen and in college, she needed a summer job and went looking on Craigslist. She ultimately started working at a "pay-for-play" fetish party, which she described as "super seedy."

The first activity in which she participated at one of these parties was a spanking session "with this little man." She was comfortable with spanking because it was something she had done in her personal life. The management neither encouraged nor discouraged "extras," like hand jobs, oral sex, and "foot jobs," since the money they made was from the cover charge at the door. "So they didn't care if you were fucking people or not fucking people, or giving hand jobs or not giving hand jobs." She added:

> There wasn't really pressure from the other girls, either, except that people wanted to make sure that you were kind of having a baseline price. Like I remember once I was in one of the little gauzy booths, which were semi-sheer, and I had someone—I was sitting down, and I had someone kneeling in front of me, and I was doing nipple torture on him. And one of the girls saw the position from the back, and she thought he was, like, going down on me. And afterwards she said to me, "I just wanna make sure—like, you got at *least* eighty bucks for that, right?" [*laughs*]. So, you know, it was really seedy. It was a place where you could go down on somebody for eighty bucks.

She worked at the pay-for-play parties once a week for about two months before going back to school in the fall. At the parties, she had been introduced to a man in the lifestyle ("He would get super drunk and just like rant about how all the girls were strippers and hookers and that it wasn't real BDSM"), who encouraged her to become a professional dominatrix and told her how to apply to Houses. When she returned to school in Chicago, she took his advice. Although she had participated in BDSM in her private life, she told me that her first session at the House was a kind of trial by fire. The client requested something she had never done in private play—a session in which the dominatrix wears a dildo and penetrates the man anally:

> This guy came in; he wanted to do a strap-on session. [The other girls] were like, "You can go do it." I was like, "No! I've never done a strap-on session! I don't know what I'm doing! I don't know how to do it!" And they're like, "It's not rocket science. You just put on the harness. You put on the dildo. You stick

it in there." So, um, that's what I did, and it was just *awful*. It was just *so* awful. They gave me these, like, eight-inch platform heels to wear, and I fell on
them in the session, and I got this enormous bruise on my calf. We did it in
the cross-dressing room, and in the cross-dressing room there was this raised
platform with a stripper pole on it, for the guys to twirl around, which was
really fun to do. And I tied his wrists to the stripper pole, and he was down on
all fours, and I came up behind him. And I couldn't get the angle quite right,
so I took a step down on the stairs that led up to the platform, and I fell. And
he was still tied to the pole, so he couldn't see, but he was like, "Mistress! Mistress! Are you okay?" [*laughs*]. And I'm like, "What? What? You think because
I fell down I'm going to cry, because I'm a little pussy, like you are?" Like, I
tried to make it part of the session. But it sucked [*laughs*].

She told me that the House wasn't "shady," in that "the girls didn't do
nudity, [and] no extras." However, she concluded that, overall, working there
was a negative experience for her. "We didn't really have a training program,"
she recalled. "The turnover was really high, so that there weren't a lot of people who'd been there a long time to learn from. By the time I left, I'd been
there the longest out of anyone, aside from the Head Mistress, who was also
the owner." After she left, she went indie in Chicago for six months and then
moved to New York, where she continued to work independently. When I interviewed her, she had been doing dominance work professionally for about
two and a half years.

While this domme's prior experience with erotic labor was in an area
closely connected to professional dominance—and other pro-dommes had
worked in related fields, such as fetish modeling, before entering the industry—I interviewed women who had come to BDSM from a diversity of erotic
industries. Some had been exotic dancers or peepshow performers, and a few
had worked the phones for different sex industries, including escort services
and massage parlors. However, only one reported having had sex for money
prior to becoming a pro-domme. Additionally, while the woman described
above had both a background in BDSM and a history with erotic labor before moving to professional dominance, more often, lifestylers in this sample
lacked backgrounds in sexually oriented industries. Their experiences with
unpaid D/S led them to pursue careers in the dungeon.

I interviewed one woman from this latter group over lunch at a Thai restaurant in Midtown Manhattan. An indie in her early thirties who had been
a pro-domme for about six years, she recalled that the first D/S relationship
that she had witnessed was between her grandmother and a male admirer:

He'd come over, they'd have coffee, and he had to come over with a tribute.
She didn't call it a tribute but, my God, he better show up with whatever she

told him to buy, whether it was coffee, paper towels—whatever she needed. Maybe twenty bucks. Maybe a Metrocard. Whatever the hell it was. And I was very, very young at the time, so I didn't quite understand their relationship. He wasn't a boyfriend; it was clear about that. There wasn't any sex. I mean, he would love to see her naked, but she wouldn't allow him to see her naked. The best he ever got was her in the bathtub covered up by, like, bubbles and a washcloth, so all he could see was her from the neck up. Now as an adult I realize that's a D/S relationship. Hell yeah, grandma! [*laughs*]

The woman also personally experimented with dominance at an early age ("In grade school I used to tie up other children and stuff like that."). By the time she was out of her teens, she had had begun translating that childhood play into erotic D/S in her personal relationships as well as out in the Scene. She also started going to swingers clubs. Around the same time, she began working at a series of jobs—waitressing, temping, secretarial work, and for a few years, stand-up comedy ("By the way, all the comics you see on TV, I know their kinks. I know who likes cross-dressers and transvestites. I know all that dirty stuff."). She felt dissatisfied by "vanilla" work, however, "because I don't like people telling me what to do, especially when they don't know what the fuck they're doing."[1] Hoping to turn her hobby into a career, she began answering ads for mistresses and ultimately went to work in one of the New York Houses. "And the problem was that they expected me to do hand jobs or show my tits and I was like, 'Wow, that's so not D/S. That's a hooker and a stripper.'" She "jumped" to another dungeon where those practices were not going on, but eventually she realized that she would prefer working for herself, and she went independent.

BDSM Kindergarten: Professional Debut and the Larger Dungeon

As suggested by the career trajectories traced above, while women can enter into this industry "cold," without prior experience with BDSM, experiential training is generally considered necessary for one to gain comfort with, and excel at, the profession. Like all three of the pro-dommes discussed above, many women gain entry into the field of erotic dominance by working at larger dungeons before going independent. This trend mirrors the career trajectories that appear within other service industries. A friend of mine who is a personal trainer, for instance, told me that it is common in his profession to start out working for a larger gym, gain experience and a client base, and then go work for oneself. Hairdressers, in the same vein, can also work at salons, building up knowledge and clientele, before becoming free agents.

As discussed, the primary distinction between an indie and a dungeon domme is that a dungeon domme works for a particular House and is hired by the owner or manager. The House takes a cut from every session she does there, supplies her with equipment, advertises, does initial client screening, and books her sessions. Indies are self-employed and do sessions at one of three types of spaces. (1) Most Houses, in addition to being staffed by dungeon dommes, rent out rooms to independents, for a flat, per-hour rate. Less commonly, there are also Houses, usually run by pro-dommes or former pro-dommes, that rent only to indies and do not have permanent staffs. (2) Some women rent apartments or rehearsal spaces for sessions. (3) Rarely, pro-dommes use their residences as their primary session spaces. Three individuals in the study fell into that category.

Independent dommes for the most part do their own advertising and booking, though some who rent space at unstaffed Houses get business through those locations. The pro-domme who rents space at the House described in the introduction, for instance, says she does 80 to 85 percent of her own booking and the remainder through the House receptionist.

The number of professional dominatrices working in either New York or San Francisco at any given time is almost impossible to determine because there is such a high rate of employee turnover at the larger Houses and some "retired" dommes continue to advertise but rarely take sessions. For about six months during my field research, I joked, with only slight exaggeration, that I couldn't go to any social events in my personal life without meeting someone who had some kind of a social tie to a current or former professional dominatrix. Perhaps this is unsurprising given the homophily of my crowd of twenty-something liberals and the sample, but this also included family events and academic functions. At a dinner party in Washington, DC, for instance, I found myself seated next to a young conservative lawyer in a bow tie who told me that he had once "accidentally" gone out on a date with a dominatrix. He added that, although he "obviously" could not continue dating her, he prolonged their dinner because he was fascinated by the details of her profession. One study of BDSM participants from the early 1980s estimated that there were about 2,500 pro-dommes in the United States at any given time, and that approximately 100,000 to 150,000 men visited them in a given year (Scott 1997, xii). In November of 2008, an industry directory on the Internet had active listings for 184 pro-dommes based in the New York City metropolitan area and 47 based in the San Francisco Bay Area. There were active listings for eleven Houses in New York and three in San Francisco.[2] This directory is not exhaustive, however; some of the women whom I contacted through snowball sampling, for instance, are not listed on it.

At the time of their interviews, eleven (16.7 percent) of the women in this sample were working in larger dungeons. Fifty-five (83.3 percent) were independent dommes, but twenty-five, about half of them, had worked in at least one House before becoming self-employed. In sum, more than half—thirty-six (54.5 percent)—of the women I interviewed were working, or had worked, in the larger dungeons. However, because the sample is skewed toward those with longer career tenures, and dungeon dommes are more likely than indies to "burn out" and quit after relatively short periods of time, this sample likely underestimates the percentage of all pro-dommes who have worked at Houses.

Why do so many dominatrix careers begin at the Houses? First, working at a House allows a woman to enter into the industry with little financial investment on her part while creating a name for herself within the community. The dungeon provides her advertising, client base, and tools of the trade. Many indies included the tagline "formerly of" in their Internet advertisements, promoting their ties to particular Houses. Larger dungeons also provide free on-the-job training. Because it was so common to gain basic proficiency at a dungeon, then to expand upon one's repertoire as an indie, pro-dommes on both coasts referred to the Houses as "BDSM kindergarten." One thirty-four-year-old independent domme who had begun her career at a House told me, "There's this whole sort of hierarchy, where that's supposed to be kindergarten, and you graduate to high school or college or whatever. When you're independent, you can be a star." Another indie, recalling her prior work in a larger dungeon, explained, similarly:

> It was like BDSM kindergarten in a way. You learn the basics of a lot of things. There was no one there doing electrical play. We didn't have the equipment to do—well, we could do *pretty* heavy bondage, but we didn't have, like, a lot of really expensive equipment. We didn't have, like, a rack to stretch people on. We weren't supposed to do suspension in the space. Only two of us did piercing, and there was no wax play. . . . It's just not as edgy. We didn't really push people as much. It was more like your friendly neighborhood grandma's dungeon.

Her assertion that larger dungeons do not "push people as much" may explain why the client profiles from the New York dungeon demonstrate an aversion to "extreme" forms of pain. It also suggests that individuals involved in commercial BDSM—both from the demand and production side—begin their tenures in the industry by participating in less extreme forms of play and then move on to "edgier" or "harder" activities as their endurance and tastes develop. Thus, indies (who have typically been in the industry longer) are likely to play harder, and clients who are into harder play may be more likely to visit them.[3] During interviews, both pro-dommes and clients repeatedly made this observation.

Over the period of time that they are in the industry, then, it appears that not only are dommes trained to be dommes but clients are trained to be clients, typically starting slowly and developing their knowledge about their own erotic tastes over the course of time. While sometimes a House client is "loyal" to a particular woman in that House, more often such clients tend to "hop" from domme to domme. In contrast, indies are more likely to have clients who see them exclusively. Some indies in my sample explicitly requested that their clients be loyal to them. It seems that, over time, not only does knowledge increase but the cathexes of particular domme/sub dyads grow stronger.

Another reason to begin one's career at a House, my informants told me, was because getting a job at a dungeon was relatively easy in comparison to other avenues of employment. One woman, who had been in charge of the hiring for a New York dungeon, told me, "Really, as long as they knew what it was, and as long as they had a schedule that we could work around, I'd hire them. We were desperate. . . . As long as you look all right and you're not, you know, completely pathological, you're gonna get the job."

In part because it was common to use the expertise one had gained in a House as the springboard for an indie career, employee turnover at the larger dungeons was high. The standard amount of time women spend at the larger dungeons is about a year, according to my interviewees. At the end of that time, more often than not, they leave the industry. One pro-domme, who had worked in a House for about six months before going independent and now shared a space with several other indies, told me,

> It's interesting. If you're at a House and you've been working there for six months, you're *super* experienced compared to most of the people there, 'cause most people don't work at a House for more than six months. But, as an indie, I really feel like the baby here. The woman who owns the space has been working for, like, fifteen years and a lot of the other women who rent here have been working about that long.

Pro-dommes in this sample who had worked in Houses generally had done it for at least a year, however, suggesting that those who ultimately go indie tend to stay at the dungeons longer than those who leave the industry.

In addition to losing dommes who go independent, Houses have high rates of turnover for several reasons. The first is that employees become disenchanted when their experiences do not match up with their financial expectations. At the Houses, women are commonly expected to come in for long stretches of time, and they only get compensated for the hours they actually spend in session. An employee could conceivably come in for a full day shift, see no clients, and leave empty-handed after eight hours. One indie in her early twenties, who had formerly worked at one of the larger dungeons, explained,

> We would tell people who interviewed at my House, "Oh, you make seventy-five dollars an hour." And people would think, "Oh! Well, the shifts are like eight to twelve hours. That means I'm makin' bank!" And it's, like, no. No. No, you're not. 'Cause you might only be working two hours that day. You don't get *anything* for just being there. . . . People come in, and they think they're going to make a ton of money really fast, and it's just not like that. I think a lot of people quit because they're just not making enough money.

A New York dungeon domme explained, similarly, "I feel like that can be really tiresome, when you waste your time and leave with nothing. I just feel sometimes like that's going to make me quit one day, but it hasn't happened yet."

Others quit, according to my informants, because they grow weary of splitting their session fees with the House. Still others leave the Houses because they realize BDSM, or commercial BDSM, is not for them. Some also leave because they have romantic partners who disapprove of their jobs or because of "drama" among the employees. As one woman recalled, "I mean, in Houses, you've got a lot of strong personalities together in a small space. You're mostly hanging out together all day. You can't leave. At least where I worked, there was a lot of drama, a lot of personal drama."

An additional reason for the high turnover rates was the practice of "dungeon hopping"—as illustrated in the case history above of the domme who "jumped" to another House when she was asked to do nudity and hand jobs. It was particularly common for a dominatrix to switch Houses when, as in her case, she was working at a place where "extras" were part of the deal. Oppositely, some left to pursue other avenues of erotic labor. Informants commonly made references to former colleagues from the Houses who had gone on to become strippers or escorts. One former dungeon domme from San Francisco told me, for instance, "For a lot of women at [the House], it was just one stop in their whole journey through sex work."

The Role of the Internet in Professional Debut

There is currently an online infrastructure—including, but not limited to, chat rooms, message boards, listserves, e-zines, pornography, shopping, social networking sites, and blogs—that has a role in organizing real-life D/S. Web advertising is also a key part of a domme's entry into the current market— a development that distinguishes this project from earlier studies of BDSM communities, many of which were based upon pre-Internet fieldwork. In her participant-observation and interviews from the early 1980s, for instance, Scott found that pros largely advertised in local "sexually oriented" news- papers (1997, 209). Today few women advertise in any kind of print media, and those who do also maintain presences on the Internet. This shift from print to the web, some women suggested, has created a threat to the larger dun- geons. "It's much easier for a girl to start off independent now," one woman told me. "A lot of girls do it on Craigslist." Many women who had been in the Scene for a relatively long time spoke disdainfully of women who, with little or no prior knowledge of BDSM, start off indie by buying basic equipment and advertising their services online. Such statements were key elements of their narratives about what constitutes an "authentic" pro-domme.

Women who came to the industry prior to the advent of the Internet reported fundamentally different experiences with professional debut than those who had become pro-dommes more recently. Not only had the Old Guard debuted through a different medium, but their initial access to infor- mation about the business—and their clients' access to information about them—had been significantly more limited. When asked how she found out about professional dominance, a Bay Area pro-domme in her late fifties replied:

> How did I find out? There was no finding out. There was no Internet. There
> was not anything like that. It was 1981. How did I find out? I found out by
> coming out into the Scene and finding out that I really enjoyed playing, and
> I found out that I could bottom and top and that I really enjoyed the energy
> of topping and so I set myself up with [another domme], and there were very
> few women doing that. There were maybe about ten women in all of San Fran-
> cisco. You wouldn't know that now, right?

Her estimate of "about ten women" may be on the low side; Scott—who was coincidentally doing fieldwork in San Francisco in 1981—estimated that there was an average of twenty dommes per major city at the time (1997, xii). Regardless, as noted, in 2008 I found forty-seven Bay Area dommes who had advertised on just one website. It is clear that, at least in part because the Internet has facilitated professional debut, there are larger numbers of pro- dommes competing for clients in American cities.

A common contention among older informants was that the Internet has "killed the business." While I observed a thriving industry during the period of my fieldwork, their claim makes practical sense. Today, as many informants pointed out, potential clients can meet play partners on the Internet or have "cyber D/S" relationships in lieu of visits to the dungeon. On the other hand, because the population of pro-dommes has increased, it is also likely that individual dominatrices perceive a diminution in subs because there is increased competition for clients.

The web has also greatly increased the accessibility of dominatrices to potential clients. A potential client may now find out detailed information about most professional dominatrices, including reviews, from any personal computer, without having to subscribe to a specialty publication. "The Internet has taken the place of community in that you can ask around about somebody and check their reputation," one woman told me. "Pre-Internet, it was hard to get background information about people." Specialty websites also nurture the fetishes that support the industry; becoming part of online communities may make men more comfortable with their predilections and more likely to explore them with professionals.

In short, the Internet arguably *creates* clients. One male client and participant in the Scene who identifies as straight but plays with both men and women described to me a rendezvous he had arranged via America Online in the late 1990s:

> When I was eighteen, I was looking for anyone to play with, really. Anybody who would play with somebody who was friggin' eighteen. And so I went to play with this guy and it just turned really awkward. He took me to McDonald's for dinner, and then we went back to his place and I realized—oh my God, I'm in, like, Joe Schmoe's house. He could be like any guy on Long Island. But it was *better*. He was a politician. . . . And all of his reelection posters were, like, on the walls of his house. And the magnets were covering his fridge. And there's photos of his family, his wife, and I'm like, "Oh my God, what am I doing here?"[4]

This informant told me that, while he had struggled with his fetishes as a young teenager, he became more comfortable because of the Internet. "AOL in its heyday—it was like the only thing," he recalled. "It was the breeding ground for sexual deviance. It really was. Now it's everywhere. It's so easy."

Session Fees

Despite the accessibility to both pro-dommes and clients that the Internet facilitates, it is relatively unlikely that a woman will be able to make a living only by working as a dominatrix. Most women claimed not to know how much money they take in from professional dominance in a given year, indicating that it varies widely on a weekly basis. Those who answered the question cited gross estimates averaging about $1,000 a week, but these also tended to be the women who were logging more session time.

In the dungeon, payment is referred to as a "session fee" or, more commonly among independent dommes, a "tribute." Independent dommes, who have higher overhead costs, charge more than the average dungeon domme. The independent dommes in this sample charged an average of about $250 per hour.[5] The dungeons charged, on average, about $180, from which the dommes took home about half. Some Houses have payment systems tiered by tenure; the longer a woman works there, the higher the percentage of the fee she takes home. Some informants also told stories of bargaining with dungeon owners for a higher percentage of their session fees.

Additionally, dommes charge more for certain types of sessions. As one twenty-year-old dungeon domme told me, "The place that I work at, it varies because for certain activities you get a specific amount of money. So for example, if you do a regular session, which is basically just like corporal or foot worship, then you get $65 an hour, but if it's more sensual then there may be some nudity . . . and then it's $85 an hour. If it's anal play, which is, like, fisting or dildo play, then you get $105 an hour." (The numbers she cites are the domme's cut; the House charges "anywhere from $165 to $200 an hour.") Charging more for nudity is standard among dommes who do nudity, but the activity which most often garners higher session fees is defecating on a client—known as "brown showers," or simply "brown." Of the women in this sample who did "brown" (the majority told me that they did not), all charged more for it, except for the one self-proclaimed "toilet mistress," who said it was her specialty.

It is also common practice to charge more for sessions with clients who have been difficult to deal with in the past, for wrestling sessions, which were also typically shorter sessions, and for sessions requiring a more elaborate setup. One Manhattan-based indie, for instance, told me she charges more if she needs to purchase equipment: "Like, if I'm doing a mummification that's a hardcore mummification, I might need to get equipment for that." She specified that she typically uses duct tape and plastic wrap to mummify her clients, but that "hardcore" sessions may involve medical gauze and plaster of paris; she added, "Would you go to your doctor or dentist and expect to pay the same for an implant as you would for a cleaning? No." Finally, the price is often elevated if more intensive cleanup is required. An independent domme told me that she charges more for messy scenarios like "splosh":

"Splosh" is playing with food usually; it's getting messy. The funny thing is that it's more fetish than—well, it *can* be power play, I don't know why I say that—but more often than not it's not about power play, it's about playing with food and getting messy. The guy has a fetish for watching girls smear creamed corn all over [themselves]. Or pieing. Who knew? The day I got an e-mail about *that*, I had no idea, and I was like, "You wanna throw pies at me? Yes. Let's do it." I was all for it.

At the other end of the spectrum, some dominatrices set lower fees for sessions that are less labor-intensive for themselves. One interviewee told me, as we sat in her basement dungeon on Long Island, "If the guy really wants to be tied to that table and I'm not doing anything except monitoring him for safety—I never leave the room but I'm not hands-on and I'm not using equipment—then I will charge the full rate for the first hour, and then however many hours he wants to be tied up with minimal contact I'll charge a lower rate for that." Another interviewee explained, similarly, "The only time I've gone lower [in price] is when someone just wants to be babysat in bondage, so I'm not really doing anything except making sure they don't die in their bondage [*laughs*]. Which is fine with me! Or, like, if they're sleeping overnight in a cage or something."

The larger Houses also had promotional deals. For example, according to one informant, her New York City dungeon had a "two-for Fridays" package, which meant that "for $185 you either got two girls together for an hour or one girl for two hours." Another dungeon offered a "Coffee & Discipline" deal, advertising on its website "Fresh Coffee and $20 off all appointments from 10:30 AM to 1:00 PM!" And, one winter, an independent domme in New York gave discounted sessions to clients who brought in coats, which she then donated to a holiday clothing drive.

Finally, on top of their session fees, it is also a common practice for clients to give dommes tips. Dungeon dommes are more likely to get tipped than independents, perhaps because their session fees are generally lower. Tips typically range from $20 to $100, though they vary widely; the women with whom I spoke reported having received everything from a $3,000 "Christmas bonus" to a roll of quarters ("That was in a session where I got paid in rolled coins. He'd been saving his coins for a long time. It was so sweet!").

About half of the women I interviewed indicated that sessions were their primary sources of income, but for only about a quarter of the sample—many of whom were also attending school—sessions were their only form of income. Among the half of the interviewees who had other primary sources of income, jobs in offices and hospitals were most common.

Interviewees also commonly asserted that they brought in additional income by translating their knowledge of BDSM into related fields—for instance, fetish modeling, hosting Scene parties, making and selling tools of the trade, teaching workshops, or producing BDSM and fetish videos. Throughout my fieldwork, I attended the tapings of several of these videos. In one, for instance, a real-life female lawyer in a cheetah-print thong leotard wrestled a real-life doctor in spandex shorts, pausing occasionally to tell the camera what a weakling he was.

While professional erotic dominance could be a lucrative profession, and there were women who claimed to be making upward of $100,000 a year, women who made such claims were the outliers. More commonly, pro-dommes described their work as hand-to-mouth, and indies, particularly, emphasized their large overhead costs in the form of space rental and tools of the trade. While a handful of women had regular clients who provided them with living stipends, everyone else described the business as cyclical. One woman from Manhattan whose primary form of income is professional erotic dominance, which she does for "at least ten hours a week," described it as "a roller coaster," adding, "One week you're riding really high and fast, and then you're down. Financially it all evens out at the end of the year." A Bay Area indie told me, similarly, "I like making a lot of money for a little amount of time, although it's still totally feast or famine. Like, you really have to *love* it to make it your primary source of income, because you don't know where your next dollar is going to come from."

"New Girls" and the Structure of the Scene

Most women begin in professional erotic dominance on the crest of the career roller coaster ride. When one debuts in the industry, it is common to experience a "feeding frenzy," as local clients gravitate toward the novelty of a different dominant. Pro-dommes who had started out as indies told me that, at the beginning of their careers, they had been deluged by calls from clients with "outlandish" or "crazy" requests and those hoping for sexual extras. One pro-domme who specializes in wrestling sessions explained, for instance, "Especially when you first put your profile up, you get the crazy inquiries. The people that, like, just wait to see if the new girl will do the thing that no one will do. So you get, like, competitive boxing [requests]—where I'm not a competitive boxer and of course I'm not going to let you hit me, when I have an office job where I can't be bruised to high hell." At the other end of the spectrum, informants who'd had relatively long careers spoke about the effect of their decrease in novelty. While a prolonged career helps one to build up a foundation of regular clients, it can also limit the number of clients one ultimately sees. One indie, whose client volume had tapered off in the decade she had been working professionally, told me that she attributed this not to her age, but to the fact that she was "old news." Contributing to this effect was the fact that women who had been in the business for a number of years sometimes refused to take on new clients at all.

One might wonder what is to prevent a particular pro-domme from reinventing herself with a new name and identity in order to reinvigorate her own appeal and increase her client volume. The fact that this strategy simply does not work is a testament to the fully integrated nature of the Scene. The Scene is made cohesive not only through the constellation of social networks that exist within it but also via the overarching concept of BDSM that, along with its particular mores and argot, shapes these interactions on a macro level.

BDSM's practices, terms, and mores are solidified and reaffirmed through books on the subject, as well as by print magazines and websites devoted to kink—ranging from BDSM as a whole to highly specific fetishes, such as body trampling and pedal pumping.[6] Howard Becker, examining sadomasochistic photographs in a catalog, makes the point that BDSM adherents have their own argot to describe their particular social organization. "Ordinary words were used in a technical shorthand designed to whet specific tastes," Becker explains. "One does not acquire a taste for 'bondage photos' without having learned what they are and how they may be enjoyed" (1963, 31). There is an international market for these kinds of pictures and for the practices they depict. One dungeon owner in New York City, for instance, also manages dungeons in other cities and has organized theme parties in Los Angeles, San Francisco, Amsterdam, the Caribbean, and Thailand. Some of the women in this study talked about having worked on BDSM-themed cruises, as well as abroad. Many more of them described having traveled to other US cities—most commonly New York, San Francisco, Los Angeles, and Boston—to offer sessions. This circulation of key players facilitates the flow of information between local pockets.

The core terminology involved in this social world thus transcends location and even temporality, which explains why most of the concepts found in the Weinberg, Williams, and Moser study of nearly thirty years ago are still applicable today and why the results of studies of SM participants display uniformity across cultural contexts. In an analysis of questionnaire data from a self-identified sadomasochistic sample of 178 men in the United States, for example, Moser and Levitt (1987, 325) point to the "striking" similarity between their results and the results of Spengler's study a decade earlier in West Germany. To be clear, I am not arguing that BDSM communities are always structured in the same way across historical circumstances and social environments. For instance, the Internet aided in vastly expanding the scope of professional D/S in the United States. I *am* making the point, however, that many of the core terms and procedures (for instance, the use of safe words) that make up BDSM culture remain the same across these contexts.

Successfully appearing "new" within this social sphere by changing one's identity without, for instance, switching cities would be virtually impossible. As one pro-domme put it, in the New York BDSM Scene, "Everybody knows everybody." Although it is a rarity, an identity change is not unheard of. One trans male involved in the industry, for instance, changed his Scene name after he transitioned. While he was able to successfully switch personas—aided by a dramatic change in self-presentation, including a double mastectomy—he reported that he would occasionally be told, "You look familiar. Don't you have a sister in the Scene?"

Easing into the Industry

Pro-dommes' recollections of their first session experiences were generally connected to the pathways by which they had entered into the business. Unsurprisingly, those with some lifestyle experience indicated that they had been more comfortable with the technical aspects of their first professional scenes than those with none, although they were sometimes innocent about the sexual aspects of the industry. One woman, who had gone to a House with a lifestyle, but not a sex-work, background, recalled, "When I first started out, I was really naïve about all of this. I didn't even know the guys would be naked. I didn't even know that they could touch themselves. . . . And they're there in a condom so they're not dripping, but I didn't know they could masturbate. I thought it would just be me prancing around in fetish clothes." Further, even if they had lifestyle experience, new pro-dommes could be asked to perform specific acts with which they were unfamiliar, like the strap-on scene described earlier in this chapter.

To ease new dommes into the industry, some Houses initially gave them less demanding scenes. The former dungeon manager explained, "We'd always try to start girls off with an easy session. The idea was we'd always have the first session be, like, a foot-worship [session], or a smoking session where they just blow smoke in the guy's face."

They'd do that for the whole hour?
Yeah. It was always hard on the nonsmokers. They'd come out looking green.
  At the same time, though, it's a bit easier than doing some complicated bondage thing that you're not even sure how to do.

Those who had consented to do switch sessions often started out either entirely as pro-subs or by switching; such sessions are deemed less technically challenging for the woman. Some dommes who had started out by subbing emphasized that they had gained a unique perspective from being on the opposite end of the action. One Bay Area woman told me that she used to volunteer as a "bottom"—the recipient of actions such as whipping and spanking—for BDSM classes early in her career: "The experience of bottoming, you get so much out of it that, if you're smart, you can translate it to topping."[7] For similar reasons, a number of the dommes in my sample said that they would try out new implements on themselves before using them on clients.[8]

Professionalizing Erotic Dominance: Training and Expertise

Bottoming was just one activity in which pro-dommes engaged in order to increase their level of expertise. Some pro-dommes also indicated that, at the beginning of their careers, they had familiarized themselves with the literature on BDSM—most commonly Wiseman's *SM101*, Larry Townsend's *The Leatherman's Handbook*, and the erotic novel *Story of O*. They also talked about attending demonstrations offered by local organizations or private classes from more seasoned dommes, as well as traveling to BDSM-themed conventions. One informant, who began her career as an indie, recalled, "When I hit the ground here [in San Francisco] I was taking every class I could—sometimes three times a week—and I was reading and just learning as much as I could." I spoke with a woman in San Francisco who runs an annual workshop for professional female dominants. She explained that, in addition to teaching skills, "We have business and law and safety and taxes and how to present yourself," adding that they also instruct in everything from "negotiation skills" to "what archetype you are in Jungian thought." Other pro-dommes had taught classes on specific aspects of D/S such as wax play (dripping hot wax on a submissive), rope bondage, mummification, genital piercing, electric-shock stimulation, and medical-fetish scenarios, as well as general BDSM classes with titles like "How to Do a Scene."

While there is no formalized apprenticeship program within this industry, some of the women I interviewed had entered into "apprenticeship" or "mentorship" relationships with more experienced dominants, either to get started in the business or to learn a specific skill. One pro-domme, who rents dungeon space in her mentor's house, explained.

> She's taught me a lot. Just talking to her, too, she's always coming up with, like—"Well, have you tried *this*?" I'm like, "Really? That's *sick*! Yeah, I'll try

that next time. Thank you." And you get ideas, too, just playing with other
women. And that's part of the fun of having the Girl Gang and getting in touch
with other women because everybody's a little different. Everybody's brain is
gonna come up with something slightly different.

Learning skills from other dominatrices with whom one socialized—as in the
case of this informant's Bay Area "Girl Gang"—was far more common than
apprenticing. An indie based in New Jersey who is active in the New York
Scene told me, similarly, "I've never taken an actual class. It's more through
other mistresses; we all teach each other stuff. 'Oh, I'm using this now—
wanna try it?' Or, 'Here's a technique,' and we show each other stuff. But
it's always a learning process." Some of those who had worked in the larger
dungeons also had begun their careers by "co-topping"—dominating a client alongside one or more other mistresses— or sitting in on other women's
scenes. I spoke to a dungeon domme, for instance, who had learned how to
play with electric shocks by watching one of her housemates do a session:
"She explained to me how it worked and what to do and certain spots which
I should use it on, and certain spots don't use it on."

A common sentiment among the women with whom I spoke, however, was
that many women in the industry—particularly at the Houses—lack the necessary skill to be doing this work. The contention that, among dungeon dommes (especially younger women), skill is not held as sacred as it is by the older
indies, is supported by the dungeon employee's statement that "as long as you
look all right and you're not . . . completely pathological, you're gonna get the
job." However, even at her dungeon, new employees were required to attend an
interactive instructional session with an experienced dominatrix. In fact, most
dungeon dommes who sat for interviews with me had gone through some type
of training—even if it was just in the form of co-topping with or watching
other dommes in the House, as in the electric-play session described above.

Once she gains expertise in a given area such as electric play, a pro-domme
may go on to become known for that particular activity and carve out a niche
market for herself. Others specialize based upon skills they have acquired
prior to becoming pro-dommes (for instance, a woman who spoke Japanese
and Russian became known for her interrogation scenes) or by virtue of the
pathway by which they entered into the profession. One woman recalled that
she took her first step toward becoming a domme when she was in her forties
and was employed at a massage parlor:

> And one day a regular customer called and asked if any girls would give an
> enema. And I asked the girls, and they were all like, "Ick!" So I said, "Sorry,

nobody here will do that." And he said, "Well, what about you?" And I said, "I don't work the rooms." Because I worked the phones. I was married then. But no one was doing the enema. So he came in. He had his own equipment. I did an enema. That was that.

Although she engages in other aspects of D/S, she identifies and advertises primarily as an enema domme.

Other women become known not for particular activities but for their wardrobes or their session personas; there are "latex dommes" and "mommy dommes," for instance. Some entire Houses cater to niche markets, as well. The most prevalent of these are "session-wrestling" companies,[9] but there are also foot-worship Houses, as well as a House that specializes in cross-dressing scenarios and one staffed only by Asian women.

The emphases on training and expertise distinguish professional BDSM from other forms of erotic labor. Various organizations within the Scene offer classes, panels, and demonstrations on aspects of BDSM, and some of these cater specifically to pro-dommes. In contrast, while Bay Area attorneys give classes on the legal aspects of sex work, there are few classes on how to improve one's technical skill as a prostitute.[10] Further, there is evidence that professional erotic dominance is viewed as a technically complex profession, even by people working in other erotic industries. As one of Chapkis's informants, a woman who had transitioned from stripping into professional dominance, recalled, "Lots of strippers fantasized about becoming a pro-dom[me], having this mysterious lifestyle, handling all these implements of torture, having men groveling at your feet and calling you 'mistress.' Being a regular prostitute had no mystique associated with it at all. It was like you got dressed up and fucked a guy. Big deal" (Chapkis 1997, 192).

Chapkis's informant's comment leads logically to a basic question about the two industries: if strippers "fantasized" about becoming pro-dommes, why did they not pursue this route? Based upon my interviewees' narratives about their industry, the answer lies, in part, in the fact that professional erotic dominance involves a kind of expertise that is learned. The industry holds a "mystique" because the "implements" are foreign to many people and the actions involved do not appear to be intuitive.

To be clear, I am not making the claim that prostitution or stripping require less technical know-how than commercial BDSM, but rather that these industries do not include the same emphasis on expertise or the internal training mechanisms that professional erotic dominance does. Further, the rhetoric pro-dommes use to describe their experiences in the industry—for instance, "learning a craft," "developing my skill," "It's a learning process," "I had to be trained"—heavily emphasizes professional development in ways that women doing other kinds erotic labor do not.

To illustrate this point about the unique relationship between professional D/S and expertise, it is useful to draw a contrast with Katherine Frank's work on female strippers. Frank has found that, at least in the strip club industry, there can actually be an inverse correlation between the precision of a woman's routine and the success of the performance. Signals of a lack of professionalism, such as wearing her everyday underwear because she had forgotten her g-string, or appearing nervous onstage, could work to a stripper's benefit by increasing her perceived authenticity:

> Nervousness or awkwardness would . . . signal the fact that a dancer was genuine, more like a "real girl," as did *mistakes* (sometimes carefully crafted) in performance or attire. . . . The lack of "professionalism" exhibited by dancers new to the business implied to some men that they would not be as skilled at manipulating them out of their money. To others, it seemed to provide a balance between purity and defilement that was particularly exciting. (Frank 2002, 209; emphasis in original)

Sometimes seasoned dancers worked these "mistakes" into their routines in order to earn extra money (209).

While mistakes can humanize strippers, contributing to their appeal, my informants told me that their own success hinged on their ability to appear polished, professional, and in control at all times. This difference comes into focus when we contrast Frank's observations with the words of a pro-domme: "There's a discord between me—someone's who's a real amateur, coming from a feminist background, and doing this for fun—and meeting these men who assume, 'You must be a seasoned professional. You must know how to do all those things.' Everything I do must be very calculated. Because they *assume* that." Another informant, echoing this sentiment, told me that sometimes when clients tell her to do whatever she wants to them, she will threaten to take out a BDSM book and do a three-hour rope bondage session by painstakingly following the diagrams. She laughed and added, "Because nobody wants that. They don't want that. They don't want you to be *learning* how to do something. They want you to already know how to do it and be good at it and to be a professional at it. And it bothers them to think that you're gonna, like, not be sure about it."

This particular difference between the strip club and the dungeon tells us something distinctive about the fantasies underlying professional D/S, in opposition to those sustaining some other forms of sexualized labor. The concept of technical mastery plays into the idea of female dominance in a unique way, while the archetype of the amateur can prove particularly titillating within other forms of erotic labor. Frank, for instance, writes about the appeal of "amateur nights" at the strip clubs. Consider, also, the cultural success of "amateur porn." There are no "amateur dominatrix" nights at BDSM clubs, however, because the "amateur dominant" is not a category that can be sustained within the gendered construction of the D/S fantasy. The appearance of calculation and professionalism increases these women's appeal to clients, whereas, in the strip club, appeal is bound up in a different kind of authenticity.

Although the rise of the Internet has made it easier to break into the commercial D/S industry with no prior knowledge about its practices, prodommes indicated that success in the industry is strongly linked to proficiency. One client, for instance, described a session with a woman on Long Island he had seen only once. "She wasn't a real domme," he told me, rolling his eyes. "She didn't know how to do anything. She couldn't even tie [ropes] worth a lick!" To be an authentic dominatrix, one must be authentically *dominant*—or at least convincingly act the part—not the fallible "real girl" giving an unpolished performance to a sympathetic male crowd.

"Dommie Knows Best": The Professional Model and the "Whatever You Want" Problem

Commercial BDSM is an industry that relies heavily upon its practitioners' claims to professionalism; this facet of erotic dominance can be useful to investigate, in that it sheds light on professional relationships outside of the dungeon. In making this point, I draw upon Everett Hughes's concept of the "professional claim." "Professionals *profess*," Hughes explains. "They profess to know better than others the nature of certain matters, and to know better than their clients what ails them and their affairs. This is the essence of the professional idea and the professional claim" (1963, 656; emphasis in original). Thinking about what pro-dommes do in the context of their claims to professionalism and expertise opens the door for unfogging the nuances of service-industry exchanges more generally. Erotic dominance is particularly useful for thinking about professional claims within other forms of labor because the domme/sub relationship is structured as a unidirectional power dynamic, which makes the disjuncture between that claim and the actual tension that exists between professional and consumer in determining the conditions of the exchange all the more salient.

To be clear, professional erotic dominance does not fit the classic sociological characterization of a "profession," for a variety of reasons.[11] There is no licensing involved in commercial D/S,[12] and, unlike the professions Hughes discusses, it does not confer upon the practitioner high social prestige. Additionally, once one has been trained as a pro-domme, it is relatively easy to leave the industry, whereas a "man who leaves a profession, once he is fully trained, licensed and initiated, is something of a renegade in the eyes of his fellows" (Hughes 1963, 657). It is not an unusual occurrence for a dominatrix—even one who has been working for decades—to drop out of the industry. This is undoubtedly because pro-dominance neither requires the financial input (years of expensive schooling) nor, as a general rule, yields the financial output of a "true" profession, like medicine. That women who drop out are not viewed as renegades, further, may have something to do with the fact that many of them remain in the lifestyle and continue these activities in the absence of financial exchange. That is, many of these women still identify as dommes and continue to play privately or in the Scene. In contrast, one cannot give up her license to practice medicine but continue to be a doctor "for fun." In fact, of the four structural attributes of the professional model described by Harold Wilensky in a 1964 *American Journal of Sociology* article, only one applies to erotic dominance: the creation of a full-time occupation.[13]

The professional model is nonetheless useful for describing erotic dominance, and its utility lies in the distinction between attitude and organization. Previous authors have argued that attitudinal attributes of professionals, such as "a sense of calling to the field" and "a belief in self-regulation" are as important as the organizational features of the professional model (Hall 1968; see also Gannon 1971 and Hughes 1966). Such attitudinal attributes are also useful for theorizing microlevel interactions within nonprofessional service industries in which the service providers make the claim to professionalism. While commercial BDSM is not organized as a profession, many of the women who do this kind of work frame themselves as professionals—a discursive move that fundamentally influences how their industry functions on the ground.[14]

This claim to professional status manifested itself in interviews with pro-dommes, in particular, in these women's discussion of the "whatever you want" problem. Nearly everyone I interviewed told me that they get many clients who declare that the dominatrix is free to do anything she wants to them. Pro-dommes made the assertion that most of these clients, in fact, would not be satisfied with just any aspect of D/S, and that, as women with experience and expertise, they needed to be able to discern their clients' individual desires. In essence, they indicated that, in many cases, they possessed the ability to understand clients' fantasies better than the clients themselves. One woman, who had been in the industry for decades, exemplified the professional claim when she discussed her conversations with clients prior to session:

> Ask the people what they really need out of the scene. And then you have to pull it out of them, because a lot of people don't know. The basic answer is, "Whatever you want, mistress," which is completely not true. So you start saying, "Well, fine," and you can volunteer information about yourself. . . . "I really like to do spanking, paddling, blah blah blah." "I like to do nipple play." "I like to do cock-and-ball bondage." "I might wanna use a blindfold on you." And then you just see how they respond. "Oh, no no no," "Oh yes, I like that," or "I'd love a caning, but I can't have any marks because my wife doesn't know about it." [I say,] "No, you can't have a caning, but maybe you can have a—a little taste of it. But not a caning; that's gonna leave marks!" [*laughs*]. So you pull the information out of the people.

One concept that emerged repeatedly in my interviews was that, as one woman put it, "Dommie knows best." Sometimes, even when they did get specific session requests, dommes professed to know clients' tastes and limits better than the men themselves. A Manhattan-based indie recalled, for instance, "I saw somebody a couple of weeks ago, and they were really bugging me. They wanted a play piercing, which is more extreme play. . . . I knew this person, and I knew this person couldn't take a lot. But he was like, 'You gotta do it. You just gotta do it quickly.' And I bring it out and they go, 'Oh, no no no no!' See? I knew you couldn't handle it." Such narratives were common among the women I interviewed. As individuals who professed to be professionals, they felt it was necessary to be able to handle the disjuncture between abstract fantasy and the physical reality of what a client will enjoy. Their professional claim caused them to question clients' requests, particularly the "whatever you want" request, rather than immediately accepting them at face value and behaving accordingly.

One useful way to think about the exercise of the professional claim in this context is that pro-dommes work to generate preferences in their clients. This ties into my earlier argument that a long-term client will typically pair up with a particular dominatrix who will help him to develop his erotic tastes over the course of time. In this way, pro-dommes are similar to a variety of other service providers. In his study of New York City doormen, for instance, Peter Bearman argues that one of a doorman's main tasks is "inducing clients to have and communicate preferences." "Repeatedly," Bearman explains, "doormen will work to find just that mix of services that tenants want. When they find it, they stick to it, often reminding the tenants that this is in fact what they want" (2005, 100). In the same way, while clients come into the dungeon with specific fantasies and fetishes, pro-dommes teach these men to mobilize and articulate their desires, as well as building upon them over time with additional activities they feel the men will enjoy. Their ability to do this successfully helps to sustain their claims to professional status.

Beyond dominatrices and doormen, we can see echoes of the professional claim, and the struggle for control over the interaction that it involves, within other service industries that are not, strictly speaking, "professionalized." A hairdresser, for instance, may claim to know better than a client what cut will best frame her face, or what cut will be in line with the latest trends, and he or she will offer advice accordingly. During one of my own recent trips to the salon, the woman cutting my hair told me a story about a client she had "fought with" because the client had wanted bangs and the hairdresser had felt that bangs were a mistake with curly hair. This is a particularly interesting case because the hairdresser's assertion of the professional claim went against her own financial interest, since maintaining bangs requires more frequent trips to the hairdresser. Ultimately, she ceded to her client's demand and gave the woman bangs.

Along the same lines, the popular television show *What Not to Wear* is essentially an hour-long assertion of the professional claim, as the stylists tell so-called fashion victims why their personal choices for wardrobe, accessories, and makeup do not really flatter their particular bodies, as well as asserting that they do not reflect the victims' "true" personalities. The episodes in which the fashion victims repeatedly butt heads with the stylists make for particularly good television, as the victims stand their ground and fiercely cling to vestiges of their old wardrobes. Consider, as another example of the same dynamic, the physical therapist's battle with the stubborn client who needs the rehabilitation but resists the treatment because it is painful or does not give it her full effort. In this case, the client resists doing "what's good for her," both in the sense that she does not submit to the rehabilitator's expertise and in a literal, physiological sense, since she does not heal as quickly. Reverberations of this struggle within other areas of life are countless, as individuals whose wants dictate the exchange butt heads with service providers who make claims to expertise that may or may or may not be compatible with these wants. Commercial D/S offers us a unique window into this process because it is a service industry interaction in which power exchange is made explicit, so the disjuncture between the dramatized unidirectional dynamic of control and the actual jockeying for control between the professional and the client is particularly pronounced.

Using the professional model as a tool for theorizing commercial D/S also sheds light on some of the particularities within different forms of sexualized labor. In the past, erotic labor—especially prostitution—has been characterized as unskilled or low-skilled work (Edlund and Korn 2002, 181). Yet, as pro-dommes show us, the extent to which practitioners of erotic labor themselves agree with this categorization can vary across types of erotic labor. When pro-dommes talk about themselves as professionals who "know better" than their clients, they suggest that, in some ways, they have more in common with vanilla service providers, like hairdressers or physical therapists, than with individuals who engage in other forms of commercial erotic activity. These women's narratives about their work suggest that erotic dominance looks like other nonprofessionalized service-sector occupations we have seen before. Further, its overt dramatization of the power dynamics between professional and client helps us to better understand power relations in those other occupations.

"I Was *Born* a Domme": Cultural Capital and Naturalizing the Dominatrix

In addition to emphasizing occupational training and expertise, my interviewees engaged in a parallel narrative, in which they attributed their skill to aspects of their personalities that existed before they had learned about D/S. These included both an innate "domminess" (a term I have just conjured up, for lack of a better word) and the cultural capital that is required to do an effective scene.

These two elements were sometimes interwoven in the pro-dommes' narratives, as they connected the "inherent" ability to be a successful dominatrix to social class. Some women—particularly those who had studied psychology or had been medically trained—specifically linked their capabilities as dommes to their educational backgrounds. The idea that a particular kind of cultural capital is necessary to be a successful dominant may explain why so many professional dominatrices are well-educated white women. However, most informants described the intellectual capital required for this occupation as integral to one's personality. Discussing a woman from her House who had since gone independent, for example, one woman clarified that the kind of intelligence required to be a successful dominatrix was not necessarily the result of schooling:

> She was *extremely* good at what she did. I mean, she was *ridiculously* good. She hadn't done it before. She came in and within two weeks was just kicking ass. She was amazing. She was someone, though, she might not have had the formal education of, you know, going to university and all that stuff, but she was really in tune with the intellectual qualities of it. The psychological stuff.

> She was brilliant. And see that's the thing—it's not that the girls are now less educated. It's just that they're less sort of aware of the intellectual side of it.

At the same time that this description naturalizes this particular domme's talents, it is revealing that the speaker clarifies that the woman was not formally educated, as though one would assume that formal education and competency at this form of erotic labor would go hand in hand. This default assumption that higher levels of education make for a better pro-domme was a common contention among my informants, and it finds expression in the relatively high levels of education within my sample.

Other women connected competency in the industry to innate as well as achieved traits. They naturalized the capacity to engage in the psychological aspect of dominance, as well as the ability to communicate effectively with one's submissive within the context of a scene. One pro-domme from a Manhattan House told me, "I feel like it's more about a personality, and I think if you don't have one then it's just nothing and it's just basically a woman with a whip. . . . Even if technically they're good at what they do, if there's no connection then it just doesn't work out."

The sentiments "There are just some things you can't learn" and "Some women are *born* dommes" emerged frequently in interviews. Some of my informants, like the following two women, embedded their own childhood recollections within this naturalizing discourse:

> I'm a natural domme. It's something that comes absolutely natural to me. There's a picture of me, [at] three or four years old, and I actually remember—maybe five or six years old—and I actually remember the incident. I was braiding a girl's hair, and she didn't want to because of all the knots, and there's a picture of me with my hand up like this [raises hand as though to strike]. And so it's—it's a *personality*.

> I think I was born a domme. I really do. 'Cause in kindergarten this little boy was annoying the hell out of me and I said, "You need a spanking" and he went, "So give it to me," and I grabbed his arm and I said, "Get in the position." And I had him in, like, a cross shape. You know those paddle-balls? I snatched the ball off and started to whack him a couple of times. And my teacher sat there and watched for a couple of minutes before she said, "Okay, we can't play like that." Then, after that, that little boy got my milk for me. He carried my cookies. He was a natural sub.

The idea that D/S personas can emerge early in the life course is nothing new. Scott (1997, 23), for instance, interviewed adult submissives who recalled having felt excitement at being tied up during games of Cowboys and Indians as children. A few of the women with whom I spoke, however, described their identities and play personas as inseparable. When asked whether she referred to herself as a "dominatrix" or a "mistress," for instance, one woman replied, "Well, I *am* a domme. I don't call myself a domme. I *am* one."

These dommes' naturalizing accounts of their life trajectories can be usefully analyzed as narratives of fate: stories in which the end state defines the overall plot. In making this argument, I draw upon Peter Bearman and Katherine Stovel's analysis of autobiographical accounts of becoming and being a Nazi. Bearman and Stovel describe this process by which "standard life-stories produce their end (the life realized) by accretion of specific relational events to the life-world of the narrator: roles, people, and places" (2000, 85). Accounts of "becoming" and "being," moreover, are intertwined. As Jerome Bruner points out, "It is always a moot question whether the actions of persons should be attributed to circumstances or to their 'enduring dispositions'" (1986, 37). For Bruner, to attempt to sever the two would be to create a false cleavage, as both inherent character and the process of becoming are always involved in the outcome of a narrative. Within the context of her larger narrative of fate, the interviewee who got a boy to carry her milk and cookies, for instance, was not only *disposed to be* a domme but was also *produced as* a domme later, when she happened to encounter a fellow student in a university class who introduced her to that world. In the case of many pro-dommes' retellings, these women both are dommes essentially and become dommes through an accretion of events that, within the context of their stories, have produced their current state.

Another helpful way of conceptualizing pro-dommes' naturalizing discourse is to return to the dramaturgical frame for a moment. Specifically, the distinction between a woman who feels she is inherently a dominatrix and one who views the role as a persona she can put on and remove at will is akin to Konstantin Stanislavski's distinction between "surface acting" and "deep acting" (or "method acting"). In surface acting, a performer assumes a role and behaves as that character for the benefit of an audience. In deep acting, the performer becomes so immersed in a role that she feels what the character feels and reacts as the character would. She becomes that character. In *The Managed Heart: Commercialization of Human Feeling*, Arlie Hochschild (2003, 43) riffs on Stanislavski's dichotomy, arguing that service providers and other individuals use a kind of method acting as a technique for managing emotion. If they feel they are not acting appropriately within a given context, people evoke feelings in themselves to produce the emotions that are socially mandated by their circumstances. While those women who maintain that they are inherently dominatrices would no doubt object to the categorization of their work as "acting" at all, the concept of "deep acting" is nonetheless useful for thinking about how these women characterize their involvement in BDSM. It also came across very clearly in my own interactions with these particular informants—recall, for instance, the male dom who threatened to put me up on the rack or the pro-domme who described me as "Little Red Riding Hood coming to see the Big Bad Wolf" when we were on the phone setting up an in-person interview. Another informant, whom I had contacted via e-mail about doing an interview, wrote back, "If you wish to speak with Me, you must abide by the following conditions . . ." Her adoption of the dominatrix persona, and specifically her use of the capitalized "Me," a convention of the industry that some other potential informants deployed in their correspondence with me as well, suggested that she did not always remove the dominatrix mask outside of sessions.

Some dommes and subs view BDSM as a frivolous leisure activity. Others put forth narratives that describe their roles in the D/S exchange as unshakable, emanating from the cores of their personalities. These narratives are structured around early childhood stories, as well as around the accumulation of knowledge, both of which tie into pro-dommes' conceptions of their own authenticity as pro-dommes.

As an erotically oriented career, commercial BDSM has its perks. Pro-dommes seldom engage in intercourse or oral sex with their clients, so the risk of disease transmission is lower than within, for instance, prostitution. Dungeons are indoors and relatively clean, and clients are, at least to some degree, screened before sessions. To return, then, to the question posed earlier in reference to Chapkis's informant: why do all erotic laborers not aspire to become dominatrices?

Of course, it would be naïve from a demand-side perspective to suggest that it would be possible for all erotic laborers to transition into professional erotic dominance. Pro-dominance is a more specialized form of erotic labor than prostitution, which has its own market constraints. Clearly there is not unlimited demand for professional dominatrices. However, the question remains why all erotic laborers do not at least attempt to become pro-dommes, if the lure of the industry is so appealing.

I have argued that pro-dommes are perceived as possessing (and generally do possess) a certain type of cultural capital as well as needing to undergo training in order to gain expertise in the industry. While women can and do go into the dungeon knowing little about BDSM, comprehensive knowledge about these activities is valued in the industry, both by other dommes and by clients. Commercial D/S thus can emit an aura of unattainablity for those without prior knowledge of its implements and practices.

Another possible explanation for the fact that all sex workers do not aspire to become dominatrices is that there is generally, if not always, comparatively less money to be made as a pro-domme than in other sexually oriented industries. Strippers, for instance, can make $200 to $300 a day (Barton 2006, 93). Nevertheless, although on the low end of the pay scale, a domme will make $60 for a one-hour session, on the upper end, she can make upward of $300 for the same amount of time. Thus, depending upon her place in the pay range and her number of clients, a professional dominatrix can either earn more or less than women who work in strip clubs. On the other hand, those pro-dommes in the highest pay brackets are typically indies, who have high overhead costs, thus potentially nullifying their financial edge over exotic dancers.

While financial concerns may play a role in the fact that not all erotic laborers attempt to become pro-dommes, it is clear that the industry also projects an aura of unattainability due to the technical know-how involved. When we start to think about pro-dommes as professionals who make claims to a particular type of expertise, we can begin to see that their interactions with their clients have reverberations within many spheres of life that are not erotically oriented. What is important to take away from this chapter is the fact that, although pro-dominance is an industry uniquely organized around the production of subversive sexuality and a dramatized inversion of the gender/power hierarchy, it is useful to look at partly because it illuminates the tension between expert and client that is involved in these more "typical" transactional relationships.

Further, commercial D/S is uniquely positioned to shed light on the nuances of control within these other realms because it is ostensibly structured as a unidirectional power relationship. In the salon, it is not necessarily obvious whether the hairdresser or the client is "supposed" to be guiding the interaction. In commercial D/S, we know who is intended to be dominant— her very title signifies her role—so the instances when she relinquishes her claim to professional expertise to accommodate her client's demands are all the more striking. In the next chapter, I will more fully examine this dynamic in which client and domme vie for control over the circumstances of their interaction, specifically in the context of pro-dommes' characterization of their work as "art."

Will the Real Pro-Domme Please Stand Up:
Art, Authenticity, and Pierre Bourdieu

Since 2004, a crowd of "rope artists" and bondage enthusiasts has gathered in Chicago for a BDSM-themed convention known as "Shibaricon." The four-day event includes workshops on various aspects of shibari—the Japanese art of binding bodies with rope—as well as social events and the sale of BDSM-related implements and clothing. "Come to Shibaricon," the event's website advertises, "to experience this unique, ancient, ever-evolving art form that binds the body, releases the soul, and allows one to touch the depths of sensuality that many only dream of!"[1]

This characterization of shibari as an art form resonates with the way many pro-dommes discuss not only rope tying but other facets of their industry as well. While, initially, there were no questions on my interview schedule about BDSM as an artistic enterprise, a salient and unexpected discourse emerged during the ethnographic process: pro-dommes who were also in the lifestyle repeatedly legitimated their sessions with clients as artistic, interpreting their own work as "real" and drawing a distinction between themselves and those pro-dommes who work solely for the purpose of financial gain.

In this chapter, I use one of Pierre Bourdieu's theories of art as a structural analogy for thinking about the discourse whereby pro-dommes legitimate themselves as "artists." The way that some pro-dommes speak about themselves as producers bestowed with motivations specifically disconnected from profit, despite the fact that they themselves are earning money to dominate men, can be usefully interpreted through the lens of Bourdieu's theory of "the anti-'economic' economy of pure art" (1996, 142). Bourdieu argues that individuals on the "autonomous end" of the artistic spectrum (for instance, avant-garde artists) ritually renounce economic criteria for success as a means to symbolically distance themselves from the "heteronomous" end (commercial artists). "Purist" dominatrices not only participate in this same symbolic distancing, but they exhibit other key characteristics of avant-garde artists, from the "mutual admiration societies" they form for the purpose of cultural legitimization to their complex relationship with an "audience" (their clients) whose tastes they often denigrate while on whom, to some extent, they must rely for professional success.

In drawing this theoretical connection between Bourdieu's artists and professional dominatrices, I pick up and tie together two discursive ropes that have run through this text thus far: authenticity in the dungeon and the struggle for control within the domme/client exchange. What does it mean to be a "real" dominatrix and a "real" submissive? What is the relationship between these distinctions and the dynamics of control within the interaction? Finally, what can this purity regime within commercial D/S tell us about power exchange within other occupational spheres that are considered "artistic" by the professionals who inhabit them?

From the outset, because I am using Bourdieu's theory as a frame for this chapter, it is important that I address my lack of attention to his central concept of "field." Whether professional erotic dominance represents a Bourdieusian "cultural field" in a meaningful sociological sense is not a question that is fundamental to this analysis. Bourdieu's "anti-'economic' economy" is an apt metaphor for the discourse of artistic purity employed by pro-dommes whether or not this corner of social life is truly a "field." My point about commercial BDSM is not that it fits Bourdieu's schema like a glove but that a number of Bourdieu's terms and conclusions can be used effectively as a structural analogy to highlight a basic tension of the industry that is at the center of this book.

Previously, social theorists have taken Bourdieu's theories about art as a point of departure for fruitful analyses of various creative industries, ranging from gastronomy to experimental film (Ferguson 1998, Wheeler 2003, Bayma 1995; see also Jameson 1990, 15–16). Although these other scholars have applied Bourdieu's writings on art to cultural forms that may appear more apparent as art, pro-dommes' narratives about their work hold the potential to push his theory beyond the boundaries of what is traditionally considered "artistic." Further, though previous literature has drawn upon the sociology of work to characterize the social organization of art (H. Becker 1978), pro-dommes allow us to invert the paradigm and look at self-identified professionals within the context of art-world theory.[2] I thus use Bourdieu as a tool to investigate the social organization of professional erotic dominance, in turn shedding light on purity regimes within domains that are conceived of as artistic by their practitioners.

Professional Erotic Dominance as an Artistic Pursuit

Perhaps I should have predicted that many of the women I interviewed would speak about their work as "artistic," since the interpretation of BDSM as a creative enterprise has precedents in social scientific literature. As discussed, for instance, Thomas Weinberg uses Goffman's "frame analysis" as a tool for conceptualizing SM as dramaturgical. Pro-dommes in my own study not only used the same dramaturgical argot but also engaged in a discourse legitimating BDSM as a kind of art in its own right, not a variant of theater. Again it should be emphasized that they engaged in this pervasive rhetoric despite the fact that I did not ask them any questions about erotic dominance as an artistic pursuit. When I asked her what first attracted her to the Scene, for instance, one woman explained, "I'm intrigued by the art of it . . . I mean, I find shibari really beautiful, and I'm—and I think it's a really cool-looking thing, and I like just that. But I don't really get off on tying someone up; I like the aesthetic." It was common for interviewees to refer to shibari in their discussion of BDSM as a form of artistic expression. A client in his late twenties, for instance, speaking about the appeal of shibari, explained, "It's aesthetic for me, so I always want the tough positions that I'm put in to be photographed."

Other pro-dommes went as far as to call not only bondage, but the entire practice of erotic dominance, a form of art. One pro-domme in her thirties, when asked if she found her work erotically stimulating, explained,

> Some people find this incredibly sexual. To me it's erotic, but I find it mostly stimulating from the neck up. To me it's an art form. I have to know that I can step on a person without breaking a rib. I know that I have to be incredibly careful and delicate because something could bruise when it's not supposed to and do real damage when it's not supposed to. I have to know what I know.

Here, again, we see a pro-domme draw upon the professional claim in characterizing her interactions with clients. These kinds of assertions about knowledge and training were crucial to the rhetoric of aestheticism that pervaded my interviews.

Other pro-dommes drew parallels between BDSM and specific forms of art outside of theater, such as literature and dance. A man who had been working as a pro-dom for decades explained, for instance, "When I do a scene, it's like a book. There's a beginning, a middle, an end. You want it to *flow.*" And a pro-domme drew a connection between the practice of erotic dominance and her personal history in the ballet:

Can you list some of the things you do in sessions?
Corporal. I'm big on corporal punishment, because it is a dance. . . . That's
   why every time I'm at a play party and I do my corporal, people come up
   to me and go, "My God, that was beautiful." I actually was a dancer, you
   know, so I absolutely feel their energies, and I meld with it.

Whether framing their work as an artistic pursuit in its own right or drawing parallels between their sessions and various art forms, pro-dommes engaged in a discourse conceptualizing BDSM as art. Only when I took my informants' lead, and began to think about professional erotic dominance as a form of artistic expression, did this revealing parallel to Bourdieu's artists become apparent.

An Anti-"Economic" Economy

"In the struggle to impose the legitimate definition of art and literature," Bourdieu explains, "the most autonomous producers naturally tend to exclude 'bourgeois' writers and artists, whom they see as 'enemy agents'" (1993, 41). In the BDSM world, a similar struggle takes place between indies, who work for themselves and are more often in the lifestyle, and non-lifestyle dommes, especially those who work in larger dungeons, who are perceived as only participating in commercial BDSM for the financial rewards. Though all pro-dommes receive financial compensation for BDSM activities, the former perceive the latter as participating in erotic dominance *only* for economic reasons. One interviewee explained this opposition:

> Some of the younger girls who have been coming into this in the last few
> years—they don't want to do this stuff. It's not something they've always been
> fascinated by. You know, they weren't kind of reading the *Story of O* when they
> were fifteen. You know, stuff like that. They're not—they don't have a kind of
> intellectual interest in it. They just want the money. . . . The girls who were re-
> ally into the BDSM Scene and were really intellectually stimulated by it didn't
> like those girls at all. . . . I don't think that [lifestyle dommes] see what they
> do in that world as being kinda economically based. . . . But they are getting
> money.

Her rhetoric places lifestyle dommes at the "art for art's sake" end of the aesthetic spectrum and the girls who "just want the money" at the commercial end—a conceptual orientation that repeatedly arose in interviews with lifestyle pro-dommes. This discourse is in line with what Bourdieu terms the autonomous principle, which is based "on the obligatory recognition of the values of disinterestedness and on the denigration of the 'economy' (of the 'commercial') and of 'economic' profit (in the short term)" (1996, 142). One pro-domme, who had also been in the lifestyle for over thirty years, positioned herself in opposition to the women she termed "hoochie dommes," whose interest in BDSM was exclusively financial. She indicated that she had largely stopped doing sessions for money:

> Because *now* you have the hoochie dommes and places like ——, which are just factories for stupid chicks to get taken advantage of. You know, they're going, "I'm puttin' myself through school. I'm making sixty bucks an hour. That's a hell of a lot [more] than makin' forty-eight dollars a *day*." I understand that. But . . . they are contributing to the deterioration of the *honor* of what being a domme is and what being a mistress is. I would be fine if they didn't use the term "mistress" or "domina" or "goddess." If they used a different term, I would have no problems with them. . . . But the idea that there's some little hoochie and she's calling herself "mistress" and then *I* say, "I'm Mistress ——," somebody gets the idea that I can be bought for *whatever.*

Here, she symbolically distances herself from the hoochies who "can be bought" by emphasizing the noneconomic facets of erotic dominance (the "honor" of the profession) and disavowing her own commodification.

In this "competition for cultural legitimacy" (Bourdieu 1969, 90) within the world of professional BDSM, the question of who may be considered a dominatrix is salient. Through a discourse spattered with terms like "real," "fake," "phony," and "actual," participants in the Scene legitimated lifestylers against the backdrop of the more commercially oriented pro-dommes. The following discussion is taken from an interview with one male submissive, who described a conversation he'd had with the proprietor of a local fetish store:

She hopes—her hope was that, in your interviews, you would be able to figure out which ones were real and which ones were the phonies. Which she thought would be an interesting take for you, because there are a lot of phonies.

What's the difference between a real and phony?

Basically you've got girls that realize they could make money by calling themselves dominatrices. Okay? Because they look good in some tight clothes and they could try to boss a guy around by being generally mean. But it's always sloppy, and anybody looking in can tell, that knows anything about the Scene—they can just tell that it's a hodgepodge mixture of un-organized actions, and it's usually pretty terrible looking.

Note the emphasis on aesthetic ineptitude ("terrible looking") linked with the perceived "phoniness" of pro-dommes who inhabit the commercial end of the artistic spectrum.

Participants in the BDSM Scene characterized non-lifestylers using negative descriptions that were notably similar to each other. One lifestyle pro-domme discussed her perception of the typical dungeon domme in comparable terms:

> Instead of working at McDonald's for ten dollars an hour, she can work at a dungeon and make sixty bucks an hour while the dungeon's making two hundred [or] two twenty-five. These girls really have no clue, and they're young, inexperienced, lack techniques, and basically don't know the etiquette and protocols that come with being a domme. Or a sub, for that matter.

Again, these descriptions interpreted the—often younger—dungeon dommes as artistically inept ("lacking technique") and positioned them at the purely economic end of the artistic spectrum, thus symbolically displacing the lifestyle pro-dommes' own financial benefits from D/S.

Some of my informants accounted for their own declining financial success within the BDSM community as a function of the demand for these economically oriented "false" dominatrices—an interpretation that that can also be illuminated by looking at Bourdieu's rubric. In discussing the polarization of the art world, Bourdieu identifies

> the heteronomous principle, favourable to those who dominate the field economically and politically (e.g. 'bourgeois art') and the autonomous principle (e.g. 'art for art's sake'), which those of its advocates who are least endowed with specific capital tend to identify with degree of independence from the economy, seeing temporal failure as a sign of election and success as a sign of compromise. (1993, 40)

Several women attributed their own loss of economic capital to the rising influence of the Internet, particularly to the increasing appearance of "phony" dommes' advertisements on public domains such as Craigslist. One woman, who had been doing commercial D/S for six years, complained that business was "not nearly as good as it used to be a few years ago. . . . For one thing, [because of] Craigslist. 'I'm a mistress,' and it's some girl who bought a five-dollar fake whip. Who's really a hooker. They're the ones who do full service."[3] She interpreted her "temporal failure" as an indication of her "election" as a real dominatrix—a "purist," as she described herself at another point in the interview—not a "hooker" brandishing a false idol: the "fake whip" of erotic dominance.

One staple of Bourdieusian theory should be explored, as a possible reason for this tension between those lifestyle pro-dommes who see themselves as purists and the "hoochies" in the larger Houses: the concept of habitus.[4] We might expect to find differences in habitus between these two groups because lifestylers repeatedly spoke about dungeon dommes using derogatory epithets such as "twits," "nitwits," and "idiots," suggesting that these "hoochies" lack certain socialized cultural and intellectual characteristics apart from the industry itself. However, among the women I interviewed, I found no appreciable differences in social background between dungeon dommes and indies. Dungeon dommes tended to have slightly lower levels of education than women who worked for themselves, but this is likely because they were also younger.

Further, as discussed in the chapter 2, it is common for a dominatrix to begin her career in a House and then "go indie" after gaining clients and expertise. As noted, about half of the indies I interviewed, twenty-five women, had at some point in their careers worked in Houses. The cultural capital that dungeon dommes lack, in the eyes of their indie counterparts, appears to be connected to their location in their career trajectories, as well as to their ages, not to their position within the larger social hierarchy.

One major difference between indies and dungeon dommes, however, is unexpected, in light of the discourse being explored here. Given the former dommes' symbolic disavowal of the economic component of their profession, one would expect that they would charge less than their "hoochie" counterparts.[5] However, those pro-dommes who eschewed the notion of purely commercial D/S were oftentimes the ones asking higher prices for their sessions. That is, independent mistresses typically charged more than dungeon dommes.

One reason for the existence of pro-dommes with both high cultural and economic capital within this social world is that, since lifestyle dommes—the ones who denounce purely economic motivations—are more likely to work for themselves, they must contend with higher overhead costs than dungeon dommes. Indies rent or buy their own spaces, supply their own equipment, and finance all of their own advertising. Pro-dommes' economic stratification is isomorphic with their stratification within the spectrum of "authenticity," but not only because of this difference in their purity status.

Still, claims to purity were part of the reason that some dommes said they charged higher fees, as is evidenced when we look at the market for professional erotic dominance from the demand side. Several of the clients interviewed for this project indicated that they were willing to pay more for sessions with "real" dommes. In the same vein, the lifestyle pro-dommes in this sample put forth the idea that their status as authentic dommes should entitle them to higher session fees.[6] Through this seemingly paradoxical discourse, lifestyle dommes complexly expressed their authenticity by charging more than their non-lifestyle counterparts, while at the same time expressing a lack of interest in their own financial benefits from doing sessions. This phenomenon is not without parallels in other social spheres that are considered artistic by those who inhabit them. One need only to consider the discrepancy in prices between cheaper, mass-marketed ready-to-wear fashions and haute couture to find a correlate.

Watching the Clock

One discursive strategy pro-dommes used to symbolically distance themselves from the financial benefits of their labor was to emphasize their own freedom from time constraints when it came to sessions with clients. "Watching the clock" during a session was interpreted as indicative of crudely economic motivations, and some pro-dommes counteracted this either by charging a flat rate instead of a per-hour fee or by failing to charge an additional fee if a session went beyond its agreed-upon time limit. A male dominant, for instance, explained, "I try to give [BDSM] a good name. Doing what I love. Living what I love. . . . There's no love in what [people who are in it for money] do. They're always looking at the clock." Despite the fact that he charges a flat rate for a two-hour session, he emphasized, "I'm not really on the clock. I never rush. It's not just about the money. It's about giving back a little. I don't rush them out the door when they're done. We chat, watch TV. They go to my refrigerator without asking!" [*laughs*]. A female informant explained her orientation toward temporality in a similar way: "I do a lot of talking with them before and after. I never, never, never, never, never watch the clock. If they come to the door and spend two hours or two and a half hours, that's cool. Especially if I'm having a good time." This rhetoric about "watching the clock" allowed some lifestylers to demonstrate their personal interest in BDSM and the relative unimportance of money by emphasizing the recreational, rather than financial, aspects of the exchange.

Here it is instructive to consider Georg Simmel's work on the intersection of sex and money. Simmel argues, for instance, that prostitution differs fundamentally from other sexual encounters in the sense that financial compensation ensures an unequivocal end to the exchange: "The relationship is more completely dissolved and more radically terminated by payment of money than by the gift of a specific object, which always, through its content, its choice and its use, retains an element of the person who has given it" (1990, 376).[7] By allowing scenes to continue beyond their agreed-upon time limits, some interviewees here symbolize that their relationships with clients are not radically terminated by monetary exchange—that dominance is personal and that financial compensation is not the defining feature of the interaction. By allowing his clients to "chat and watch TV," for instance, the dominant above demonstrates his unwillingness to frame his work *as* work—as a clinical financial transaction. In this way, lifestylers symbolically enact their freedom from the entanglements of purely economic enterprise.

This act of symbolic distancing is not unique to commercial D/S; it is important within other erotic industries as well. Exotic dancers, for instance, experience pressure to establish their authenticity through their indifference to the financial component of strip club interactions. Discussing private lap dances, Frank contends that "the point at which a dancer is asked to 'prove' her disinterestedness in financial gain or be labeled a hustler comes quite early on in the interaction. . . . [E]ven men who knew that they would be paying for their interactions in the clubs and who desired this state of affairs often sought signs of a dancer's sincerity before they interacted with her." One strip club patron, for instance, tells Frank, "I don't like anything synthetic, artificial. . . . I don't want someone who's doing this just to make money" (2002, 205). Within the walls of the strip club, dancers are thus required to "prove" their genuineness by demonstrating that they do not strip for crudely economic reasons—that there is a kind of "love in it for what they do." In strip clubs, we see this discourse about proof emanating from the customers—not the dancers—but the concept carries over to the rhetoric of the lifestylers examined here. Further, my own interviews with subs provide evidence that, within commercial BDSM, some male clients, like lifestyle dommes and strip club patrons, also look for "authentic" women, as opposed to "hustlers" conducting cool financial transactions. "She is a real dominatrix. She's not a clock watcher," one male client told me, for instance, about a New York dominatrix.

Symbolic Disavowal and the Payment Ritual

One way in which clients and dominatrices work together to disavow the economic component of their interaction is by engaging in a ritualized system of payment that symbolically decontaminates the money being exchanged. The majority of pro-dommes only accept cash and take the money up front for pragmatic reasons. Those who did not do this, or had not in the past, recalled having been shortchanged on occasion. However, it is rarely a money-in-hand transaction. Dungeon dommes generally receive payment through a middleman—a dungeon manager or receptionist who accepts the payment prior to a session. Independent dommes take the money themselves but, for the most part, do not handle it. They displace it by requiring their clients to deposit it in a box, dish, or envelope—sometimes in another room.

One indie who works out of Manhattan explained, for instance, "I have them get changed, undressed in the bathroom [before the session] and I have a little tray and I have them leave [the money] there, because it would be tacky and weird for them to hand me the money." She told me, as many informants did, that she "sneak[s] out" during session, if the client is new, and confirms that he has deposited the appropriate amount. Another indie, who had been in the industry for five years, similarly described her feelings about overt monetary exchange: "I always ask for [the money] in an envelope. I really hate guys, like, taking out their wad of cash and, like, peeling off the money. That's just tacky [*laughs*]. . . . The really nice ones and experienced ones put it in a card—write a little thank-you note or something. And that's really nice." In this way, my informants indicated that they enforce a separation between their hands and the money, as though connection between the two would expose the financial element of the interaction and contaminate the scene. In one case, thank-you notes function to emphasize that the pro-domme/client encounter is not an impersonal exchange of money for labor. Slipped in with the money, these cards, in Simmel's words, "retain an element of the person who has given [them]."

When pro-dommes call their payment a "tribute," it also deemphasizes the commercial aspect of the D/S exchange. During interviews, indies were more likely to refer to their payment as "tribute," while dungeon dommes tended to call it a "session fee." This difference seems to support lifestylers' contention that sessions at the larger Houses are framed as more overtly economic transactions, as "fee" rings of compulsory monetary exchange, while it is ambiguous whether a "tribute" is voluntary or required. According to the women I interviewed, this linguistic disavowal of the compulsory economic aspect of the exchange benefits the client as well as the domme. An indie who works in San Francisco explained:

> There's usually intricate game playing around the exchange of money. It can be very interesting as far as how—because it's technically "sex," even though you're not having sex, it's still very emotional and related to sex, and people don't really want to pay for sex. They do it all the time, but they don't *want* to, so they'll try to get out of it. So instead of paying money, they'll want to

pay in gifts. . . . Usually there's a tradition of calling it a "tribute," rather than a "charge" or something like that. So it's like paying an *honor*, if that makes sense. That makes it easier for most people to deal with.

Her description resonates with Simmel's characterization of prostitution in the sense that the clients of dominatrices go to lengths to avoid those features of the exchange that would mark it as a purchase. While money radically terminates an economic exchange and explicitly denotes that exchange as economic, a gift does not. Calling the payment a "tribute," furthermore, implies that the sub is paying for the experience of the session, or the honor of a domme's company, rather than the specific erotic labor being performed on the dungeon floor.

Just like the use of the word "tribute," the receptacle holding the money serves as a barrier between pro-dommes, their clients, and the obligatory economic facet of the exchange. Pro-dommes and their clients engage in this symbolic distancing partly in order to perpetuate one of the underlying fantasies of commercial D/S: that a real domme is engaging in BDSM with a submissive because she wants to. Money ruins the fantasy because, as in the strip club, money is the ultimate signifier of inauthenticity.

The Extremes: Lifestyle Dominatrices and "Financial Domination"

At the tails of the commercial spectrum are dommes who are purely lifestyle and not professional and those who engage in "financial domination": a practice in which the economic facet of the encounter cannot be symbolically displaced because monetary exchange *is* the act of dominance.

At the least commercial extreme are women who self-identify as dominatrices but who only play in their personal lives and do not engage in paid D/S. Just as there exists a division between lifestyle and non-lifestyle pro-dommes, there also exists a division between dommes who are *only* in the lifestyle and those who engage in commercial BDSM, including lifestyle pros. Although nonprofessional dominatrices were not the focus of this study, a common theme that emerged in my interviews with pros was the antagonism of people in the Scene toward individuals in the industry. "There seems to be a schism between lifestyle and pro-dommes," one pro-domme who is also in the lifestyle explained to me. "A lot of people in the lifestyle community look down on pro-dommes as money-hungry whores and bitches."

To some extent, my informants seemed to exaggerate this divide. In New York City, for instance, pro-dommes are integrated into the Scene; they participate in workshops about the industry and serve on panels for the Eulenspiegel Society (TES, pronounced "tess"),[8] and they attend and even host parties regularly attended by lifestyle dommes. On the other hand, this kind of rhetoric exaggerates sentiments that do exist and that came out during my encounters with lifestyle players. I received one angry e-mail, for example, from a woman who was upset that, upon seeing her name and e-mail address on a pro-domme website, I had contacted her about being a potential interviewee. She asserted that she was lifestyle and not a pro. "I'm sorry to tell you I'm not a whore," she wrote, concluding, "Get your facts straight next time!"

Another time, I was at the local BDSM club in New York City doing field research, and the acquaintance who had brought me to the club, a male-to-female cross-dresser, was complaining about the lack of attractive women in the Scene. I gestured toward the half dozen or so beautiful women in skimpy fetish clothing. "Those are pro-dommes," she told me. "They don't count." Though my acquaintance's comment suggested that, in the Scene, there is a rift between those who play purely for fun and those who also do it for money, those two groups are also enmeshed in many ways. The club adjoins a commercial dungeon, which explains why the pro-dommes were there that day; spending time at the club is one of the ways they bring in new clients. This physical connection between the club and the dungeon underscores the embeddedness of professional erotic dominance within the New York Scene. While purely lifestyle dominatrices' animosity toward pros works logically as an extension of the Bourdieusian schema being explored in this chapter, it is striking given the significant overlap between the world of commercial BDSM and the Scene.

At the most commercial end of the spectrum, on the other hand, are non-lifestyle pro-dommes who are involved in D/S only for money, as well as those who engage in a practice known in the industry as "financial domination" or "financial blackmail." This practice has a variety of manifestations and can range from dominating a client over the phone to being compensated for attending an event with a client. A salient feature of this activity is that the transfer of money from client to domme *is* the D/S interaction. One interviewee defined the term for me:

> Financial domination is when—so there's no, like, physical domination that occurs. And the two parties don't even have to meet. And there's a lot of—so a lot of girls who were dominatrices sort of set up websites and just call themselves financial dommes now and basically they will e-mail the guys and talk to them on the phone and kind of subjugate them through e-mail or phone conversations and then expect payment in return. And some of them do quite well out of it.

She went on to explain what she perceived to be the appeal of these types of exchanges:

> So the guys who are into it as, like, clients don't—they're turned on by the fact that they're just providing for someone. So the girls just sort of have to tell them what they want—you know, "I want this, that, and the other, and this is how much it costs and this is how you get the money to me." So the guys are turned on by the fact that they can sort of be this father figure type thing.

Many of the women who considered themselves "purists" were highly critical of pro-dommes who engaged in financial domination. During my interviews, financial domination was the practice, other than sexual extras, that my informants most often criticized. Their disapproval makes sense in the context of the treatment of money within this industry. Because the fetish is the economic exchange itself, symbolic displacement of the monetary element of the exchange cannot possibly occur. Financial domination thus ruptures the barrier between dominatrix and currency that functions to authenticate the interaction.

Legitimacy and the Public

In discussing the social dynamics involved in the art of writing, Bourdieu argues that "the fundamental stake in literary struggles is . . . the monopoly of the power to consecrate producers or products (we are dealing with a world of belief and the consecrated writer is the one who has the power to consecrate and to win assent when he or she consecrates an author or a work— with a preface, a favourable review, a prize, etc.)" (1993, 42). Although there are no "prizes" awarded to outstanding pro-dommes, professional erotic dominance is embedded within an interlocking series of social relations that confer legitimacy upon its "worthies" in a variety of ways.

At local events, those pro-dommes who are in the Scene interact with other pro-dommes and sometimes acquire new clients or lifestyle play partners. These events also may involve demonstrations on the part of particular players, during which elements of BDSM are displayed and admired. "There's play parties, there are fetish parties, there's the club," one pro-domme from New York City, who has been in the Scene for a decade, explained, "It's nice to show off." Here, she distinguishes between "play parties"—at which attendees engage in "play"—and "fetish parties"—where play may occur, but which are more about socializing while dressed in fetishistic attire. Intercourse or oral sex rarely occurs at these public events; many have nudity restrictions, especially if they take place at public venues. However, sex and nudity are more frequent at smaller private parties. These types of events are distinct from the various local discussion panels and how-to workshops—some of which are run by TES—with titles such as "Traditional Discipline: Spanking That Special Playmate" and "Play Piercing for Fun and Fashion."

As of 2011, there was only one permanent-structure BDSM club (as opposed to traveling party) left in New York City. It was open two nights a week and typically hosted a demonstration or workshop on Fridays. There used to be other local clubs, but they closed, according to participants in the Scene, owing to a combination of legal and financial issues. The club is a place where participants can come not only to have fun, but to see and be seen, socialize with their friends in the lifestyle community, and to demonstrate their technical proficiency. The following is taken from my field notes at the club in December of 2007:

> On the small stage in front of me an older man with a long white mustache is being flogged by a twenty-something domme in see-through lingerie. He is naked except for a Santa hat. In an adjoining room, past the bar (which serves no alcohol), three people are being spanked. Upstairs, a domme is eating dinner from a foil take-out tray while a male sub lies at her feet, bound and gagged, and porn plays on a nearby television set. Elsewhere in the club, a middle-aged man is tied to a bar suspended from the ceiling; his nipples are being twisted by a domme while a "sissy" (a man dressed like a toddler girl, in a lacey dress and bonnet) looks on. It's a slow night, but it's early still.

Later, the crowd picks up:

> Here come the "New Jersey Guys," which is what some people call the middle-aged men who always look like they've wandered out of a Jets game. It costs more to get in if you don't wear fetish clothing, but they still show up in jeans and football parkas, circulating the club but rarely playing.

On the local level, the BDSM population includes a relatively small social network of highly involved core participants as well as a broader web of occasional players. One female submissive in the New York Scene explained, "There's a lot of consistent faces, especially if you're older. Younger people, they come and go, but if you're older and you're in, you're in for a while." A San Francisco interviewee asserted that this holds true for pro-dommes in the Bay Area in particular: "Here, all the dominatrices—we all know each other. . . . There are some dominatrices that play well with others and some that do not [*laughs*]. And I think the ones that do play well with others, we do have a tendency to share information and watch out for each other."

New York's pro-dommes, too, had developed both alliances and hostilities. Many lifestyle pro-dommes were friendly with each other, facilitating

my snowball sampling, and they socialized outside of Scene events. My informants often wanted to know whom else I was interviewing, and when
I explained that I could not reveal the names of other participants in the
study, regularly added their personal thoughts about other dommes I might
encounter. "Did you talk to ——?" one pro-domme asked. "She's a cunt!
Oops! [*laughs*]. But she is really a horrible bitch, and what she doesn't know
is people do not like her." When I interviewed the woman to whom she was
referring, she cautioned me about potentially interviewing the other domme,
"Stay on her good side."

Within each local Scene are a series of smaller groups, which are in line
with Schücking's conception of "mutual admiration societies," upon which
Bourdieu draws:

> The exclusion of the public and the declared refusal to meet popular demand
> which encourage the cult of form for itself—an unprecedented accentuation
> of the most specific and irreducible aspect of the act of creation, and thus a
> statement of the specificity and irreducibility of the creator—are accompa-
> nied by the contradiction and intensification of the relations between mem-
> bers of the artistic society. And so what Schücking calls "mutual admiration
> societies," small sects enclosed in their esotericism, begin to appear. (Bour-
> dieu 1969, 94; citing Schücking 1966, 30)

"Mutual admiration societies" appear within the Scene when participants co-
alesce for particular parties or events, based upon a shared philosophy about
BDSM or their mutual interest in a niche aspect of the scene—for instance,
groups for pro-dommes who specialize in wrestling or "Lesbian Sex Mafia,"
a group for lesbians interested in BDSM. Other societies form on the basis of
the perceived attractiveness of their members, closing ranks on the "trolls"
whom their members describe as populating the larger events.

In symbolically distancing themselves from economically oriented pro-
dommes, these women were also inherently distancing themselves from the
public world of BDSM, as portrayed in "mainstream" culture, including television, film, and pornography. Many informants spoke negatively about their
presentation in mainstream media. One indie, for instance, declared, "I think
it would be kinda fun to be a consultant for movies and TV shows and stuff
like that. I know people who've done that. I think it would be fun because I
see stuff and I'm like, 'That's so wrong. That doesn't happen.'"

Could you give me an example?
Nobody wants to be down on their hands and knees and bark like a dog. Nobody wants to be called a worm. I mean, I'm sure there's somebody. But

that's not real. Nobody really wants to be shouted at. Who does that? . . . I'm sure some people shout, but they're not very good.

Again, the rhetoric of authenticity permeates the discussion; this informant implies that pro-dommes influenced by the media have lost the competition for cultural legitimacy within the BDSM world. That is, "nobody really" behaves this way, and those who might are "not very good." Other women specifically linked economically oriented pro-dommes to these mainstream influences. "They see it on TV and think they can make a quick buck," one lifestyle pro-domme explained, about the "hoochie dommes." Like avant-garde artists disassociating themselves from the "enemy agents" of commercialism, lifestyle dommes thus authenticated themselves partially because they were autonomous from the influences of the mass markets.

The pinnacle of this cultural legitimacy in the autonomous sector, according to Bourdieu, is the "capital of consecration," since the "only legitimate accumulation" in this sector "consists in making a name for oneself" (1996, 148). Indeed, "consecrated" pro-dommes and other BDSM participants had gained a kind of celebrity status within the scene. Seven informants, for instance, mentioned the same domme's name during interviews, though only one of them was a personal acquaintance of hers. This fame becomes concretized through displays of skill at parties and other events. One pro-domme, describing the workshops held at a Manhattan fetish store, explained, "It's kind of interesting because you get to meet people that you might have seen on the net or heard about, that are kind of famous within the S&M world. It's like, 'Whoo hoo! Let's go see what she's got to show us!'" Women who specialized in less common practices, such as electric shocks or enemas, often earned names for themselves because of this specialization. Their names became linked to these particular practices in the Scene the way Andy Warhol might be associated with pop art or James Joyce with stream-of-consciousness fiction. In the absence of an emphasis on financial gain at the autonomous end of domination, the BDSM community thus consecrates those who win the competition for cultural legitimacy by demonstrating particular expertise.

The "Ideal Reader"

In the art world, the competition for authenticity extends not only to the artists but to the audiences for particular works as well. Bourdieu indicates that the intellectual increasingly has "the declared intention of refusing to recognize any but the ideal reader, who must be an *alter ego*, that is, another intellectual, present or future, able to assume in his creation or comprehension of works of art the same truly intellectual vocation which characterizes the autonomous intellectual as one who recognizes only intellectual legitimacy" (1969, 94). Just as they forged a discourse about "real" and "fake" pro-dommes, informants described their customer bases in similar terms. They conferred cultural legitimacy upon particular clients, denying it to those who did not have the intellectual capital to make the exchange worthwhile, who viewed commercial BDSM purely as a form of sex work, or who were not real submissives in the sense that they tried to seize control of the session.

One indie, describing why she'd had a difficult time working at a larger dungeon, explained:

> [The House told me,] "We're getting some complaints from our clients." Now, to me, that sounds ridiculous. The fucker is a *submissive*. How *dare* he complain. "Well, yeah, he's not getting exactly what he paid for." Like, well then go to a hooker. Don't come to me. I have training in this, I have an education, I know the psychology behind this, I've studied this *in college.* . . . They're thinking it's bad business for them, and I'm thinking, you're not getting real submissives. You just want a quick buck.

"Real" submissives, the "ideal readers" within this discourse, receive pleasure solely from being submissive to a dominant—not from having their needs fulfilled in a manner they themselves have determined. Topping from the bottom, then, is anathema to some pro-dommes not only because it disrupts the encounter and is an attempt at getting over but also because it is evidence of a sub's inauthenticity. Just as they spoke frequently about the inauthentic nature of other dommes, informants frequently spoke about "fake" subs during our interviews.[9]

One Major Tension of the Domme/Client Exchange

Now that I have identified what it means, within pro-domme narratives about the profession, to be a real dominatrix and a real submissive, I turn to the relationship between these distinctions and the struggle for control over the interaction. A major tension within the domme/client exchange is that pro-dommes, while "dominant" in a session, must also to some extent rely upon their clients—even the ones they feel are lacking in authenticity within their schema. Bourdieu makes a similar observation about individuals at the autonomous end of the artistic spectrum. While he distinguishes between "a cultural production specially destined for the market and, partly in reaction against that, a production of 'pure' works destined for symbolic appropriation," Bourdieu reasons that neither extreme is ever attained, "either total and cynical subordination to demand or absolute independence from the market and its exigencies" (1996, 141–42). Pro-dommes who used the rhetoric of purity and artistic expression themselves admitted that they were subject to the constraints of their clients' demands.

Here, the financial component of professional erotic dominance becomes salient, as pro-dommes contrasted their experiences of dominating clients for money and playing purely for recreation. Recall the male dominant who declared, "Clients are a lot of work. . . . You always do what they say." He indicated that his lifestyle play partners were much less likely to top from the bottom and that there were "no scripts" for these interactions. Another informant described a particular scenario in which a client kept her actions in check:

> Some gentlemen get really annoyed if you go out of character. One time I answered the door, said, "Come in, come in," and this guy went right into *mode*—calling me "My Lady." For some reason people fall back into that kind of Renaissance, medieval kind of thing. He said something and "My Lady" and I was chewing on jelly beans because it was Easter and I had all these jelly beans in my mouth. And he's going, "Ugh, what are you doing?" And I said, "I'm eating my jelly beans." And he goes, "Oh. Oh. I'll come back." And he did. He *walked out* and he came back twenty minutes later. And I knew he wanted me to finish my jelly beans. Me eating jelly beans while he's trying to be Sir Galahad or court jester or I don't know what the hell—I learned a lesson on that one.

Although the informant was the "dominant" partner in the scenario, she ceded to pressure from her client, whom she knew was not pleased with her departure from character. Here was a struggle for control in which the client, though ostensibly the bottom, taught her a "lesson" about how he expected her to behave in the future. As another pro-domme explained, about her paid sessions, "You have to be careful because there's a certain element of—of course you're dominant, but then they're paying you for a certain thing." Though she participated in the discourse on "fake" submissives who top from the bottom, this interviewee also acknowledged that she would typically continue a session, even if the client was being demanding in this way. Discussing what she called her high-maintenance clients, she indicated, "[They'll say], 'Okay, I like this, this, this, and this.' We call them 'McSessions'—burger-flipping sessions—where they're just work. You're just like, 'Eh, I'm gonna pay the bills with this.'"

Several pro-dommes drew similar parallels between the fast food industry and commercial BDSM. As one informant summarized, "Pro sessions are to

BDSM what McDonald's is to food." Pro-dommes' use of the burger-flipping metaphor signifies that, despite their claims to artistic purity, they felt that the exigencies of the market had the potential to turn them into automatons, slinging a commercialized and homogenized product. The analogy thus exemplifies Bourdieu's description of the "creative project," as "the place of meeting and sometimes of conflict between the *intrinsic necessity of the work of art* which demands that it be continued, improved and completed, and *social pressures* which direct the work from outside" (1969, 96; emphasis in original). Although the "McSessions" domme quoted above, for instance, interpreted her work as art and described sessions as "a way to express [her] creativity," the implication was that if she only dominated "pure" submissives who never topped from the bottom, her career no longer would be financially viable.

Along the same lines, one dominatrix who had stopped doing paid sessions indicated one of the reasons she left the industry: "I'm revolted by who shows up, pretending they're a submissive." Nevertheless, she asserted, she might have to begin again owing to financial troubles. Howard Becker, distilling art to the quest for material benefits, explains, "Audiences select what will occur as an art work by giving or withholding their participation in an event or their attention to an object, and by attending selectively to what they do attend to" (1982, 214). Commercial BDSM, similarly, is not economically feasible without consumers, and being "dominant" does not make the women here immune to these external pressures. Vanina Leschziner, in the context of a discussion of high cuisine, explains that in artistic realms "where products are judged by lay critics and audience, conformity and originality are two imperatives coexisting in tension" (2007, 81). The exigencies of their particular market require dominatrices, like Bourdieu's artists and Leschziner's chefs, to cater to both purists and uninformed clientele. Popularity with local submissives may not confer cultural legitimacy upon pro-dommes in the same way that consecration by participants in the Scene does, but it provides them with necessary economic capital. To keep afloat, most pro-dommes must satisfy both "real" and "fake" submissives.

Continuing on the theme of cuisine, looking at the dominatrix/submissive relationship alongside the producer/consumer relationship in the culinary world is particularly illuminating, not only because can we draw parallels between these two spheres, using chefs to better understand pro-dommes, but also because pro-dommes can also help us better understand professionals such as chefs, who think of their work in artistic terms. In the restaurant world, as Gary Alan Fine explains, professionals view their work in terms of its "aesthetic value," which functions as a marker of a chef's competence. Yet,

Fine points out, culinary production "is not unbounded, as client demands, organizational efficiency, and the organization's resource base have effects" (1992, 1268). For instance, in restaurants, as in larger dungeons, there may be friction between management and labor, and food preparers must, to some degree, suit the needs of their superiors. "Although there is a possibility within the kitchen for negotiation or at least a questioning of higher authority, an obdurate power structure determines what is served" (1287). Power operates similarly in the Houses, where as we have seen, managers and dungeon owners require dungeon dommes to perform sessions that the women themselves find distasteful or contrary to their own narratives about purity. While this is not the case for indies, their work is akin to culinary production in that they engage in labor about which they have a specific aesthetic discourse but must express their creativity under market constraints.

The way that pro-dommes speak about their interactions in the dungeon—face-to-face encounters located explicitly within the context of power exchange and discussed in terms of aestheticism—brings the tension between laborer and consumer in other aesthetically oriented fields into crisp focus. Even in the absence of managerial oversight, a pro-domme's ability to conform to her own narrative about aestheticism is curtailed by pressure from her clients. Chefs, like pro-dommes, have both individual and collective narratives about what constitutes "good" work in terms of aesthetic quality: for instance, whether grapes have "bad lines" or crepes are "lopsided" (Fine 1992, 1276). Though chefs do not usually engage with their customers face to face, their work may be influenced by the hierarchical structure of their establishments and by restaurant patrons who can decide whether or not dishes are to their liking. As for Bourdieu's example of the "favourable review," some BDSM websites and the websites for the dungeons themselves do contain reviews of various dommes. Subs who post on Internet message boards also relate their experiences in particular sessions. Restaurants, of course, have food critics.

At the same time that they are subject to market constraints, chefs and pro-dommes also have a degree of control over their clients as they develop arguments about what constitutes aesthetic quality and work within their constraints to bring these ideals to fruition. Further, the culinary world is like professional erotic dominance in that each customer puts his safety in the laborer's hands, whether it is by allowing himself to be bound and whipped or by ingesting a morsel of food. In short, pro-dommes and their clients unfog the role of control in this push-and-pull space of commercial aesthetic production, shedding light on the amount of control that each party has within these types of embattled purity regimes.

Deviations from the Bourdieusian Framework

While I have only made the claim that Bourdieu's rubric works as a structural analogy for the organization of this particular artistic realm, rather than a perfect box into which it fits, it is still illuminating to look at how the competition for cultural legitimacy within the BDSM world differs from that within more "traditional" art worlds. First, and perhaps most salient, is the unique genesis of professional erotic dominance as an industry. While avant-garde artists seek to distance themselves from the preexisting sphere of commercial art, it seems that, here, the chicken came before the egg. That is, based upon pro-dommes' characterizations of their industry, "avant-garde" ("purist" or "Old Guard") pro-dommes were around before the "phonies" came along. Pro-dommes indicate that they are seeking to symbolically distance themselves from commercialization now primarily because the quantity of "inauthentic" dommes in the industry has swelled in recent years.[10]

The second complication to the Bourdieusian frame is that the potential for serious bodily injury sets BDSM apart from some aesthetically oriented pursuits—though not, for instance, culinary production or dance—and the ability to play safely is inextricably linked to authenticity within my informants' narratives. One pro-domme, who had been in the Scene for over thirty years, described an incident at the local BDSM club in which she felt a player's safety was at risk:

> [Technique is bad] if you do not know where you're hitting, how you're hitting. You hit someone on a bone or you hit someone where there's a concentration of nerves or lymph nodes, you're gonna damage them. I saw a guy take a cane and hit someone on the neck. That's when I said, "Okay, that's it. I cannot take it anymore. That is *dangerous* and it's irresponsible." We got in a *huuuge* fight. [He said,] "How dare you interrupt me in my scene?" I said, "I appreciate that. I apologize for interrupting your scene. But that's dangerous, and if you paralyze that person, I am never going to be okay with the fact that *you* are irresponsible and you don't know what the hell you're doing. Here's my card—take my class. But don't you ever let me see you hit her again on her neck. . . . You could paralyze her and the fact that you don't know that makes you incompetent as a dom. You shouldn't even call yourself a dom. Read a book."

This description was representative of many accounts from informants who associated the technique and artistry of dominance with knowledge of the body and the minimization of permanent damage. Because she perceives this participant as an unsafe player, the interviewee denies him status within the community by telling him, "You shouldn't even call yourself a dom." In this sense, the stakes within the competition for cultural legitimacy are higher in erotic dominance than in some other artistic arenas, as not simply reputation or financial solvency are on the line but also the physical well-being of one's clients. However, although this emphasis on safety does not have correlates within any of the forms of art Bourdieu discusses in particular, there are correlates in the art world. BDSM is comparable, for instance, to some of the martial arts, in which the ability to strike without causing permanent bodily harm in one's opponent is sacrosanct.[11]

The element of eroticism also complicates an application of the Bourdieusian frame to this particular social world. Legitimacy as a dominatrix, within the discourse here, is connected to the unwillingness to perform sexual extras. "Purist" dommes, as has been demonstrated, authenticate their own work by contrasting themselves to the "fakes," the "hookers," "hoochies," and "prostitutes" who may perform these acts during their sessions. As one male client explained, "That's tip number one for you: if they're having sex, they're probably not dommes. . . . That would be a phony domme. That would be a prostitute." Partially this distinction arises because purist dommes perceive the submissive who comes into a session with the expectation of a sex act to be not a real sub, in the sense that he requires pleasure from the interaction beyond the gratification from being topped. Also, purist dommes perceive dommes who perform these particular sex acts as exceeding the proprietary boundaries of artistic expression. One interviewee, indicating that for legal reasons the women in her dungeon did not perform sex acts, told me, "The ones who are purists and who are practicing this art form would be offended by the insinuation that they would do [these sexual things]." (For more on legal issues, see appendix B.)

Again, although Bourdieu does not specifically discuss types of artistic expression that navigate the boundary between sex and art in this way, this does not mean that there are not correlates in the art world; a useful parallel to draw here is the boundary between "legitimate" acting in art films and acting in pornographic movies. It is also significant that those who engage in commercial art are sometimes described as "whoring themselves out" to the masses for financial gain.

It is clear that while all of the women in this study were paid to dominate men for money, through the rhetoric of the anti-"economic" economy, lifestylers repeatedly legitimated themselves as producers who possessed symbolic capital disconnected from profit.[12] In the chapters leading up to this one, I have made the claim that pro-dommes' conceptions of their professional expertise have a role in producing a contest for control between themselves and their clients that belies the image of the woman who is completely dominant in the encounter. Their claims to artistic purity function in much the same way. It is hardly a stretch to extend Hughes's characterization of the client who "may want an impossible result, and be bitterly resentful of the professional man's judgment that it is impossible" (1971, 361), to both the topping-from-the-bottom submissive and to the purchasers of services in other domains where creative process is in contention. One could imagine an interior decorator, for instance, engaging in the rhetoric of artistic purity while attempting to wrangle a demanding client who repeatedly tries to top from the bottom.

In this light, the fashion designer who asserted her professional claim when she reacted to a demanding customer by grumbling that she was "not a dressmaker" can be framed as a woman who was taking part in a particular purity regime continually put in peril by commercial demands. The customer who had requested the "disgusting" wedding dress was clearly not someone whom she considered to be her "ideal reader," yet the designer had to work with that customer to create a final product.

Using Bourdieusian theory as a structural metaphor for the world of professional erotic dominance thus brings into sharp relief a key tension within service industries that have aesthetic components. Additionally, this discourse of authenticity in which pro-dommes engage sheds a unique light on erotic labor, complicating its popular characterization as low-skilled work by interpreting at least this one industry as requiring a high degree of creativity and artistic technique. In the next chapter, I continue this discussion about conceptions of real and phony within this industry when I argue that, paradoxically, professional dominatrices' authenticity is determined by their ability to effectively play make-believe.

4

Playing Make-Believe: Fantasy and the Boundaries of Commercial Intimacy

I'm sitting in a basement dungeon in Queens, and the first thing I notice is the cheerleading outfit emblazoned with the word "SLUT" hanging on the back of the door. The wood-paneled room itself is unremarkable, reminiscent of many basements I encountered during my childhood in suburban Long Island, but its perimeter is organized into sections, each with its own theme. Along the wall to the left of me is the medical section, complete with a doctor's table and an assortment of gleaming tools. The far left corner is organized into a kind of schoolroom, with a desk, a blackboard, a dunce cap, and a round wall clock with a languid second hand. The domme who works out of this space—an indie in her forties—has devoted another area to "puppy play"; it includes a large cage, a dish, squeaky toys, and dog treats. The main feature of the prison-themed corner to my right is a seven-by-four-foot functional jail cell with bricks painted on the inside wall. The dungeon also contains, among other accoutrements, a swing, an OTK (over-the-knee) spanking bench, hoods, gas masks, whips, canes, leather restraints, dildos, a foot-worship throne, and a number of floggers. Finally, there's a television set. The domme tells me she often plays "very tasteful" pornography in the background during sessions.

This is in the spring of 2008, toward the end of my fieldwork for this project. By this point, I've seen most of these accoutrements of the trade before, in various combinations, at other dungeons. What strikes me in particular about this space, however, is the unique way in which it is so neatly compartmentalized, like a patchwork quilt of the major role-playing fantasies that sustain commercial BDSM. Each section tells its own story about the particular masks pro-dommes and their clients put on as they produce scenes in the dungeon.

In this chapter, drawing upon the sociological literature about "play" and "the game," I contend that these scenes can contribute to our knowledge about the social importance of make-believe outside of childhood. What is it, I ask, about the erotic sphere in general, and the world of BDSM in particular, such that participants "play" in them in a way that they do not within the other areas of their daily adult lives? In answer, I return to one of the central arguments of this text: part of the appeal of the dungeon is that it allows individuals to explore alternative aspects of their personalities. The dungeon brings out the subordinated facets of their gendered sexualities, thus illuminating them. At the same time, in weaving the tapestries of fantasy that underlie their dungeon interactions, pro-dommes attest to the durability of the gendered character of professional interactions. They produce a companionate femininity that is common within erotic labor in particular and traditional "women's work" more generally. I conclude the chapter by investigating the permeable boundary between professionalism and intimacy in these fantasy-sustained interactions.

The Social Functions of Sadomasochistic Play

Since at least the 1930s, social scientists have been concerned with play, but they have limited their scope to the importance of playing in the social lives of children. Perhaps most notably, George Herbert Mead viewed "play" as a period in human development through which young children get a sense of themselves as actors within their social worlds through games in which they imitate particular characters or roles: "Children get together to 'play Indian.' This means that the child has a certain set of stimuli which call out in itself the responses that they would call out in others, and which answer to an Indian. In the play period the child utilizes his own responses to these stimuli which he makes use of in building a self" (1967, 150). Mead views this "play period" as specific to young children.[1] As children mature, he argues, they move on to increasingly complex organized games, like baseball. In these games, according to Mead, the child "must be ready to take the attitude of everyone else involved in that game, and . . . these different roles must have a definite relationship to each other" (151; see also Lever 1978, 471, and Piaget 1962).

Other researchers concerned with the social role of play, however, have problematized Mead's distinction, suggesting that childhood play may have more in common with higher-order games than Meadian developmental theories would have us believe (Whalen 1995, Garvey 1974, Corsaro 1979). By challenging Mead's linear model and identifying this blurred boundary between childhood "play" and "the game," these scholars open the door for thinking about the leisure activities of adults in new ways. In short, acknowledging the gamelike features of play facilitates an acknowledgment, on the flip side, of the playlike features of games—specifically, erotic games between adults.

While a BDSM scene is like a game in that it is an organized encounter that involves a definitive role structure, it is also nothing like baseball. It is a form of make-believe in which actors assume roles and interact with each other with varying degrees of spontaneity, within boundaries but without any clear victor or goal within the scenario, other than arousal.[2]

Looking at play as not just the province of children, then, sheds light on a unique function of the erotic sphere in general, and BDSM particularly, within adult social life. Elizabeth Wilson briefly touches upon this point in an article about the 1982 Barnard College conference on sexuality. She muses that "from the way some sado-masochistic and similar sexual practices are described it is tempting to suppose that individuals find an outlet for the playful in these 'sexual games.' After all, for adults in our society there is no place where they can really 'play' other than in the intimacy of a relationship that is designated 'sexual'" (1983, 38). Wilson illuminates something specific to the erotic realm as a site for adult leisure: while adults regularly engage in games, they seldom play, whether because of lack of opportunity, lack of interest on the individual's part, or social unacceptability. In short, the erotic realm may provide access to play in a way that other areas of adult life do not.

This linkage between sex and play has, in the past, been touched upon conceptually (Foote 1954), but it has rarely been explored on an empirical level. One notable exception is John Alan Lee, who, citing Ovid and de Sade, has observed that historically "sex has long been fun and games" (1979, 92). Lee argues that the playful aspects of sex are particularly apparent in the context of homosexual sadomasochism because, like homosexual sex, SM is a purely recreational sexual act. It is divorced from the function of procreation. "Gay sex has long been playful sex (probably one of the reasons for the intense disapproval of it by those who valued only procreational sex)," Lee explains, "So it is not surprising to find a greater evidence of S/M sex among contemporary homosexuals than among heterosexuals. *S/M sex is the epitome of recreational sex*" (92; emphasis in original). It also bears repeating that participants in BDSM frequently refer to their interactions as "playing."

The practice of BDSM and the practice of play both involve the production of fantasy; thus, is it any wonder that dungeon interactions are so "playful"? Early twentieth-century historian Johan Juizinga has made the point that the quality of play is fundamentally different from that of "ordinary" life (1955, 4). This argument about play is substantively the same as the argument I have been making about BDSM throughout this text: it allows people to engage in activities and roles that are inaccessible during the everyday courses of their lives.³ In making this point, I draw upon Foucault, who has observed that, within SM, "sexual relations are elaborated and developed by and through mythical relations" (1997, 151).

Foucault brings us back to the first argument of this chapter. Pro-dommes' narratives about their encounters in the dungeon suggest that, in some sense, these interactions are a fiction. They involve the changing-up of social roles and reconfigured, "mythical" relationships because this reconfiguration *can* happen—because, in the erotic space of the dungeon, play is contextually acceptable. The dungeon thus provides a venue for a unique form of adult leisure. It is a venue in which individuals can become who they are *not.*

Playing Make-Believe in the Dungeon

Who are clients *not?* One way in which submissives alter their personas in the dungeon is through the experience of dressing up, for instance, in cross-dressing scenes, in which clients don articles of women's clothing. One independent pro-domme told me that she had disliked doing these sessions at the beginning of her career but had grown to enjoy them: "I like cross-dressing as a transformation—like, taking a guy and really, completely changing the way that he looks and then playing with personas. Seeing if I can bring the female persona out, which gives him a break from his regular life." Her description plays into a pervasive discourse about BDSM as a psychological escape—it is a "break" and a "transformation"—in addition to characterizing dungeon activities as playful.

At the same time that such scenes are evocative of early childhood play activities (for instance, a young girl trying on her mother's heels), they are reconfigured by gender (a grown man becomes the little girl) and have an underlying structure that distinguishes them from childhood play. As discussed, pro-dommes and their clients contextualize their interactions within larger fantasy scenarios through scripting conversations. Describing her pre-scene negotiation with clients, one Manhattan-based indie told me:

> I find out ahead of time: Is there anything you want to hear me say? Is there anything special you want me to do? Then we go to the particulars: what kind of scene. What have you done wrong? Why are you here? Why were you sent to me? If you're an adult, were you sent by management because you were disrespecting women? Or were you sent by your doctor because you were overeating? You know, that kind of thing. There usually has to be a reason that they're there. And that's when I work my best.

Through the scripting process, clients are given the opportunity to provide narrative frameworks for the make-believe that will occur in the session. A woman who had been working in a larger House in New York, for instance, recalled a recent client who had provided a specific context for their fantasy scene:

> The last guy I saw was into some kind of school role play where I was the soccer student and he was the coach who was spying on me in the locker room. And he wanted that I would find out and blackmail him, by basically saying that he would be my slave and, if not, then I'm going to tell the school principal and my parents and show all the pictures he has of him spying on all the girls. So we basically made him do our chores and our homework and basically ride him around like a pig and take, like, really obnoxious pictures of him and show it to the rest of the girls on the team, which were the other girls I was working with that day.

Here, there are roles, interaction, and reciprocity, but there is no winner or loser, no rules for interaction—only boundaries—and no turn taking; it is not a game in the Meadian sense. The participants immerse themselves in their roles and engage in make-believe in a way that has few counterparts in other areas of adult life. Similar examples may be found in the fantasy-related organizations that overlap with the BDSM world—the Renaissance Faire circuit and live-action role playing (LARPing) events. However, the latter, at least, are structured as games. For instance, they have a rule structure and turn taking.[4]

These fantasy scenarios in the dungeon can become highly particularized to meet the demands of individual fetishists. A Bay Area woman in her mid-twenties described an encounter with one client who had provided not only specific dialogue but also a costume for their session:

> One of my favorite clients ever, ever, ever was this really funny British guy who had a fetish for the Revolutionary War. . . . Like, he had written a comic book and what he wanted me to do was read the comic book on camera and dress up in the outfit that was like one of the characters, which is almost like a fetish-looking version of a Revolu[tionary War uniform]—like, a thong, but uniform on top, like with the helmet with the plume and everything. And there's Liberty Girl and the nasty Redcoat. I was Liberty Girl, and he really wants us to crush those nasty Redcoats. . . . And it was just—he was aroused by it. And the fact that he was aroused by it, I love thinking about, where does that *start*? Where *are* you when you think, like, "The Revolutionary War is *hot!*" [*laughs*].

This is a good example of a scene that is not SM oriented, or even about the client's submission, but that is structured around a particular fetish. The informant brought up this scene in the context of a discussion about the fact that "there's someone with a fetish for everything." When I made the point that outliers are commonplace, this is what I meant. One informant, for instance, described a leprechaun fetishist. Another client was aroused by a Hillary Clinton mask. These scenes differ from childhood play not only because they are in response to certain fetishes, and not only because these are adults at play, but because these interactions are paid exchanges. To meet the demands of these more highly individualized fetishes, dommes must carefully tread the line between commercial appeal and playful spontaneity in their sessions.

During these commercial interactions, not only do fetishes mature over time, as I have discussed, but sessions also tell more complex stories over time, as dommes and subs work together as scriptwriters, "unwinding [their] own reel[s]" (Goffman 1974, 133). As noted, my informants described some clients who remain with them for extended periods of time as progressing to both more intense behaviors and more intricate scripts. Based on these characterizations, the dungeon becomes a space not only for the development of these behaviors but also for the development of punishment narratives. This becomes apparent in an account from one Manhattan-based indie, whom I had asked to describe a "typical scene": "I'm the neighbor lady and you've been looking through my window, so your mom sends you over to do errands for me but instead I punish you. And you can't tell anybody that I'm punishing you. And, strangely enough, some of these people return to me and the story continues to develop." The accumulation of scenes over time within a particular pro-domme/client pairing can be iterative—reproducing the same scene during each interaction—but it appears, more often than not, to be generative to some degree. It is not just that clients can handle more pain over time and that their tastes expand over time, but their stories can also develop over time, as domme and sub go on a journey together, unwinding their reels of fantasy.

Maintaining the Fantasy

Because BDSM is founded on a set of "mythical relations," within which clients can engage in behaviors that are atypical for them, it is important for pro-dommes to preserve the fantasy character of their exchanges and to safeguard their interactions against intrusions from the "real world." In some cases, the men who come to see dominatrices have highly particularized fantasies that, these clients assert, can only be maintained through the use of specialized props or attire. Dommes spoke about the specificity of clients' fetishes in a way that played into the discourses about topping from the bottom and problem clients, as well as about the authenticity of their submissives. Pro-dommes told me that cross-dressing clients, in particular, required highly specific accoutrements in order to sustain their fantasies. "A lot of major cross-dressers aren't submissive," one Manhattan-based indie told me. "A lot of [the] time those people tend to be really high-maintenance. Divas. 'Do you have this color of a blonde wig?' and 'I need a black latex skirt and boots.' I'm like, 'I can't have everything in everybody's size!'" A Bay Area pro-domme explained, similarly, "For somebody who wants to cross-dress, let's say if you put them in a one-inch heel, they feel ripped off because what they really want—what their fetish is, is a six-inch [heel]. And if you tell them you have a corset but you have a little flimsy merry-widow with two bones in there, they'll never come back, because they wanted a *corset*." Because of the specificity of their fetishes, some of the more "hardcore" cross-dressing clients bring their own outfits to sessions.

Pro-dommes told me that clients with niche tastes often needed them to be specifically attired in order to elicit an erotic response. As noted, pro-dommes often discussed these particular wardrobe requests in the context of clients who were not "authentic" submissives or who "topped from the bottom." However, most accommodated such demands, at varying levels of specificity. "For some clients they have specific things that they definitely want in a session," one dominatrix who worked in a Manhattan House explained. "Like, for example, they want someone who must wear a black outfit, and if you don't have one, it ruins the fantasy for them. And they just won't pick you."

Pro-dommes create environments that nurture fantasies not only through the way they dress but also in the way they construct their dungeon spaces as havens from the everyday world. They accomplish this through various sensory devices—commonly, for instance, filling the room with music. One indie, discussing a recent session, described the lengths that she had gone to, in order to turn her dungeon into a kind of alternative reality:

> I had pre-set-up my dungeon, which is done with massive beams, twelve-by-fours . . . and black velvet drapes. There's like thirty adjustable intensity lights in the ceiling. I have a $12,000 oxblood red Persian rug. I had set up the CBT chair. I had turned on the fog machine, turned down the light, and I had pre-loaded some synthesized Middle Eastern music. . . . And when you walked into the space, it was like you were stepping into a medieval Middle Eastern dungeon. And I had him sit on the CBT chair, and I hit the remote control

and the music came bursting—it's like an eight-hundred-watt sound system. And I hit the fog machine, and a bank of fog filled the room, and I had little candelabra lights. It was really a bit overwhelming. I intentionally do visual, sensory overload when the clients come in to play, to try to get them out of the real world and into a fantasy play-space, for that suspension of disbelief.

"Real-world" intrusions in the dungeon can create ruptures in the fantasy bubbles that encompass professional sessions. Recall the woman, for instance, who had been eating jelly beans when her client arrived. The fact that she was not in character upon his arrival proved so disturbing to him that he had to leave the dungeon. Other informants told me that they specifically took measures to avoid these disturbances. One House in Manhattan, for instance, was equipped with buzzers in every room; the receptionist would buzz the dominatrices five or ten minutes before a session was scheduled to end. Some of the women, however, had foregone the buzzing. They had begun playing hour-long CDs, and they timed their sessions by the tracks that were playing. This new practice, as one former employee explained, was "good because the buzzer going off was sort of a break in the fantasy."

The practice of using music rather than buzzers to signal the close of a scene underscores the importance of making a seamless transition between the end of the fantasy scenario and the client's reemergence into everyday life. My interviewees suggested that, when a transition is not made smoothly, there occurs a disjuncture that underscores the fictional character of their interaction. Their repeated emphasis on the importance of, for instance, "winding down" a scene, bringing it to "a natural end," or "ending it gracefully," tells us something about the relationship of the dungeon to the larger social world. While the dungeon is a fantasy bubble, it is a bubble embedded within reality, and reality can impinge upon it at any time. As guardians of the bubble, professional dominatrices indicate that it is their task to make certain that it is not abruptly popped but rather is gently dissolved when the session reaches its close.

Pro-dommes' emphasis on their roles as wardens of fantasy in the dungeon is also indicative of the importance of the narrative structure of the scene. Another way to think about the job of a pro-domme, who functions as custodian of narrative structure and gatekeeper between scene and reality, is as a kind of erotic anesthesiologist. An anesthesiologist's particular expertise lies not necessarily in her ability to put people to sleep for surgery but to safely and effectively wake them up afterward. Similarly, pro-dommes assert that their task is not only to lead the client into this alternative world for the duration of a session but also to successfully bring him out of it.

Negotiating the Boundaries of Intimate Labor

Within the fantasy-sustained environment of the dungeon, in which pro-domme and client go on a narrative journey together and interact physically during an erotically charged exchange, they gingerly walk the line between intimacy and social distance. In thinking about this line, it is useful to consider other types of professional exchange that require both closeness and professionalism. In *Doormen*, Bearman describes one historical strategy for maintaining this precarious balance within service industries:

> Historically, and still the case in some contexts, the sociological tension be-
> tween simultaneous physical closeness and social distance was simply resolved
> by negating the social identity of the other, through slavery or other physical
> and psychic forms of inducing social death. The sociological "trick" of such
> systems is the radical negation of the other as a strategy for neutralizing the
> intimacy that arises from close physical contact—bathing, dressing, schedul-
> ing, serving, feeding, and nursing. (2005, 7)

While, in Bearman's study, tenants and doormen manage the social space separating them "more subtly" (7), it is useful to consider this "radical negation of the other" in the context of pro-dommes and their subs. Some submissives, like some clients of prostitutes, are able to objectify their pro-dommes in this way, localizing any intimacy within the walls of the dungeon. As one purely lifestyle dominatrix at the New York BDSM club told me, echoing Simmel, "Commercial transaction is great for subs because they can get what they want with no romantic entanglement."

The element of make-believe in these interactions, however, lends an additional dimension to this neutralizing of the other. Some pro-dommes suggested that the fact that these are fantasy-sustained environments actually allows some clients to "negate" them in a unique way: by exalting them. As one interviewee explained, "There are some clients who, when they sexualize their domme it's not—it doesn't work for them to see their domme as a sexual being. They just want to see her as a goddess, pure. And to serve her. And *serving* for them is the systemic pleasure." Some clients confirmed this sentiment, telling me that they could never imagine having sex with their domme because they had placed her on a pedestal; she was their "goddess." This particular narrative suggests that, by thinking of his dominatrix as a "goddess," a submissive can manage the inherent intimacy of the exchange, creating the social distance required by the context. This disconnect is particularly apparent in the various activities of body "worship"—for instance, "foot worship," "ass worship," "muscle worship," or "breast worship"—through which the domme becomes further depersonalized. In these scenarios, the fetishist can identify the foot, for instance, as the object of adulation, rather than the woman per se. Clients can thus "induce social death" not through degradation—as in the case of slavery—but through an exalting objectification that manages the tension between the intimate nature and the practical requirements of the exchange.

While negation of the other via goddess worship is one way in which clients can manage to be simultaneously intimate and distant, more commonly pro-dommes spoke about clients who had attempted to cross the boundary between the fantasy world of the dungeon and everyday life. That is, rather than nullifying their dommes' sexuality or even personhood, they went the other way, striving to establish relationships with their dommes outside of sessions.

In some cases, maintaining a real-life rapport with clients could be part of the job. According to my informants, it is common for pro-dommes and their repeat clients to discuss non-BDSM-related topics before and after sessions. "I chat a lot," one indie told me, for example. "You see somebody for a while, you tend to develop a friendship with them. So I'll be like, 'Oh, how's your kids?' [He'll say,] 'Oh, so-and-so is in the choir' or 'taking Japanese.' [I'll say,] 'Oh, taking Japanese? I know Japanese,' and we'll talk in it." Of course, such discussions of shared interests are not unique to dommes and subs; they reflect the situational intimacy that characterizes many working relationships. Co-workers, for instance, can develop the potential for intimacy by making similar connections based upon "points of contact" such as similar demographic characteristics or shared recreational interests (Marks 1994, 846).

Clients—similarly to co-workers, in certain situations—go beyond the accepted rapport created by these points of contact, however, when they attempt to forge attachments that transcend the occupational setting. These relationships do not have to be romantic in nature for a pro-domme to perceive them as transgressive. An independent dominatrix in her fifties, for instance, told me about one client who had "kinda crossed the line" by aggressively seeking her friendship. The client was a female spanking fetishist, "And all she wanted to have me do was wale away. Just spank and spank and spank and spank. And, with her, she was a very nice person but she wanted to be my friend and that made me uncomfortable. She was always like, 'Let's go to dinner together.' And it wasn't sexual. I mean it wasn't—she wasn't gay or anything like that."

More often than not, however, this boundary crossing does have a romantic component. My informants told me that it was not uncommon, for instance, for clients to attempt to turn them into girlfriends. One woman who specialized in wrestling sessions described a sub who had repeatedly sought a romantic attachment with her: "The offer he made me was, 'Well, I think you'd make a really great girlfriend, so maybe if you wanted to go horseback riding with me this weekend, we could then do some grappling afterwards.' I was like [*sarcastically*], 'Oh, boy.'" She, as well as other women I interviewed, conceptualized these advances not only as inappropriate extensions of the D/S fantasy into real life but as ways for the client to get over on them, since boyfriends do not have to pay to play.

It should be noted that some pro-dommes encouraged these romantic advances, up to a point. For some clients, the fact that they could potentially have a transgressive relationship with their dominatrices was part of the fantasy that kept them coming back to do sessions. One Asian pro-domme from California described an experience in which comments she made about her actual romantic partner disrupted the client's fantasy:

> You get these guys who are interested in you 'cause you're Asian. And some of them have this Madame Butterfly complex, right? Which is that she's, like, the noble but fallen woman. She martyrs herself, you know? She's like, "Oooh, I'm a little butterfly!" So I had this one guy—he was an academic guy, you know, president of his society. And he would just rub my feet for hours, and then he would drink my piss. And I would lock him in chastity.[5] . . . We would talk about my life and my opinions and stuff like that. He'd go, "You're so great, you're so great," and he would send me money. And he would always be locked in chastity. The guy annoyed me because he'd be like, "You're too good! You're too good for this!" . . . And I'm like, "I enjoy what I do. I do what I want, and I'm not forced to do anything." But I just blew it off after a while because I'm like, "Well, he's nice, and this is his fantasy." And he's so generous with me; he sends me money. So that continued for a long time, and then in the meantime during these marathon scenes—you know, hours and hours, where we're talking—it slipped that I had been partnered to a man for over a decade. Do you think he ever saw me again? No. Because, for him, the fantasy was to support this woman adrift in a sea of men who just want to use her and abuse her, and he was holding me up like the angel that I was. . . . He was just another Asian fetishist.

Within this pro-domme's narrative, the client's fantasy of a paternalistic relationship between himself and the dominatrix becomes the fetish itself. In such circumstances, any introduction of real-world elements into the scenario threatens to—and, in this case, does—throw the interaction off course.

Another aspect of the industry that this dominatrix's account brings into sharp relief is that, although the nature of domme/client pairs can allow for the reconfiguration of hierarchy, stereotypical relationships of gender, power, and race can also get reproduced within these pairs. One salient theme that emerged during interviews with Asian dommes was that their sessions often played into these "Madame Butterfly" fantasies or other stereotypical images of women in need of rescue. Such scenarios play into hegemonic conceptions not only of gender—paradoxically, a kind of helpless femininity—but of a specifically racialized gender.

Intimate Exchange and the Significance of the Gift

One dominatrix's assertion that although she found her client annoying, she continued to see him because "he's so generous" is indicative of the ambivalence that dommes can feel about their clients' attachment to them, when it comes in the form of money or gifts. The same informant who had rolled her eyes about the client who asked her on a date (to be followed by free grappling) told me that she welcomes the practice of gift giving:

> I had a client who was also very much a fan—like, some are one-time clients [and] some are fans—ask me what he should get me for Christmas. And that was very early in my sessioning days, where I was like, "I shouldn't encourage him!" And now I'm thinking, like, "Damnit, I should've thought of something good."
> *Why did you think you shouldn't encourage him?*
> I was like, "Why is this guy stalking me? Oh my God!" I've come a long way since I began sessioning.

Her statement that she has "come a long way" implies that she has learned to accept a certain form of intimacy from subs while negotiating an essential social distance from them.

I characterize gift giving as a "form of intimacy," in this context in particular, for a couple of reasons. First, while some gifts given to pro-dommes are utilitarian or, by the dommes' descriptions, just plain bizarre, more often they are the traditional paraphernalia of romantic closeness. My informants described, for example, receiving very high-end "vanilla" gifts: "Great shoes—Louis Vuitton, or Guccis. Fancy clothing, great dinners, opera tickets, ballet tickets, vacations. Like, I went to Paris for five days with someone." Clients also presented their dommes with tokens representing the tools of their trade. "Often the gifts people give me are 'Gosh, this would be really fun to have you use on me,'" one woman explained, "My cattle prod is one of those. Because the guy thought it would be fun for me to have a cattle prod." One woman I interviewed around the holidays told me that she had set up an Amazon Christmas list for her clients: "My wish list is like a wedding registry for everybody else. I've got china and a TV. Rugs. A lamp. A camera. You know, sheets." Finally, I heard many accounts of strange gifts; almost all of my interviewees reported having gotten at least one present they found bewildering. One mystified fifty-four-year-old dom told me that clients regularly send him dolls ("Don't ask me why"). A twenty-six-year-old Caucasian domme also had an experience that was puzzling to her:

> There was a guy who was very intent on bringing a gift, but it was like a cleaning-out-his-apartment kind of gift. So I got an old throw pillow and a highly offensively racist decanter of, like, a Caribbean-style peasant character sitting on a cask of rum and you could pour out of his cigar. And I was like, I have a feeling that that's worth a lot of money, in an antique, vintage sort of oh-my-God-that's-from-his-grandmother's-cabinet sort of way. It's also highly offensive and really tacky.

She told me she ended up leaving the decanter in a phone booth.

While most of my informants had stories about receiving strange tokens of appreciation, the most common gifts that they reported receiving were the kinds of things that one might purchase for a lover: candy, flowers, wine, and lingerie. One indie based in Manhattan, listing the gifts she most commonly received ("wine, flowers, earrings, crystal boxes . . ."), trailed off, musing, "They're kind of romantic gifts when you think about it." Another woman pointed out that most of the gifts she gets from clients are "the usual things you'd take on a date, basically." The gesture of gift giving can thus play into the client's fetish of the relationship itself. "It's as much for them as it is for me, I think, when they give gifts," a Bay Area woman explained, "because it's their *fantasy* of gifting."

The second reason that I describe gift giving as an "intimate" exchange within pro-domme/client relationships is that, in the context of erotic labor, gifts of any kind produce intimacy in a way that cash does not. Here, again, it is useful to reiterate Simmel's argument that money, not a gift, is exchanged for sex because "the gift of a specific object . . . always, through its content, its choice and its use, retains an element of the person who has given it." Through gift giving, the client may be able to symbolically transcend the boundary of the professional/client relationship rather than "radically terminating" that relationship, as he would by simply paying the dominatrix and leaving.

This transgression of the bounded intimacy within the dungeon is accepted, and even welcomed, when it remains symbolic, in the form of gifts that merely hint at social closeness or when it expresses a nonthreatening emotion. One domme who had worked out of a larger House, for instance, talked about a situation in which she was particularly touched by a trans client's gift *because* it broke down the wall between fantasy and reality; it was a gesture directed toward her as a person, rather than in relation to her play persona:

> She knew I tend to go jogging and not always in the safest places. And she gave me this fabulous knife in a sheath to hang around my neck while jogging. And my first reaction to it was, "Oooh, this is beautiful. It's so sexy!" And she's like, "Sexy? I just worry about you." And it had nothing to do with wanting me to use it in scene. She said, "Yeah, for you when you go jogging." And *that* nearly made me cry. Because that was something that was not about [me as] Mistress ——. . . . It had nothing to do with her image of, you know, this professional figure, or a desire to have me in session. It was absolutely about *me* and keeping me safe. It just blew me away as an incredibly generous, loving—it wasn't like she was trying to see behind the mask and *push* for anything. She was just caring about me.

In this instance, the giving of the gift brought the domme/client relationship into the domain of real life, but in a way that the dominatrix perceived as innocuous, just like conversations about shared points of interest. My interviewee indicated that the gesture was nonthreatening, and even "generous [and] loving," since the client was not trying to get over on her and did not "push" for intimacy.

On the other hand, because gifts so often play into the fantasy of a more intimate relationship, there can be a tension between accepting them and maintaining social distance from clients. "I used to live in an apartment that was owned by one of my clients," an independent domme in her early twenties recalled. "I had a million-and-half-dollar Tribeca two bedroom for a little while [*laughs*]. . . . That was how I moved to New York. I had a client that gave me this apartment that he owned. And he really wanted a girlfriend—or, he wanted *me* to be his girlfriend. So after about five months, you know, it was over." Some dommes do have clients (more often, personal subs) who supply various elements of their lifestyles, and the arrangement works for both parties. Other times, as in this informant's case, pro-dommes perceive such clients to be seeking attachments beyond the boundaries of these commercial relationships. In these situations, unless the domme is willing to make that leap with the client, the relationship generally cannot be sustained.

Correlates in Other Forms of Erotic Labor: "The Girlfriend Experience"

The fact that some clients seek intimate attachments with their dommes outside of the dungeon further challenges the Simmelian notion about "radical termination" of the interaction. Drawing parallels between prostitution and economic exchange, Simmel argues: "Money serves most matter-of-factly and completely for venal pleasure which rejects any continuation of the relationship beyond sexual satisfaction: money is completely detached from the person and puts an end to any further ramifications. When one pays money one is completely quits, just as one is through with the prostitute after satisfaction is attained" (1971, 121).

Prior ethnographic work on other forms of erotic labor has also problematized such claims about the disconnect that occurs at the end of these interactions. Bernstein points out, for instance, that the "girlfriend experience," (GFE) has become "one of the most sought after features" of a client/prostitute interaction (2007, 126). "Even when the encounter lasts only a few minutes," Bernstein observes, "from the client's perspective it may represent a meaningful and authentic form of interpersonal exchange. . . . For these men, what is, at least ideally, being purchased is a sexual connection that is premised on bounded authenticity." She notes that some clients "boasted of their ability to give sex workers authentic sexual pleasure, insisted that the sex workers they patronized liked them enough to offer them freebies or to invite them home for dinner, and proudly proclaimed they had at times even dated or befriended the sex workers they were seeing" (127). Frank, similarly, observes that strip club patrons attach importance to their personal connections with the dancers and value the "authenticity" of these interactions. For instance, "remembering a man's name and information about his life when he returned to the club a second time was an extremely successful strategy for demonstrating one's sincerity as a dancer" (2002, 208). In their study of Puerto Rican sex workers, Helena Hansen, Maria Margarita Lopez-Iftikhar, and Margarita Alegria observe that these personal connections can work to the prostitutes' benefit as well; clients with whom they have cultivated relationships are more likely to use a condom and to follow through with their payment (2002, 297). And Janet Lever and Deanne Dolnick describe such displays of interest, in the context of call girls and their clients, as mutually perpetuated illusions: "Both client and call girl *agree to pretend* that her caring and sexual attraction for him are real" (2000, 86; emphasis in original).

In a similar way, in the sphere of professional erotic dominance the ability to successfully pretend paradoxically marks a pro-domme as "authentic."

As I have argued, clients of professional dominatrices want "real" dommes, in the sense that they desire genuinely dominant women with professional expertise. Some of them, similarly to the clients of prostitutes or strip club regulars, also desire dommes who are "authentic" in the sense that they are really interested, or appear to be interested, in the men's lives outside of the dungeon. One dungeon domme, echoing the sentiments of many women I interviewed, told me that it is common for clients to want in a dominatrix "someone who can talk to you or listen to you about your problems."

At the same time, then, that the dominatrix's dungeon is a socially "deviant" space in that it allows men to perform submission and vulnerability, the women perform a kind of companionate femininity that is not atypical. While pro-dominance inverts the gender/power hierarchy in some ways, it is not unique in this particular sense. The companionate emotional work that dominatrices perform in order to demonstrate their authenticity, furthermore, represents a way of "doing" gender that is not confined to commercialized eroticism. Hochschild, for instance, observes that roughly one third of American workers, and one half of all women working "have jobs that subject them to substantial demands for emotional labor" (2003, 11). Professional dominatrices, like call girls and erotic dancers, but also like waitresses and flight attendants, are most successful at their work—by their own description—when they appear caring and solicitous toward their clients. Therefore, in order to preserve the fantasy sphere represented by the dungeon, pro-dommes engage in a type of work that is not unlike other, more traditional, forms of female labor.

Boundary Crossing: Personal Relationships and Role Engulfment

Thus far in this chapter, I have discussed the "mythical relations" in which pro-dommes and their clients participate, as well as the companionate work that pro-dommes must routinely do in order to mark themselves as "authentic" and preserve the fantasy element of the exchange. This combination of a fantasy-sustained environment and elements of the "girlfriend experience" during the interaction between dominatrix and client can lead to moments in which the boundary between intimacy and professionalism becomes blurry. Pro-dommes strive to manage points of contact with their clients, maintaining a social distance despite engaging in various forms of interpersonal exchange, ranging from erotic touching to intimate conversations.

They set up these boundaries between themselves and their clients in a variety of different ways. In addition to not performing certain sex acts with clients, pro-dommes who are also in the lifestyle sometimes save certain aspects of play for their personal relationships. Spitting, for instance, was one act commonly reserved for intimate partners. One informant also told me that she refuses to do face slapping in session because "that's a private play thing."

In addition, several women indicated that they refused to take on clients to whom they were sexually attracted. While the majority of women I interviewed indicated that doing sessions was not sexually exciting for them,[6] some discussed instances in which their arousal threatened to disrupt the dynamics of the exchange. Asked if she ever became aroused during a scene, for instance, a Manhattan-based indie in her early thirties responded, "Not professionally, because I'm really good at compartmentalizing. And if I ever find myself really attracted to a client, I have to send him away. . . . I dated one client—everybody's dated a client—but I dated one client, and I'd set up my psychological barriers so specific that it just really messed with my head. It was so hard for me to make the transition. I have to keep my boundaries." As her story illustrates, it is not only clients whose transgression has the potential to upset the precarious balance between intimacy and professionalism.

At the same time, her assertion that "everybody's dated a client" suggests that, in the BDSM world, the boundary between commercial and real-life relationships is at least somewhat permeable. Sometimes men who start out as clients go on to become personal subs or even romantic partners. One polyamorous domme from the Bay Area described a client who had transitioned into a lover:

I do have a secondary relationship with a man, that's been on and off for six years, and I met him through this.
He was your client?
Yes. At the time I was physically attracted to him above and beyond the constraints of a session.

Here, the dynamics of the dungeon interaction, in which fantasy and reality tenuously coexist, could not be sustained given the pro-domme's feelings for her client, and so they forged a different type of relationship.

Both dommes and subs also transgress the boundary between make-believe and reality during moments in which their session personas bleed over into everyday life. This phenomenon is not specific to professional BDSM; it has been observed in the lifestyle community as well. Lee, for instance, discusses this problem of "role engulfment" among the male homosexual sadomasochists in his study (1979, 91). Moreover, lifestylers use the term "top's syndrome" or "top disease" to refer to an individual who has become so identified with her dominant role in the BDSM scenario that she begins to take on "an unwarranted attitude of superiority" (Wiseman 1996, 375). The BDSM participants I spoke with described this "syndrome" as most commonly occurring among people who "live it 24/7." In the argot of the BDSM community, "living it 24/7" is used to characterize the most "hard-core" lifestyle players, whose primary romantic relationships involve continuous, routinized enactment of BDSM archetypes—for instance, master/slave, dom/sub, top/bottom. An indie based in the Bay Area told me, "I feel like a lot of clients, and a lot of pro-dommes, are more balanced than people who are lifestyle, because if you do this 24/7 it's no longer a game, and it can hide things that are not right."

However, for some professional dominatrices who are also in the lifestyle, identities and play personas are inseparable—or, at least, the line between them is blurred. In our e-mail correspondence, a few of my potential informants used capitalized pronouns to refer to themselves, even during banal discussions about topics such as where to meet up ("You will find Me at the Starbucks at the corner of . . ."). It is not clear, of course, to what extent these potential informants were simply playing into what they thought my expectations of a dominatrix might be, or whether they were—like the dom who told me his wife would put me "up on the rack" for spilling my glass of water in his living room—having some fun with me. Regardless, it is clear that a small minority of dommes, even pros, are fully engulfed in their play personas. One of my informants, describing a well-known professional dominatrix in the New York community, told me, "She *is* a domme. You can go to her house at 2 am, and she's a domme." Another pro-domme explained that, for some women in the industry, there is no separation between their professional and private lives: "'Lifestyle' means 'I do this 24/7 and I have a whole stable of slaves and they live with me and I use them for sex.' I mean, wow. I don't wanna do that. Too much work."

This range in the extent to which professional dominatrices perceive their play personas as real sheds a new light on the different expectations that they have from their subs, in terms of topping from the bottom. It is instructive to compare the domme who said that she hangs up on potential clients when they say "Mistress, I *want*," to the one who shrugs off her clients' desire to control the scene, noting, "They're not my [lifestyle] submissives. I don't require that they submit to me." While the former is "really" a domme, from the moment she picks up the phone, the latter insinuates here, and states directly elsewhere in her interview, that her interactions with her personal subs are more "real" than the commercial transactions in her dungeon. This distinction tells us something interesting about conceptions of authenticity within professional erotic dominance as opposed to within other forms of sexualized labor. In prostitution, for instance, authenticity is "bounded" (Bernstein 2007) within the context of the interaction; some pro-dommes, however, "are" dominatrices, even outside of the session room. Even though interactions in the dungeon are constructed as play, for some women there is nothing under the mask.

The attitude of the woman who observed that being a domme 24/7 looked like "too much work," however, was the most common among my interviewees. The majority of my informants—even the lifestyle players—drew clear boundaries between their BDSM roles and everyday behavior. "I feel very strongly that, out of scene, my clients are my equals," one informant told me. "I don't believe the propaganda. I'm not really, you know, the evil bitch-goddess on my pedestal [laughs]. I'll be happy to play that for you, but I don't actually believe that." And one indie pointed to the untenability of role engulfment in an everyday context, noting that, in real life, "I'm just me. What can you do? If you go to the florist and say, like, 'I demand tulips, slave!' that's just ridiculous. That doesn't work."

Many pro-dommes not only indicated that they thought of their session personas as masks that they took off when they left the walls of the dungeon, but they maintained a lightheartedness about what went on within those walls. Lee suggests that this sense of humor among SM participants is beneficial to the participants' well-being because it strengthens the barrier between reality and the play context: "The safe partners are . . . those not taken in by their own act. . . . As Goffman first illustrated with the joking surgeon, humor is a great role-distancer. Master and slave must be able to laugh at themselves" (Lee 1979, 91). One thing that is particularly apparent in my interview recordings is the good-natured laughter that can be found throughout the interviewees' responses.

On the flip side, in the absence of this role distancing, BDSM interactions can become potentially unsafe. On December 4, 2008, the *New York Post* splashed a headline across its latest edition: "Lawyer's Deadly Secret: Slain by S&M Madman Obsessed with Victim's Whip-Mistress Girlfriend" (Schram and Fermino 2008). Melodramatic newspaper diction aside, here was a situation in which role engulfment ended in tragedy. A sub, who had transitioned to a lover and become obsessed with his dominatrix had shot her other lover and then himself. People in the New York Scene told me that they had seen the warning signs of his becoming too absorbed in his fantasy-based relationship with the domme before this incident occurred.

Because role engulfment can become unsafe, pro-dommes told me that they are often alert for such warning signs when they screen clients. A woman who specializes in wrestling sessions described one situation in which she had been candid with a client about her concern that he was too engrossed in the fantasy:

> I had a client who was very much into the trash talking beforehand, and at one point during negotiations for that session I was like, "You can play whatever game you want, but I need to step out of this for a moment and just know that we both know that it's a game and you're not a lunatic." And [my manager] got in on those negotiations as well, and we both got on the phone and we said to the guy, "Before you go on playing your trash-talking scenario that we understand is important to you, we need a *sane*, upfront guarantee that you know it's a game." Which the guy was like, "Of course! Of course!" And when I showed up at the session, it was actually perfectly fine.

Significantly, in the context of potential role engulfment, the clients I spoke with were less likely than dommes to classify sessions as "theatrical" or "performance." One client in his early thirties told me, for instance, "To me when you're actually playing, it's too real for it to be theater. At least for when I play. What you feel is too intense for anything to be dramatic." Such comments from this admittedly small sample of clients suggest that the commercial BDSM interaction is more of a reality for subs than for dommes, who function as the custodians of the series of boundaries that underlie the exchange: between intimacy and professionalism, between themselves and their clients, and between fantasy and reality.

The Significance of Plausibility

I'm in the basement of a Moroccan restaurant, and two dommes in skimpy outfits are sitting opposite each other at a table, trading insults and downing shots while a camera rolls. Today they've rented out this space to shoot a video commissioned by a Wall Street trader with a shot-drinking fetish. The plot of the video consists of the two women drinking in turn (the "liquor" is, in fact, white grape juice) and becoming increasingly "drunker" until one "passes out" and the other emerges the victor. It's one of those situations in which—like the Revolutionary War scenario—the erotic component is not necessarily evident unless one has the particular fetish. I watch the shoot and hang out, mingling with others who've come to watch and hang out, including a tall, muscular pro-domme who self-identifies as gender queer. We get to chatting, and at one point she mentions that although she does fantasy, not competitive, wrestling sessions, her clients have told her that they come to her because she looks as though she could physically overpower them.

Fantasy wrestling, in which the domme and client pretend to grapple but the domme always emerges the victor, is a particularly interesting case within the context of play and the game, because it is play that is framed as a game. Whereas in Mead's model, mastery of play is a stepping-stone to mastery of the game, here participants have already mastered the concept of wrestling and incorporate its elements—its role structure, its positions, its "trash talking"—into the make-believe scenario.

The gender queer dominatrix's comment speaks to the fact that, for some clients, wrestling fetishists in particular, the roles within the make-believe scenario must be filled by plausible players or the fantasy cannot be sustained. Along the same lines, one client told me that he prefers to visit pro-dommes who specialize in wrestling sessions because he likes the feeling of being "actually overpowered," rather than being pinned in a stylized way. "I go to dungeons, and they're tying me up," he told me. "They haven't beaten me so I'm like, 'Why are they tying me up?'" One session wrestler told me that she describes her martial arts background in her advertising, in order to draw in those clients for whom a fair fight is important:

> The way I list and the fact that I *am* athletically trained gets me a lot more competitive sessions than other session wrestlers will get, who will flat-out say, "I do fantasy role play, yadda yadda yadda sessions." Not as many people will say that they do competitive [wrestling], which means that competitive guys come to me. At least the ones that can look at my stats and then look at my training and *believe* that a 5′4″, 125-pound girl can beat the crap out of them. Some people are really just into the *idea* of the big, scary strong woman. Those people don't like me.

As she attests, some clients are seemingly less selective in their choice of domme, as they have less specific criteria for fulfilling their fantasies. This explains why some prospective clients try to solicit even the House receptionist for phone sessions. Others "cast" their dommes based upon attributes that would locate them within their fantasy narratives.

This casting process is by no means limited to wrestling sessions. Some informants told me that, in general, taller women with more commanding presences did better within the industry. And other interviewees noted that various features of their self-presentations—for instance, age, race, or a foreign accent—rendered them more suited to particular fantasy scenarios. One woman in her fifties who specializes in "domestic discipline" scenes, for instance, asserted that her age and appearance put her in high demand for such sessions. "I am a grown-up, you know," she explained. "I *could* be your mom. I *could* be the babysitter."

Within the walls of the dungeon, what "*could* be" becomes important to some, though not all, clients. Most sessions, however, are embedded in some sort of fantasy context. Despite the fact that the relationships within these fantasies are structured around mythical relationships of gender and power, to produce these myths, pro-dommes participate in a distinctly nonmythical, "female" variety of labor. Previously I have argued that the pro-domme/client relationship represents an inversion of the gender/power hierarchy, insofar as it typically involves the image of a woman in control over a man. I have gone on to interrogate the one-dimensionality of this assertion, noting that this encounter involves a struggle for control that can be framed both in terms of pro-dommes' claims to professionalism and their claims to artistic purity. Looking at play illuminates both sides of this coin: both the production and reproduction of categories of gendered power that exist in the real world. At the same time that the dungeon provides a venue in which men can be who they are not (puppies, horses, little girls, lecherous soccer coaches, nasty Redcoats) and what they are not (feminine, submissive, vulnerable), dommes and subs are not fully exempt from the gendered expectations that pervade other spheres of social life. In the chapter that follows, I will elaborate this point by looking at pro-dommes' discourse about themselves as "therapists"—an orientation toward their labor that is transgressive in many ways but mimetic of real life in others.

"The purpose of playing," Hamlet said, "was and is to hold as 'twere the mirror up to nature" (*Hamlet* 3.3.16–23). In the dungeon, this both is and is not the case. On the one hand, the dungeon represents a fundamentally alternative space not reflexive of everyday life; this is part of the reason why pro-dommes so carefully monitor the boundary between session room and outside world, guarding against the contamination of one by the other. While the playing done in sessions can be transformative, however, it can also reflect "nature"—and I mean that not as a biological category, but in terms of the nature of roles and relationships as they exist in the larger social world we all inhabit.

Whip Therapy

It's a windy day in San Francisco, and I've just made my way through the swirling eddies of garbage outside the Civic Center Starbucks. It's late in the afternoon, so the place is crowded and other seat-vultures are milling around, waiting to swoop down upon a chair. I begin to worry about finding a place to sit for the interview, until I see the woman I'm supposed to meet camped out at a table by the window. She has four different books splayed out in front of her, and she's gazing intently at one of them.

If it weren't for the photos on her website—from which she is still barely recognizable in her casual clothing—I wouldn't have picked out this woman as the dominatrix in the room. When she talks, she's soft-spoken and polite, with a kind of earnestness about what she does for a living. She's forty but she looks younger, and she's wearing an oversized cable-knit sweater and leather pants, her hair pulled back into a tight ponytail. She begins to move the books and tells me she's been studying for a psychology exam.

Later in the interview, we get into a discussion about how sadomasochism is framed within the discipline of psychology. The *Diagnostic and Statistical Manual of Mental Disorders* (*DSM-IV-TR*) happens to be one of the books she's brought with her. We look through it together and learn—well, *I* learn—that, while both "sexual masochism" and "sexual sadism" are listed as "disorders" in the text, the psychological community only recognizes certain manifestations as problematic: "The diagnosis is made if the person has acted on these urges with a nonconsenting person or the urges, sexual fantasies, or behaviors cause marked distress or interpersonal difficulty."[1]

While the manual does not necessarily pathologize the work pro-dommes do, as long as it does not create "distress" or "difficulty" for them or for other people, the incorporation of these concepts into the *DSM-IV-TR* at all speaks to the manner in which the medical community, historically, has conceptualized sadomasochistic practices. Psychologist William Stekel's assessment of individuals who engage in SM was typical of initial reactions to this practice from the psychiatric community. "The investigation of the sadomasochistic paraphilia is like a journey through the inferno of human brutalities," Stekel wrote (1929, 409). Likening his analysis of the sadomasochistic subculture to "wandering through [the] kingdom of hell" (409), he called the sadomasochistically oriented individual "a criminal" (410) and linked his actions to "cannibalism, necrophilism, and vampirism" (ix). Krafft-Ebing, as discussed in my introduction, characterized the practice as a "perversion" and an "affliction" (1965, 53)—a view shared by Freud (1938, 569). Nicholas Avery (1977) has interpreted sadomasochism as a "defence against object loss" that should be subjected to therapeutic treatment, and Theodor Reik (1941, 368–72) has indicated that all neurotics are masochists. Further, while in recent years, researchers have begun to classify BDSM participants as psychologically healthy individuals engaging in a form of harmless recreation (Sandnabba, Santtila, and Nordling 1999, 273; Scott 1997, 289; and Stoller 1991, 21), pathologizing attitudes continue to permeate accounts of these practices (Goldman 2008).

Thus far, one of my concerns has been to show how pro-dommes discursively constitute their work in various ways—for instance, as theater or as art. In this chapter, I examine a particular folk narrative that pro-dommes deploy in opposition to the pathologizing discourse. Rather than wholly rejecting the medicalization of their eroticism, these women discursively constructed the "symptoms" of this "disease" (participation in acts that reflect an erotic predilection for sadomasochistic and fetishistic scenarios) as a psychological *treatment*, framing their sessions with clients not only as healthful but as beneficial for the men involved. Like other conceptions of their work that they mobilized through discourse, informants' rhetoric about themselves as "therapists" surfaced unexpectedly during the ethnographic process. There were no initial questions on the interview schedule about the therapeutic benefits of professional erotic dominance.

Here, I interrogate not whether pro-dommes are "correct" that their work is therapeutic for their clients, but rather what is significant about the fact that they *call it* therapeutic.[2] Ultimately, this chapter speaks to the argument made throughout this book that the dungeon functions as a space that is at once transgressive and mimetic of real-world relationships and processes. The significance of the therapeutic discourse is that it offers a window into one particular way in which this dualism gets produced. Through "therapy," clients can become emotionally open, revealing the repressed facets of their "complicit" masculinities. At the same time, as "therapists," pro-dommes engage in nurturing practices that have traditionally characterized femininity and female labor forms.

Pro-Dommes and the Therapeutic Discourse

Pro-dommes' rhetoric about BDSM as therapy emerged independently of any questions on the subject. When asked, "Would you consider yourself a sex worker?" for instance, one New York City–based informant in her mid-forties replied, "No. I've told numerous clients, 'Think of me as your thera-pist.' Because it is therapy for clients." Another New York domme, apropos of the same question, replied, "No. And I've had people ask me, 'Do you think you're a therapist?' No. But what I do is definitely therapeutic. Absolutely. . . . When you're dealing with actual SM play, where you're getting the endorphin release and all of that, there's a physical benefit to it. They go out of here feel-ing relaxed and refreshed and happy."[3]

My informants' descriptions of the therapeutic value of erotic dominance may be broadly categorized in four overlapping ways. They discussed sessions as healthful alternatives to sexual repression, as atonement rituals, as mecha-nisms for gaining control over prior trauma, and in the case of "humiliation sessions," as processes through which clients experienced psychological revi-talization through shame.

First, pro-dommes spoke about their clients' visits to the dungeon as an alternative to sexual repression, which they discussed as leading to psycho-logical problems. "It's *not* therapeutic to, like, hide a part of yourself forever because society says it's wrong," a Bay Area domme told me. "It's therapeutic to let that part out and enjoy yourself." Other informants listed the negative consequences that could result from repressing one's erotic proclivities. Dur-ing one interview, the informant—a Bay Area pro-domme in her thirties—leaned forward and told me, intensely, that she truly believed some of her clients would be rapists and killers were it not for their visits to her. Another interviewee, who had been in the industry for six years, explained, similarly:

> I mean, how about the people who snap and kill somebody? This is part of the reason why this is therapeutic, 'cause you're getting to control it. You're taking the power back. Even as a submissive, you're taking the power back because it's still under your terms. You're *choosing* the person who's dominating you and you're *choosing* to give over the power, and you're hopefully doing it in a controlled, good way. And that's a whole lot better than somebody who ends up mutilating animals and killing hookers.

This narrative was often combined with the assertion that many men seek out professional dominatrices either because they are unable to find romantic partners or because they have romantic partners who are unaware of their fantasies. For these individuals, the dungeon may be the only place in which they can discreetly enact these fantasies; pro-dommes thus interpreted their sessions as important outlets for the expression of these men's sexual desires.

Dungeons were also spaces in which clients could "atone" for wrongs they had committed in the real world, according to my informants. Often this ritual of atonement was the focus of the scenario enacted in the session. Informants commonly described one type of atonement scenario that involved the client doing penance for being unfaithful. A woman in her early twenties who works in one of the New York Houses, for instance, described the last session she had done prior to being interviewed:

> I don't know if he made it up or not, but he told me, "I cheated on my wife. I want you to punish me for that. Do whatever you want." So I pretty much did just a heavy corporal session. I also did some breath play with him, and I tied him up in a noose but I didn't hold it for very long for obvious reasons. But what's important is the fantasy.

Her caveat "I don't know if he made it up or not" is typical of pro-dommes' skepticism about the real-life relevance of these scripts. However, while they acknowledged that they may not be punishing a client for exactly what he had done in the real world, many felt that they must be punishing him for something he had done in the real world. A Bay Area informant explained:

> A lot of times a lot of people are exploring their own dark sides or learning things about themselves. I certainly do some—some of the beatings I do are very clearly atonement ritual things. "I feel guilty about something. This is the only way I know how to let it go—to be punished for it so I can be forgiven." And sometimes I don't even know what I'm punishing them for. Or it's this role-playing thing and it's for, you know, making paper airplanes out of the collection envelopes in church and you're a naughty, naughty boy. And clearly that's not what it's *really* about. But that psychological ritual is powerful and useful, even if you're not doing it about what it's really about. So clearly a lot of times it's very therapeutic.

Informants indicated that clients not only came to their dungeons to atone for things they had done but to work through wrongs that had been inflicted upon them. That is, pro-dommes argued that men came in to relive traumatic experiences in order to gain control over them. One woman, for instance, described a middle-aged client who had been spurned by a female lover in his early twenties and was still "working through some abandonment issues" from the incident. In their session, she tied him up and told him she was leaving to go to the bar downstairs. She then retreated out of sight but remained in the room:

> And he's saying, "Please don't leave me. Please don't leave me." And this is coming from his *gut*, you know? I was a little bit afraid to go so deep into therapy; I'm not trained as a therapist. But I opened the door, and I shut it, which is kind of hard to do, because the person here is in pain. And then he broke out. I was really staying inside the room, and I wasn't really going out. You couldn't see the door from where he was, and it was completely silent, so he thought that he was alone. He really sobbed—you know, a heart-wrenching sob. So I think that that was therapy. I think that allowed him to get something out. As to what to do with it after it comes out—which I think would be a second part of therapy—I suggested he *see* a therapist. Sometimes I think it's therapy for people that—when they have a driving desire to experience some emotional, or even physical or sexual, experience, I think it's best just to give it to them. If they want it, and if I can do it, let them have it.

By reenacting the scenario on his own terms, and being able to free himself from his bondage ropes, she indicated, he was able to take the first step toward working past the trauma.

While this pro-domme indicated that her client came to the dungeon to work through an incident from his adult life, other women told me that "age play," in which the client regresses to infancy or childhood, is also a common session request. My informants indicated that some of these scenes involved their submissives dealing with real-life childhood ordeals. One indie in her early thirties, for instance, contended that many men come to her to work through their feelings about having been physically punished as children:

> If you get somebody that's been hit as a child over the knee, there's a good chance that, God forbid, it was the hot babysitter or somebody that they kinda liked but at that age they didn't quite understand what that is. You're touching bare flesh in usually a no-no place, because of sexual overtones as an adult, and this person—now they associate the sensation of spanking as being comforting and loving. And also her knee might have been in the nether regions, kind of stimulating. So it's almost Pavlovian.

The informant who specializes in giving enemas made a similar argument about her clients who had received enemas as punishment when they were growing up:

> Just inserting a nozzle, to a small child, is a big thing. To us it may look like nothing, but to a child to be kind of in that position where they can't move and this thing is being inserted into you just because mommy or auntie or

whoever's taking care of them says so—scary. Really scary. And yet, most of them [say], "Oh, my mother was a good woman. She really didn't know. She wasn't doing anything bad. She didn't mean to be mean." And they make excuses. . . . It's really a scary thing. "They didn't know any better." And now, uh . . . and now I make a living because of that [*laughs*].

She also recalled being asked to perform many extremely elaborate scenes involving age-regression play. One of these scenarios, in particular, stood out in her mind:

I had a cross-dressing adult baby once at the —— Hotel . . . I called to say I'm leaving and I'll be there in about twenty minutes. The guy said, "Okay, listen, you know my friend may answer the door." He goes, "Don't worry." And I think, oh okay. And I'm thinking, oh my God, is there gonna be an-other guy there? I get there; this *beautiful* woman opens up the door. *Beauti-ful.* Sophisticated. Like, a white silk blouse. Trousers. This guy—*fantastic.* . . . And I came in, and he's like—I forget what the adult baby's name was. Jessie or something. You know, "Jessie's not here." Or, "Jessie's taking her nap and I just wanted to tell you, she has her dress clothes here." And, you know, he's telling me all this stuff as if it's a mother leaving her child to a babysitter. And he goes, "Just relax." You know, it was a man. "Just relax. She'll call to you. You'll hear her crying." So I said to him, "How old is she?" Nine months. Which is terrible because that means they can't verbally communicate. . . . But this guy was *gung ho*. I loved it. I mean, if you're gonna do something, he did it, boy. And so he said, "You'll hear her. She'll kind of cry or whine and you'll go in there." And I think he said [to] change her diapers or whatever. "Dress her up. Read her a story and then when she's ready to get in bed, give her a bubble bath before she goes to bed." And I'm in there for, like, an hour and a half or something [*laughs*]. And sure enough, I hear this, "Wah wah." I go into the bathroom, and in the back of my mind I *knew* that it was the same person but it was like two different people. I go in there and there's this, like, Shirley Temple blond-haired little girl in a little Shirley Temple dress sitting on the floor. And I'm like [*uses baby voice*], "Oooh, Jessie, hi, are you gonna come outside?" And I couldn't—you know, of course you can't communicate with a nine-month-old. And I'm, "Okay, come on with me. Do this, do that." But this guy had a wardrobe to kill for. I mean, if you're gonna be an adult baby—*beautiful*. White Mary Jane shoes. Little socks. Panties. Little slip . . . I mean, I changed him like into three different outfits. Put him to bed twice. Gave him a bath once because that was almost impossible; he wanted to splash. And he just went on and on. And I kept giving him a drink, giving him his bottle and then he'd wet his diaper and it just went on and on. And then finally I said to him, "Now, Jessie . . . I don't know where your auntie is, but I have to go now. There's other children I have to take care of,' and he's like [*whines*].

[*She laughs.*] He started crying. And I said, "Will your auntie be back? Can I leave you here a little bit until your auntie comes back?" She's like just crying, and I was like—because he had given me the money ahead [of time] in an envelope—I put on my jacket and I walked out. That was really peculiar because that was like one of those Baby Jane things. It was just so unbelievable. This was the same person and so evolved in his scene. Unbelievable.

Another context in which informants engaged in the therapeutic discourse was during their descriptions of "humiliation scenes": scenarios in which the submissive is shamed, ultimately to have his worth reaffirmed. The pro-domme and psychology student described at the beginning of this chapter, for instance, indicated that she will do "humiliation but not degradation," explaining, "My intent is to always build someone up. And, oftentimes, even if you're humiliating someone, the result is, in the end, they're a stronger person. Degradation is where you're actually tearing the psyche apart, I think. And, to me, that's where the line is, so I won't go there." Another pro-domme from San Francisco explained that degradation could be therapeutic, if undertaken in an atmosphere of trust and if, at the end, the client was reassured of his own value:

Would you consider yourself a sex worker?
I wouldn't consider myself a sex worker. I consider myself a psycho-erotic worker. . . . Because there's a lot of healing in people being accepted for their taboo. . . . [It's] healing to be heard. To be heard for who you are is very therapeutic. To be dommed, to be receiving the secret fantasy that you want. "I want to be degraded. And I want to be okay when I'm done being degraded." That's usually therapeutic, rather than keeping this fantasy hidden. . . . So . . . I would tell them, at the end of the session, how much I appreciated what they were able to receive. If I was doing humiliation, I will tell them, "Okay, now come back to yourself. You are no longer a pig or a dog or whatever. It's okay. It's okay to be a slut. Now get back to yourself. I really appreciated what you let yourself be with me." So it's a whole thing about trust and letting out this part of yourself that needs to come out.

Here, the informant engages in two facets of the therapeutic discourse, combining rhetoric about the therapeutic value of humiliation with the rhetoric, explored above, about BDSM in the dungeon functioning as a positive alternative to sexual repression. It should be emphasized that pro-dommes spoke about therapy through humiliation in a way that was different from the way they spoke about therapy through atonement. In humiliation scenes, informants suggested, rather than doing penance for misdeeds, a client has his desires paradoxically affirmed and normalized through the process of shaming.

Pro-dommes contend that the process of shaming confirms what the client is not—that is, "You are no longer a pig or a dog or whatever." Under this theory, the client—in being called a slut, a sissy, a slave, an animal—ultimately finds redemption in the fact that his engagement in these roles has been ephemeral. The man being shamed for cheating on his wife, likewise, reaffirms that his ego ideal does not commit such acts.[4]

My informants' contention that shaming can be redemptive when it ultimately involves repudiation could explain why clients place particular limits on their humiliation scenes. On his client profile, one man, who indicated that he is 5′7″ and 275 pounds, specified, in capital letters, "DURING VERBAL ABUSE NO MENTION OF WEIGHT." Another indicated, "No mocking size of penis." These requests provide support for the theory that the shame mechanism has a psychological benefit because humiliation states are temporary. These clients wished to be shamed, but only in certain ways—ways they could experience as recuperative in the end.[5]

Therapy, Ritual, and Transformation

In a line of discussion that intersected with their descriptions of their work as "therapeutic," informants also characterized BDSM practices as "spiritual," "ritual," "rites," and "magic."[6] For instance, the Bay Area woman's characterization of the scene in which the client is caught making paper airplanes out of collection envelopes in church as a "psychological ritual" is typical of the way these two narrative threads could dovetail.

In making claims about their work as ritualistic, pro-dommes engage in an ongoing conversation about the transformative potential of these activities—a conversation that takes place both within BDSM communities and the literature surrounding them. Sadomasochistic practices, for instance, have been discussed as a kind of self-help, in the sense that they can transform an individual by providing a window into his or her identity. Andrea Beckmann addresses these "transformative potentials" of sadomasochistic activities in her study of practitioners of consensual SM in London; she makes the point that, for some individuals, SM provides a space that "allows for a more 'authentic' (as founded on experience) relation to 'self' and others" (2009, 80, 91). Additional authors have drawn parallels between sadomasochism and other kinds of transformative exchanges, such as those that are magical or religious in nature. Alex Comfort (1978), for instance, argues that sadomasochistic activities have similarities with magical rites in their ability to expand participants' self-awareness, and Stuart Norman (2004) links his own sadomasochistic practices to Shamanism. Gayle Rubin, similarly, has observed that, at the Catacombs, an SM and fisting club in San Francisco during the 1970s and 1980s, "some habitués reported having the kinds of transformational experiences more often associated with spiritual disciplines" (2004, 128).[7]

These intertwined rhetorics of therapy and transformation shed light on BDSM and its practitioners in a variety of ways. First, they suggest that, despite their ability to use humor as a role distancer, participants in both commercial and lifestyle BDSM can also imbue their play with a great deal of meaning and solemnity. Again, whether or not all pro-dommes who deploy these discourses really believe or are correct that their work is therapeutic, ritualistic, or spiritual is not the question on the table here. It is evident from the concordance with prior research and from my discussions with pro-dommes who "live it 24/7" that, for at least some participants, BDSM holds a kind of seriousness and significance beyond that of a frivolous leisure activity or bounded occupational exchange. These individuals speak of such interactions as solemn engagements, complete with their own moral code and history (see appendix C for more on the history of the professional dominatrix).

Second, these discourses of therapy and ritual shed light on a central paradox of the BDSM encounter: freedom through constraint. Though pro-dommes speak of their work as transcendental, and as a mechanism for the repudiation of social norms, these activities occur within settings that can be highly structured in their own right. Scenes are scripted, and the relationships that are central to these practices are often defined in terms of rigid polarities: top/bottom, male/female, sadist/masochist, mistress/slave, dominant/submissive. This can be true not only for individuals who engage in professional erotic dominance but for lifestylers as well. In sum, their narratives about BDSM suggest that there is something transformative and freeing about engaging in such practices but that this freedom is brought about, paradoxically, through engagement with multiple sets of new categories and boundaries.

Finally, returning to the central theme of this chapter, by characterizing BDSM in terms of therapy and transcendence, pro-dommes produce a discourse that not only legitimizes and normalizes these historically taboo activities but that posits them as beneficial. One particularly apt way of characterizing this phenomenon, in light of BDSM participants' emphasis on ritual, is in Durkheimian terms: they cross the boundary between sacred and profane. For Emile Durkheim, the distinction between the sacred and the profane is one crucial dichotomy that marks religious life from the secular. In Durkheim's view, the two are completely dichotomized, more so than any other two social categories.[8] One cannot exist in both categories at once; however, he acknowledges the possibility of switching completely from one category into the other (1968, 55). By deploying enmeshed discourses about therapy and ritual, pro-dommes make that switch. In addition to recasting "pathological" behavior as psychologically beneficial, they take what has been categorized as profane and kick it squarely into the realm of the sacred. Through their narratives, the pathologized becomes prescribed and the ir-reverent, extolled.

Therapy, Class, Hegemony, and Spiderman's Uncle

Another particularly salient facet of pro-dommes' therapeutic discourse is that it sheds light on the class dimensions of commercial BDSM. Informants commonly argued that clients in high-status occupations pay them for the relief of having the burden of power temporarily removed. The therapeutic discourse coincides with this argument, as pro-dommes interpret clients' dungeon visits as psychologically beneficial reprieves from the "pressure" and "responsibility" of elite life.

The pro-dommes interviewed for this study indicated that the typical client is a white male in his forties who works in a relatively high-status occupation.[9] My interviewees told me that the men who visited them ranged from blue-collar workers to CEOs, but that, more often than not, clients were relatively high earners in power positions. Toward the end of my fieldwork for this project, the news broke that New York governor Eliot Spitzer had patronized a prostitution service. The following week, I went to San Francisco, and all but two of the fourteen dominatrices I interviewed there mentioned the scandal. Though Spitzer had hired a prostitute, not a dominatrix, my informants suggested that the news was pertinent—not only because I was a New Yorker interviewing them about their participation in erotic labor, but also because they generally had some familiarity with the sexual proclivities of relatively powerful married men. When asked, pro-dommes replied that the most commonly seen clients were businessmen, academics, lawyers, policemen, men in the medical industry, and men in the financial sector. In San Francisco, this also included men in the computer industry. On both coasts, dommes' descriptions of their clients tended to cluster around the same handful of core occupations, as the following descriptions attest:

The majority [of my clients] are executives. . . . Not to say that there's not an office manager or a factory worker in there. But most of the time, it's usually suits and ties. You know, and they're scheduling me in between meetings and stuff like that. I would say in my case they're mostly executives. Upper management or whatever.

It's all about the older, white businessman. Because the thing is, I'm a luxury item. Poor people can't afford to come and see me. But yeah, that's usually it. Rich, white guys.

I live in Silicon Valley, where there's all the computer industry—Palo Alto, down there. So all computer geeks. And, before that, it was people who *became* computer geeks. University teachers—I have a few clients that are university teachers, actually. . . . Doctors, very few blue-collar workers.

I see the CEOs. I see—God forbid any one of them sue me, considering how many police officers, lawyers, and judges I see.

I would say most of my clients are lawyers. I see some people who are in finance. I have a couple of people who are random things, like a sommelier. I see some people who are academics. I see some people who write in some capacity. Most of my clients—I think, they're *all* college graduates. Most of them have some kind of postgraduate education.

The women I interviewed gave a consistent narrative of the mechanism behind these trends in occupation—a narrative I have come to call the "Spiderman's Uncle" argument. In the 2002 film *Spiderman*, the protagonist's uncle cautions him, "With great power comes great responsibility." It was a common contention among informants that men in positions of power pay for the relief of having the burden of that responsibility temporarily removed. A Queens-based indie, for instance, explained to me, over French fries at a diner, "They have to make decisions every day. Million dollar decisions. And they're always in control. Every once in a while they just wanna let go of everything and have somebody else do decisions, even if it is for an hour." A Bay Area woman in her fifties echoed this sentiment: "It's a white privilege thing. The more power you have, the more you wanna give it up. That's how it works. If you don't have any power, you don't wanna give it up. Just think about it: if you're working in a factory and somebody's bossing you around all day, you don't wanna be at your knees at some woman's feet. Granted, there are exceptions, but basically not."

Here, these women perform a classic sociological analysis. They take a phenomenon that may be perceived as a matter of individual psychology (a sexual predilection), and they demonstrate the social forces governing it by drawing out a larger social fact from a collection of individual cases (most clients are well-off white men), then extrapolate a theory of the trend using deductive reasoning (men in power pay for the temporary loss of control). Their theory accounts for individual variation—that is, not all powerful men go to see dominatrices—while emphasizing the role of their social circumstances in influencing psychical processes. This analysis is also in line with prior psychological work on sadomasochism. Psychologist Roy Baumeister, for instance, positing masochism as "essentially an attempt to escape from self, in the sense of achieving a loss of high-level self awareness," explains: "The requirements of making decisions under pressure or uncertainty, of taking responsibility for actions that may disappoint or harm others, of maintaining a favorable public and private image of self despite all threats and challenges, and of asserting control over a recalcitrant social environment can become oppressive and stressful and can foster desires to escape" (1988, 29).

It is important to emphasize that this description of the demographic characteristics of the clients is based mainly on pro-dommes' statements and only in part on my own discussions with clients at BDSM events and the small sample of clients who sat down for interviews with me. Thus, it is a less-than-perfect assessment of the men who go see professional dominatrices. This measure could be skewed both by clients who are not truthful to dommes about their backgrounds and by the potential unreliability of pro-dommes' reports about their clients.

However, there are reasons to suspect that pro-dommes' reports of their clients' occupations are generally accurate.[10] First, as indicated, there are trends in the informants' descriptions of their clients' occupations. Thus, either all clients and/or all dommes are creating fabrications about the clients' jobs consistently in ways that somehow feed into the fantasy of D/S, or they are being accurate and these trends really do exist. Second, informants indicated that on occasions when the veracity of these assertions came to be tested, clients' reporting of their occupations generally turned out to be accurate. These included barter situations (for instance, one dominatrix gets dental work and legal advice from her clients in those professions) and other real-world encounters (one domme manager, for instance, hand-delivers fetish videos to a client's office on Wall Street), as well as the rare cases in which clients gave out their work phone numbers. "We have one client where one of his favorite things to do is have the girl guess what his job is," one woman told me, "and he is a professor of computer science. It's very funny, because if you call him at the number he gives, it says University of ——. So you say, 'You're a professor!' And he goes, 'Of *what*?!'"

The other main reason to believe that my informants were, on the whole, accurately describing their clients' professions—or at least their social statuses—is that professional erotic dominance is cost-prohibitive for those with low earning power. It is not a foregone conclusion, however, that working-class individuals would visit dungeons with greater regularity if prices were reduced. Historically, BDSM has been viewed as the province of the privileged. Literary scholar Allison Pease, for instance, argues that, in Victorian pornography, "sado-masochism (in its most commonly expressed form, flagellation) is a signifier of high culture and/or high-cultural vice" (2000, 110). Steven Marcus similarly links flagellation literature in Victorian England to the aristocracy, arguing that it draws upon the audience's shared experience of having been corporally punished at school: "Indeed, for this literature perversity and social privilege are inseparable marks of distinction. We are regularly told, for instance, that 'the lower order of mankind are not such slaves to this passion as people in high life'" (1966, 253). Taking away the economic constraints of the dungeon for a moment, the people I met at Scene events—which are sometimes free, and often less than the price of a movie ticket—tended to be well-educated white people. While I make no claims here about what people do in their own bedrooms, public play appears to be more popular among those who can afford high cultural diversions, for reasons that are not entirely about economic constraint. This point is well supported by prior research on BDSM (Janus, Bess, and Saltus 1977, 50; Eve and Renslow, 1980, 103; Scott 1997, 6; see also Moser and Levitt 1987; Sandnabba, Santtila, and Nordling 1999; Spengler 1977).[11]

Whether or not pro-dommes are right that their clients are high-status individuals who come to them in order to experience reprieve, and whether or not they are right about the fact that their work is therapeutic (if, indeed, such an assertion can be "wrong" or "right"), the narrative that they tell about clients as powerful men seeking therapy sheds light on how an examination of the social contours of the dungeon can lead us to insights about gender and hierarchy in the larger social world.

First, their "Spiderman's Uncle" narrative about their clients' demographics offers a potential glimpse at some of the facets of male gender expression that have become subordinated to forms of masculinity that are dominant in our culture. Here, I draw upon R. W. Connell's conception of complicit masculinity, which Connell argues is underpinned by successful claims to authority and cultural dominance, especially over women. Some forms of masculinity—for instance, homosexuality—become subordinated to this dominant phenotype. Other forms—for instance, nonwhite masculinity—may become marginalized, Connell maintains, relative to the authorization of the dominant group (1995, 77–78, 81).

Along these lines, every pro-domme interviewed for this study said that she has mostly white clients. New York pro-dommes, however, were more likely than San Francisco pro-dommes to indicate that they have seen men of color, including Indian men, Latinos, and black men. One Bay Area woman, who had been in the industry since the 1980s, told me that she had only ever seen one Hispanic client and two black men. Another Bay Area domme, who had been in the business for four years, recalled, "I have *only* had Caucasian men as clients. Yet, when I walk down the street, I am *hit on* by older black men. But I can't get them to come in and let me beat them, for some reason." Pro-dommes' assertions that most clients are Caucasian is in line with the idea that the dungeon "works" best for men who participate in complicit masculinity in daily life.[12] In the dungeon, the client can momentarily "turn off" the expressions of masculinity that undergird his cultural authority. He can be submissive. He can allow himself to be anally penetrated with a dildo. He can be nurtured.

One useful way, then, to think about both the "Spiderman's Uncle" claim and the therapeutic discourse is that they put forth the idea that the men who see pro-dommes are, by and large, not marginalized men, because it is *complicit* masculinity that is finding its expression in the dungeon. If we extend these two interwoven narratives just a tad, they imply that, for clients, the dungeon provides temporary relief from the burden of authority as well as a reprieve from "doing" masculinity in a way that is required to remain complicit with hegemony. They suggest that clients are able to play out the alternative facets of their masculinities in a closed environment.

These narratives, furthermore, dovetail with several lines of thought central to this text. They tie into the notion of the transformative character of this erotic sphere: that is, individuals can "play" in the dungeon, engaging in behaviors and personas that are taboo in their daily lives. Men who participate in "therapy," whether in the dungeon or on the therapist's couch, produce their masculinity, within this private environment, in a way that is in direct opposition to the requirements imposed within the public sphere. Both the dungeon and the therapeutic setting allow them to engage in displays of vulnerability. This may explain why, for instance, within the armed forces—a series of organizations built upon and sustained by principles of hypermasculinity—there is often a stigma associated with going to see a therapist.[13]

To return to Connell for a moment, pro-dommes suggest that the dungeon does what the therapist's office does, in the sense that, within the context of a session, men can engage in a form of vulnerable masculinity that in daily life would be marginalized relative to the authorization of the dominant group. This explanation becomes more compelling when we consider my informants' assertion that clients are men who in daily life belong to the dominant group. Within this framework, for the client, as one of the informants quoted above contends, sessions are about "letting out this part of yourself that needs to come out." Whether or not BDSM "really is" therapy, then, pro-dommes' discourse about therapy sheds light not only upon relationships in the dungeon, but upon therapeutic relationships, and upon the production of gender more generally.

Touch Therapy / Talk Therapy: Intimate Labor and Nurturing Femininity

At the same time that the therapy discourse illuminates how BDSM interactions can facilitate the production of alternative forms of masculinity, it also sheds light on how pro-dommes draw upon conventional repertoires of femininity within these interactions. One dimension of the therapeutic discourse is not related to BDSM in particular but concerns the outsourcing of emotional and physical activities that are traditionally the functions of romantic partners. Pro-dommes, in particular, engage in two important facets of emotional labor: soothing physical contact and personal conversations.

A common contention among women I interviewed was that some clients come to the dungeon for the intimate, though not necessarily erotic, skin-on-skin experiences that they are lacking in their private lives. One pro-domme spoke to this phenomenon, as well as to the idea of the displacement of complicit masculinity in the dungeon, when she explained: "You know, people just don't get *touched*. A lot of them, especially with the older ones, it's, 'Since my wife died, I haven't been able to feel vulnerable with someone.'" Another woman described her interactions with a specific client, whose wife had been undergoing cancer treatments:

> He used to come see me to be able to dress up. He's a cross-dresser and we would put him in ridiculous slutty, slutty, slutty outfits. And he's like 6′4″ and moderately big, so he required, like, [size] "extremely husky" [*laughs*]. And crazy wigs and lots of bondage on top of that—lots of feminizing bondage. And he would see me for a two-hour session, and I would dress him up, and then I would, like, cuddle him. And, really, what he needed was to get away from the stress of being really, really scared about his wife.

Since his wife's cancer had gone into remission, the informant told me, "He doesn't see me nearly as much. He's not as stressed out as much." Here, again, we see the dungeon framed as a therapeutic environment in which clients experience relief from real-world pressures, but we also see an assertion about the positive psychological effects of physical contact. Both pro-dommes and clients regularly spoke about dungeon visits in terms of "stress relief." One client told me, for instance, that he first began to engage in BDSM activities as a teenager. "Basically, it was an escape from stress," he explained. "I didn't have to worry about how my parents reacted to my grades or about school."

This idea of escape is also inherent within the concept of "subspace": a term many BDSM participants use to describe a trancelike state into which subs sometimes enter during the course of a scene. "Subspace is when you're playing with someone who's submissive, and with the beatings or whatever they go into almost a trance zone," a New York indie explained, adding, "It is the most beautiful thing to see." In subspace, according to many of the women I interviewed, subs become so deeply engrossed in the play that they make a temporary break with the reality of the moment—a psychological escape.

The dungeon provides an outsourcing of physical affection, also, in that it is not uncommon for a client to request that his dominatrix cuddle him and speak soothingly to him. These "cuddling sessions" were especially popular with pro-dommes who specialized in wrestling, perhaps because these women engaged in more extensive skin-on-skin contact with clients in general.

One such wrestling domme indicated that talking to clients was sometimes as important as administering touch. Asked if she had ever gone into the dungeon and done anything different from the scene than had been negotiated prior to session, she replied, "Well, the one that comes to mind is the one where it was supposed to be a wrestling session and the guy was like, 'I have a cold. Let's just chat instead.' I got to hear an awful lot about being a pediatrician that day. And I sat there in my tiny little thong, and he sat there, and we just chatted, and I think he was very happy that he got a chance to talk to someone."

Other interviewees ensconced their rhetoric about the importance of conversation more explicitly within the therapeutic discourse, as demonstrated in the following excerpt from an interview with one pro-domme from Manhattan:

What do you like most about being a domme?
Mostly the power and control. And I like that you're kind of a therapist to
    these people, and we all have something in common together. And even
    if it's just for an hour, they're really going to trust me to do what they re-
    ally want done. A lot of the clients that I get, they usually talk to me about
    their problems because their wives or their girlfriends don't wanna hear
    it. So they end up telling me about their problems, and sometimes they

come just for that, instead of paying a therapist. But they also feel like there's some stuff they can't talk to their wives or their girlfriends about, like their interests and their fantasies. So they usually come to us instead, because they know that we cater to those.

Her response is illustrative not only of the precarious balance between remaining "dominant" within the exchange and providing a service but also of the companionate labor involved in this industry. As she indicates, clients come in to discuss general issues in their personal lives as well as issues directly related to their interest in BDSM—an interest about which they may experience emotional ambivalence. As one indie asserted, "I tell people, 'I'm a sex therapist.' Like, I help people fulfill their fantasies and work through their shit. And a lot of it's therapy. A lot of it is talk therapy. And I don't even have to do anything! Like, I just started doing phone sessions, and I don't even have to say anything. People just call me and wanna talk about their fantasies."

This concept of the dungeon as a confessional space in which the act of talking proves psychologically beneficial ties into my previous argument about professional erotic dominance as the outsourcing of intimate, emotional labor, and it also has correlates within other professions. Consider, for instance, the common image of the bartender as a kind of therapist who provides both alcohol and a sympathetic ear. Another parallel lies in the ethnographic process, in the relationship between the researcher and informant. In her book about sex workers, Bernstein describes an incident in which a man who had visited prostitutes "bubbled over with emotion when he noted at the end of our interview how much he appreciated talking to me, especially given how much cheaper it was than a visit to his psychotherapist" (2007, 198). Like the barfly who confides in the bartender or the informant confessing to the ethnographer, the client coming in "just to talk" gets interpreted as undergoing a healthful purging of the psyche. The therapeutic discourse suggests that, in postmodern America—in which there exist so many social prohibitions on speech and touch outside of intimate relationships—clients who do not have intimate ties, and even some who do, can purchase within the walls of the dungeon the kinds of emotional attention that such ties are expected to provide.

In making this argument about the emotional labor in which pro-dommes engage, I draw upon the scholarship of Dana Becker, who has argued that such labor—particularly within the context of "therapeutic" arrangements, broadly defined—sustains hegemonic relationships of gender and power. Describing the "myth of female empowerment" within our postmodern therapeutic culture, Becker asserts that the "repackaging of the psychological as power" has resulted in the colonization of women's psyches: "What the therapeutic culture offers women . . . is merely a type of compensatory power that supports and reproduces the existing societal power/gender arrangements by obviating the need for social action to alter them, as women continue to perform the 'emotion work' of society, both domestically and professionally" (2005, 1, 3). My argument here is not that pro-dommes' narratives about their work unambiguously reproduce relationships of gendered power; in many ways these narratives subvert such relationships. Looking at professional erotic dominance as a therapeutic practice through the lens of this theory, however, helps to bring into sharp relief the ways in which the femininity produced in the dungeon is indicative of women's roles in society more generally.

This includes women's roles within other forms of erotic labor. It should come as no surprise, in light of the previous discussion about the significant demands for emotional engagement required by sexualized work, that the concept of erotic labor as a therapeutic activity is nothing new. One faint but audible strain within pro-sex feminism has been a discussion about credentialing prostitution under the aegis of therapy. Feminist philosopher Laurie Shrage asserts, for instance, that by "redefining the 'prostitute' as an erotic artist or therapist, we hope to alter the kinds of qualities people seek and see in her, and to socially define her as a person that one can say hello to on the streets" (1994, 86). Chancer notes that the reclassification of sex work as sex therapy has been suggested by sex workers themselves (1993, 161)—a point supported by Chapkis's interviews with female prostitutes. Discussing "strategies of redefinition," which are "efforts to recreate sex work as a 'wholesome' and 'normal' service," Chapkis explains, "One such attempt involves licensing sex workers as credentialed 'sex therapists' or 'surrogates.' As licensed sex therapists, prostitutes presumably would have access to some of the authority and social status associated with those in the therapeutic arts" (1997, 193). While these authors allude to the issue of reframing pathologized erotic labor, specifically prostitution, as therapy, they touch on this concept only briefly, focusing on it mainly as a political strategy for the normalization and legitimization of sex workers. Looking at the content, rather than the feminist consequences, of the therapeutic arguments mobilized by the practitioners themselves, is useful for examining how such arguments play into notions of gendered work.[14]

The content of pro-dommes' arguments about therapy suggests that, in addition to an aggressive femininity, dungeon interactions also generate a nurturing femininity. In many punishment scenarios, the "cruelty" exhibited by the domme is tempered by her solicitous acts of caring. One Bay Area woman explained, "I spend a certain amount of time petting people's arms or stroking their backs or things like that, because so many of my clients are so touch-starved. And, you know, it's the nurse who decided you needed an enema, and while she's being mean and making you hold it, she's also stroking your arm and it's for your own good. She has your best interests at heart." As noted, some women cuddle their clients at the end of punishment sessions. Others touch them comfortingly and tell them what "good boys" they are. It is no coincidence that, in their sessions, pro-dommes often transform into female archetypes whose functions in everyday life include providing comfort. Although pro-dommes also get requests for role-playing sessions in which they are military commanders, interrogators, or police investigators, more often they take on characters such as mothers and nurses, whose nurturing gestures go hand in hand with their infliction of pain.

Connections to the Healthcare Industry

In light of the nurturing roles that pro-dommes enact in the dungeon, it is revealing that many informants had been in the healthcare industry, a sphere of social life in which pain and relief are also intimately intertwined.[15] A number of the women I spoke with were at the time of interview, or had formerly been, nurses. One woman, for instance, had worked with Alzheimer's patients before leaving to become a pro-domme. Another supplemented her income as a dominatrix by working for an in-home medical services company, taking care of a cancer patient. One woman had worked as an EMT. A few were going back to school to become psychologists.

My informants put forth several possible explanations for this overlap between the healthcare industry and professional erotic dominance. One was that an interest in the way the body and psyche function corresponds with an interest in observing how they react to various painful and pleasurable stimuli. Another possible explanation is that healthcare professionals are more likely to remain in the erotic dominance industry because their specialized knowledge allows them to excel at BDSM, in particular lending an authenticity to "medical scenes" that require them to play the roles of doctors or nurses. "I do a lot of med scenes," one woman told me, "because people love the fact that I've got a lot of anatomy knowledge, so I can use a lot of terminology and do various things. That tends to be something people like to do a lot of."

Regardless of their reasons for entering the industry, many of these women discussed their erotic labor as informal extensions of their medical

roles. They told me that they felt obligated to ensure that sessions were ultimately psychologically and physically positive for the clients. One such informant, whose business card characterizes her as a "Classic Fetish™ Therapist, Domina," remarked that she considers her sessions to be therapeutic
"because I have certifications in psychotherapy, so what I've realized is that
a lot of people do not share their fetishes with the ones they love or they're
not clearly at terms with themselves and their fetishes. . . . So when I'm seeing people we go through some serious psychological determinations before
I play with them." Others asserted that some of the work they had done in
the service of conventional medicine had been more destructive than their
activities in the dungeon. One informant made this claim in a particularly
vivid manner:

> I'll tell you something: I've hurt people far worse as a nurse than I ever have
> as a pro-domme. I was a trauma nurse for ten years. I was ICU for ten years,
> CCU for ten years. I turned off over 150 ventilators and watched those peo-
> ple die on the physicians' orders. I would plunge needles into people's veins,
> pushing those needles as far as I could. I would help pull the body one way
> while the physician pulled their dislocated arm in another. I would hold them
> down while another physician punches in chest-tubes, with blood spraying all
> over the walls. I was hip-deep in blood. Yeah. *Way* worse.

The descriptions given by pro-dommes who had been involved in the medical community suggest that these two social spheres overlap not only because
one's technical expertise in the area of healthcare can facilitate more plausible
medical scenes, or because one's knowledge of anatomy can facilitate better scenes in general. They suggest not only that techniques from one world
translate to the other. The underlying argument is that both spheres require
forms of labor that are similar in a salient way: they are about being able to
perform a nurturing role that goes hand in hand with the administration
of pain.

Potential Issues with the Therapeutic Frame

While I have indicated that the purpose of this chapter is not to determine
whether professional erotic dominance is really therapy, and I have instead
turned to what the content of the therapeutic discourse can teach us about
this industry and about gender more generally, I must nevertheless emphasize the stickiness of the assertion "Commercial BDSM is therapy." Discourse
does not happen in a vacuum, and while this particular discourse is useful in
some ways, its potential consequences are not unproblematic and should be
discussed.

First, if dominatrices were to have the option of becoming licensed mental health professionals, this might serve to delegitimize those pro-dommes who did not receive such credentials, as well as framing non-normative sexuality as the province of the psychiatric community. In making this claim, I draw upon the work of Chapkis, who discusses these potential issues in the context of prostitution:

> Many of the problems with re-organizing prostitution as a form of "sex ther-apy" resemble those associated with all forms of professionalization through licensing. Not only would such a strategy fail to address the stigmatization of those unable or unwilling to be "credentialed," it inadvertently reinforces class prejudice by assuming that professionals alone deserve social courtesy and respect. . . . In addition, redefining prostitution as sex therapy serves to further pathologize non-marital, non-monogamous sexuality by placing it under the control of medical personnel. (1997, 194)

A potential issue with the discourse of BDSM as therapeutic, similarly, is that it inadvertently pathologizes the masochistic/submissive impulse—that is, "If dominatrices are therapists then there must be something psychologically *wrong* with people who see dominatrices." Baumeister's theory, for instance, serves as an example of the BDSM-as-therapy rhetoric while containing whispers of the same underlying normativity that has historically marked pathologizing discourses. For Baumeister, masochism becomes psychologi-cally useful because life has grown "oppressive and stressful"—that is, mas-ochism is still a behavior that individuals resort to when something is wrong. Thus, he simultaneously points to the psychological benefits of such practices while leaving normative sexual paradigms intact.

In their efforts to discursively normalize BDSM, some of my informants fell into the same trap. One particularly salient example is the dominatrix who suggested that her clients might be out "mutilating animals and killing hookers" if it were not for their ability to experience reprieve in the dungeon. In a way, this informant simultaneously spoke of her work as therapeutic and located sadomasochism squarely in the pathological realm. Her asser-tion that violent behavior might be the alternative for some of these men whose desires are not "controlled" is indicative of a potentially problematic slippage within a discourse that seeks to resist medicalization *through* a kind of medicalization. Similarly, credentialing BDSM workers as therapists may potentially repathologize the very impulses pro-dommes seek to define as normal and healthy.

However, unless such a system of credentialing were set in place, classify-ing pro-dommes as mental health providers could prove potentially dangerous in that it presupposes a familiarity with principles that not all of them have. By my informants' own accounts, some of the more psychologically intense sessions can open up clients' old emotional wounds. Describing the dominatrix as a therapist implies that she has the technical training to be able to deal with these wounds once they have been exposed. Some women told me about clients who had experienced "freakouts" during sessions. The most common of these were war veterans whose PTSD had been triggered in the context of particular scenes. One informant, who had been in the industry for fifteen years, described a session she had done with a former military pilot:

> He wanted an interrogation session. And he wanted me to be in military uniform. So I made up what I thought an interrogation session was—shined a light in his eyes and asked him for his name, rank, and serial number and try to trip him up in some of his replies and insist that he say, "Yes, ma'am," because I'm his commanding officer. He started to, like, trance out. I could see a change come over his face. His eyes seemed to glaze over, and he started to say, "Yes, sir. Yes, sir." And his tone of voice came from a faraway place, which put me completely on alert, because all of a sudden I'm asking myself what's happening here. So I said, "Sir? Do I look like a sir to you?" And he said, "Oh, no. No, ma'am." But every now and then he'd slip into this, "Yes, sir / No, sir." So I knew something was up. I couldn't figure out exactly what it was. I was happy that the session was coming to an end. I think I closed it a little sooner than I normally would have and asked him what happened. And he said that when he was in Vietnam he was captured and taken to, like, a prison camp. So, I guess he was tortured and had to say "Yes, sir / No, sir" to these men who captured him. So I guess that's where that came from.

It should be noted that she ultimately felt that this session was beneficial for the client: "To me . . . if a violent situation can be sexualized, it's more palatable."

Another woman who had been doing professional erotic dominance for four years, but who had been in the lifestyle for decades, described a similar "freakout" triggered by an audio cue:

> I've had a couple of Vietnam War vets trigger PTSD. And the one that was the worst was an executive who's been playing for a long time. I told you I have this massive sound system, and I tend to run subharmonics quite a bit, because the studies show that with loud pulses of subharmonic sound—they cause adrenaline to pump up. But for *him* it was the sound of artillery shells landing all around him when he was in Vietnam, and he couldn't escape. He was tied up to a chair in bondage at the same time as the pounding sound ar-

rived. So I ended up having to do a one-hour crisis intervention with him. And I've worked suicide crisis for nine years; I was director of nursing in the psych facility. And I studied PTSD as my primary focus when I was in grad school. So we got to a good space, but I considered that a medical emergency.

This informant credited her ability to diffuse the situation to her educational background. In doing so, she insinuated that a pro-domme who had not had her kind of training might not have been in a position to deal with the psychological dynamics of the situation after triggering those memories. As one informant put it, in a common response to the interview question "Have you ever had a medical issue with a client?": "I think that the physical risks are much smaller than the psychological damage you can do to people." Another pro-domme concurred, "I'm really leery of opening up people's psyches in the way that you can with this and dumping stuff in there that isn't good for them, that isn't productive. I don't want anybody to leave sessions with me feeling worse about themselves."

A final wrinkle in the therapeutic discourse is that, in identifying as therapists, some pro-dommes felt that they were absolving clients of conduct with which they personally did not agree. Several informants indicated a deep ambivalence about their therapeutic role when it came to scenarios they found morally repugnant. One example of such a scenario was "race play." Clients who request race play ask to be disparaged through the use of ethnic stereotypes and epithets. No pro-domme I spoke with had received any requests for race play from white clients, but some had received such requests from their few clients of color.

Informants spoke of race play as sexually exciting for the clients because of the strong social proscriptions against racism. A Foucaultian might identify this sensation as transgressive pleasure. Michel Foucault argues that part of the appeal of talking about sex, for instance, is that we perceive it as "defying established power" (1990, 6). Along these same lines, one informant, when asked to explain race play, replied, "It's 'Hey, nigger,' and the guy's black. Or, 'You stupid fucking kike.' And bring out all the epithets. Everything you're not supposed to say about that race. It's taboo, and that's part of it. Because of the taboo, it becomes an erotic thing to this person. I find it humorous. Also, I'm not racist. I'll call my friends racial epithets, because I don't believe it. I won't use epithets if I don't like the person." Many pro-dommes spoke of their initial aversion to these types of sessions and, like this domme, distanced themselves from their dominatrix personas by emphasizing that they are not racist. The women in this sample tended to be well-educated, white liberals—a social group within which the prohibition against racial intolerance would be particularly strong.

Another type of session that elicited moral ambivalence from pro-dommes was "Nazi play"—an aspect of BDSM made notorious by the Max Mosley story. One informant described an experience with this type of scene:

> I mean, I have green eyes and blonde hair. I've gotten asked for an awful lot of Nazi scenes. And I took German in college. And I did one—*one*—Nazi scene, with somebody I knew well. I'd seen him a lot of times. . . . I finished it and went, "Well, that was an interesting experience. And you don't seem to be damaged by it. But I'm not doing that again. That is not something I believe in. That is not something that I think is morally right, and I don't want to be a part of it."

She indicated, however, that she experienced ambivalence about the situation, because she also felt it was wrong to judge clients for their sexual desires. "I try very hard not to give people the reaction of, 'Ew, that's disgusting— you wanna *what*? Oh my God, you freak!'" she explained, laughing. "I think it takes an incredible amount of courage to ask for what you want so people shouldn't get shot down for asking."

Some women also experienced this kind of ambivalence in atonement sessions with men who indicated that they had mistreated their wives. Several informants told me that, by allowing these men to "atone" for these transgressions, they felt they were condoning and encouraging reprehensible behavior. Describing the only session she had ever stopped during her decade in the industry, one woman recounted:

> I was a sub, and it was this guy that I didn't like anyway. He was this Indian man. And it started to feel like he was trying to make it okay—like, it started to feel like he was transferring his wife, like I was a battered Indian woman, and he was trying to make it okay. Like, he was hitting me, and I was supposed to be saying, "It's okay." And I just totally tapped into him abusing his wife, and I was like, "Fuck this. This is bad. No thanks. You're creeping me out right now." Because that was this validation that he totally needed.

This notion of BDSM as potentially validating violence within intimate relationships taps into a whole "radical feminist" literature, within which sadomasochism is conceived of as perpetuating the connection between sex and violence that is a key factor in female oppression (MacKinnon 1994). However, the pro-dommes I interviewed were, overwhelmingly, women who felt positively about the fact that they were combining physical aggression (most of them did not consider it "violence") and eroticism for a living—hence the therapeutic discourse. The sessions in which they felt that their work was normalizing unhealthy forms of aggression were the exceptions, not the rule.

The folk narrative employed by the pro-dommes I interviewed thus frames "therapy" more broadly than it has been traditionally, conceptualizing it as potentially inclusive of activities that have previously been viewed as pathological and destructive.[16] In positing commercial BDSM as psychologically beneficial, they invert the historical paradigm of sadomasochistic tendencies as a psychological condition, reconceptualizing sadomasochistic behaviors as treatment. This inversion of the disease paradigm has correlates within other socially stigmatized erotic practices. Homosexuality, for instance, which was originally listed in the *DSM* as a psychological disorder, has followed a similar trajectory. The act of "coming out," experienced by many queer individuals as liberating, is now coming to be seen by mental health professionals as one remedy for internal anguish. Prostitution, which has been an issue of concern within the psychiatric community, as we have seen, has also been reinterpreted as a form of "sex therapy" by some of its participants as well as by some feminist theorists. Female masturbatory aids are another relevant case. Elsewhere, I have noted that, in US legal battles concerning the distribution of sex toys, the courts have conceptualized these products as "therapeutic" devices. However, in framing vibrators and other sex toys as treatments for sexual "dysfunctions," they affirm normative, dyadic sex and inherently deny the validity of female masturbation as a healthful activity for "normal" women (Lindemann 2006). By reconstituting pathology as cure, participants in non-normative erotic practices run the risk of creating an even stronger link between sexual deviation and medicalization. This is a potential consequence, which cannot be ignored, of conceptualizing professional D/S as a form of erotic therapy.

Nonetheless, this discourse is instructive in that it provides a useful lens through which to view the activities that take place in the dungeon as well as relationships of gendered power more generally. Looking at therapy as a metaphor for professional erotic dominance facilitates the unfogging of complicit masculinity. It reveals alternative masculinities that, in daily life, are obfuscated by compulsory expressions of strength and aggression. At the same time, it reflects the performance of femininity within other spheres of life, particularly within service industries into which emotional labor has been outsourced. There is a clear disconnect between the nurturing femininity in which pro-dommes engage and the image of the cruel, whip-wielding woman who bellows at her cowering clients, showing them no mercy. This disjuncture provides further evidence that relationships of gendered power in this social world are far more nuanced than they superficially appear. In the chapter that follows, I will examine these nuances more closely, exploring how pro-dommes' subversive production of dominant femininity is actually sustained through their engagement with normative, gendered tropes.

"Is That Any Way to Treat a Lady?": (Re)production of Gender on the Dungeon Floor

I'm at the Life Café in downtown Manhattan, and there is a leather dog mask on the table. Everyone's brought their costumes and props with them to dinner; afterward, we're heading over to a Scene party at a nearby bar. Tonight I'm joining a dominatrix manager, his wife (herself a pro-domme), and a friend of ours who plays in her private life and is thinking about breaking into the industry. She has a notebook open in front of her—with a list of bullet points she wants to discuss at this meeting—and she's jotting down notes faster than I am.

"What's your thing going to be?" the domme manager asks her. "Your *hook*?"

"That's the thing—I don't know," she says. "What hooks do people have?"

"Danielle might be the person to ask about this," he replies.

I laugh.

Ultimately, she decides to take on the persona of a "High Lady" and perform stylized wrestling moves on her clients.

Months earlier I had been conducting an interview, coincidentally in the same café, with a pro-domme in her early forties who had been describing to me what she called her "dungeon protocol." "In my sessions, I insist that I be called 'Mistress' or 'Ma'am,'" she had explained, dipping her fork into her vegetarian entrée. "But it's not just about protocol; it's about manners. It's about respect. If they don't follow the rules for my dungeon, I will ask them, 'Is that any way to treat a lady?'"

Pro-dommes complexly produce gender on the dungeon floor in one way by integrating assertions of their femininity into their sessions. These assertions have the effect, on the one hand, of accentuating the fact that, by taking on the role of the powerful female in the D/S dyad, they symbolically destabilize gendered norms, challenging traditional conceptions of female passivity in erotic encounters as well as in everyday life. On the other hand, as in the case of the women described above, pro-dommes sometimes mobilize traditional gender scripts during their sessions.

In this chapter, I explore this process by which pro-dommes' descriptions of their labor posit it as paradoxically reproducing traditional models of femininity in the course of subverting the standard gender/power arrangement. Throughout this book, I have explored how the world of commercial BDSM illuminates both what we *are not* and what we *are*, in terms of power, hierarchy, and gender. Here, I deal most explicitly with the gendered scenarios that are played out in this erotic space, arguing that, paradoxically, pro-dommes' narratives actually indicate that they sustain their subversive femininity through the use of conventional gendered scripts and tropes. They conform to conventional standards of beauty and emphasize the femininity of their bodies; they preserve their bodily capital by withholding sex; and their protocols often rely upon an etiquette that is in line with traditional courtly modes of masculinity and femininity. Further, their sessions often involve feminine archetypes, even in cross-dressing scenarios in which the client plays the part of the female. Looking at how gender "works" in these encounters sheds light not only on how traditional gender roles can become destabilized within non-mainstream modes of erotic expression, but also, in contrast, on the robustness of normative gender paradigms, even within transgressive forms of erotic behavior.

Further, this chapter sheds light on a facet of BDSM, in general, that has been undertheorized within prior studies. Previous sociological literature has not dealt adequately with how dominants and submissives "do" their genders in such encounters,[1] leaving open the question of how masculinity and femininity get produced or reproduced in the contexts of these erotic exchanges.

While a discussion of the production of gender on a microsociological level has been absent from the social scientific literature on sadomasochistic sexuality specifically, the symbolic interactionist literature on "doing" gender within face-to-face encounters has enjoyed a long history. It is this literature I draw upon in making the claim that pro-dommes enact and produce particular kinds of femininity in the dungeon (Riviere 1966, 213; Butler 1999; West and Zimmerman 1987; Salzinger 2003).[2]

The one place in which the intersection of gender and BDSM has been a salient issue of concern is within the feminist community. Along with pornography and prostitution, sadomasochism is one of the big three sexuality-related issues that have historically proven divisive for feminists. These issues have been hashed out in a series of academic conversations that are sometimes termed the "sex wars."[3] While many "pro-sex" feminists, as Chancer summarizes, believe that sadomasochism is "a legitimate form of consensual sexual activity" in which women should be able to engage "without fear of discriminatory judgment by society or other feminists" (2000a, 79; see also Califia 1988; Rubin 1992), "radical feminists," such as Andrea Dworkin (1974, 1987) and Catharine MacKinnon (1989, 1994), have called for a ban on pornography that involves sadomasochistic acts, viewing it as a reinforcement of gender hierarchy.[4]

It is important to note that it would be irrelevant for some feminist opponents of sadomasochism that women are the dominant partners in dungeon interactions. Discussing a female sadist, for instance, MacKinnon argues that the "relational dynamics of sadomasochism do not even negate the paradigm of male dominance, but conform precisely to it" (1989, 142). For MacKinnon, even when the aggression emanates from women, SM reinforces the connection between sexuality and violence, power, and contempt that creates and perpetuates female oppression. This feminist conversation about SM as a theater for playing out larger gendered dynamics, however, has been largely theoretical. As a venue where the woman plays the dominant role in the SM interaction, the dungeon provides a laboratory in which we can evaluate claims about the connection between sadomasochism and gender display "on the ground."

The Challenge to Female Passivity

Pro-dommes' narratives about their professional activities suggest that, on the dungeon floor, gender is in many ways produced subversively—that is, in contrast to the heteronormative, patriarchal standard of the male as the aggressor, erotically and otherwise. The normative, relational paradigm of the sexually aggressive male and passive female has been well documented. Francesca Cancian, for instance, has indicated that initiating sex has been the "masculine role" within loving relationships (1986, 696). Likewise, historian Beth Bailey notes that traditionally, "masculine men are powerful, dominant, aggressive, and ambitious" while "feminine women" are required to be "dependent, submissive, [and] nurturing," and that these socialized traits translate to their roles in dating and sex (1989, 98; see also Flora 1971, Allen 2003, and Miles 1993). Pro-dommes present a challenge to this model by assuming the rule of the "top" and behaving with physical and verbal aggression toward their male clients.[5]

Gender/Power Inversion in the Dungeon

As I have stated elsewhere, it is not the intent of this book to resolve the debate about who really has the control in a paid erotic exchange (as though such a resolution were possible), or whether the commercial realities of the industry uphold conventional beliefs about masculinity and femininity—that is, to rehash the same debate that has taken place regarding most other forms of erotic labor. One point I do want to make clear, however, is that within the particular theater of the dungeon, in the scene each dominatrix plays out with each client, the pro-domme takes on the role of the aggressor. On a microsociological level, at least—as she picks up the whip or the paddle, as she places the client in restrictive bondage, as she gives him orders, as she humiliates and taunts him—she produces a femininity that is in direct contrast to conventional "dependent, submissive" femininity.

Moreover, the industry of female dominance works precisely because it relies upon the inversion of the gender/power hierarchy—a point that even MacKinnon concedes: "The capacity of gender reversals (dominatrixes) and inversions (homosexuality) to stimulate sexual excitement is derived precisely from their mimicry or parody or negation or reversal of the standard arrangement" (1994, 270). While, in MacKinnon's view, gender reversal in the dungeon ultimately reaffirms the conventional arrangement (the same way that, for her, the category of homosexuality ultimately reinforces heterosexism), her argument nonetheless rests upon the recognition of female erotic dominance as a reversal. The figure of the dominatrix has such cultural salience, in short, because it represents an interruption in the production of gender-normative sexuality.

Subversion of Gendered Norms: Dommes, Clients, and Risk

Looking at how pro-dommes conceptualize risk is particularly illustrative of commercial BDSM's uniquely explicit organization as an inversion of the standard gender/power arrangement. The element of risk "works" differently in pro-dommes' narratives about their industry than it does within the narratives of other erotic laborers, and this is partially owing to the unique relationships of gendered power that play out in the dungeon. It is telling that a female professor remarked to me, during a discussion about pro-dommes and safety, "If my daughter were doing any form of sex work, I would want it to be this."

Risk has been a pervasive theme in prior sex-work literature, which largely focuses on the potential risks to female erotic laborers of being alone with male strangers during illegal erotic encounters. Discussions about the safety issues involved in sex work have involved the characterization of sex workers as victims and have been mobilized as evidence in the historical debate between "victim" and "power" feminists (Sanders 2005, Cesario and Chancer 2009, 217). Professional erotic dominance, however, is distinct from other forms of erotic labor in that there are few, if any, victimization narratives about the women who engage in it. The inverted power relationship that is dramatized in the dungeon, and the fantasy of male submission that sustains this relationship, are crucial factors in this unique aspect of the industry.

It is striking that, when asked if they had ever experienced a safety issue in the dungeon, many of the pro-dommes' responses focused on the clients' safety. Even the question "Has this job ever made you fear for your safety?" often elicited comments about their desire to preserve the physical well-being of clients.[6] Many of my informants, for example, indicated that they had denied requests for sessions that they had deemed unsafe for the potential clients. Some said that they refuse to engage in "edgeplay"—a blanket term used in the BDSM community for an activity (such bloodletting, extreme breath play, or playing with fire) that is potentially more dangerous than the typical scene.

Other times, they engaged in negotiations with their clients that resulted in sessions they considered less hazardous. One woman from New York recounted, "A client wanted to use poppers during the session.[7] I said, 'No.' He wanted *serious* breath play. I said, 'I'm not gonna do that with you.' He'd just told me that he had [high] blood pressure and a heart condition or something. And then he wants me to do breath play with him. I don't need to be calling 911." My interviewees commonly but not universally refused to see clients who were chemically impaired, for the clients' safety as well as their own.

The other safety-related case in which dommes said they refused to see clients was when they had doubts that they themselves were in the proper frame of mind to safely perform a session. An indie who identifies as a "conscious, loving sadist" told me that she refuses to strike people she does not personally like. She explained:

> I will not hit out of anger. If I'm angry, I'll have to work through it. Part of being a mistress is also having control over oneself. And if I don't have control over myself, I can't possibly have control over anyone else at that moment. If I'm having a bad day, I'll cancel my sessions, because they should not see me like that and I should not tell them what to do. I might make a misstep. Ever hit something a little too hard because you're angry and you break it? Don't wanna do that with a person.

Many pro-dommes who were also in the lifestyle subscribed to the SSC credo—"safe, sane, consensual"[8]—a kind of Hippocratic oath for BDSM participants, which amounts to avoiding overly risky and certain kinds of morally ambiguous play—but, again, this attitude was not universal. One informant told me that if a client wishes to do something she considers dangerous, she advises him of the risks and proceeds. "I don't have a lot of nos anymore," she added. Another indicated that she once had a client who wanted to be kicked until she broke his ribs. She did it.

The majority of women in this sample, however, told me that they had never feared for their own safety because of their work as pro-dommes. Plausibly, there is a selection bias effect among subjects who are still pro-dommes, as one informant suggested. Indicating that she had never felt unsafe in ten years of being both a pro-domme and a pro-sub, she told me that her clients, in general, were extremely respectful, "Because they don't want to screw up and *lose* that sub. Or lose the ability to get back in the House." She added, "I've never had a situation where I was truly scared, or where I felt I had to protect myself. And that's working out of, like—in strange cities, out of hotels. And thank God. Of course, I know that happens. Thank God that hasn't happened to me. That's the thing, though—if it *did* happen to me, I wouldn't be in this fucking business anymore. I'd leave." A few women told stories of other pro-dommes who had left the profession after their safety had been compromised.

Nevertheless, overall, the women I interviewed for this book gave me every reason to believe that physical assaults on dominatrices were a rare occurrence.[9] The fact that women only had one or two stories to tell about clients overstepping their bounds, if they had these stories at all, is potentially indicative of the structure of the industry, both internally and relative to larger dynamics of gender and power. Bernadette Barton's work on exotic dancers provides a compelling counterexample. She observes that women age out of exotic dancing, partly because there are so many situations in which their safety is threatened. Many of Barton's informants had experienced sexual harassment and abuse and every one of the strippers she interviewed had experienced at least one "psychologically disturbing" scenario while on the job— for instance, spitting, unwanted groping, and customers who threw change at them (2006, 63). Similar stories arose on occasion during my interviews but they were the exception, not the rule. As discussed previously, the difference here lies not only in the fact that professional D/S is set up as a reversal of gendered power. Pro-dommes also screen their clients, and they have a series of built-in safety mechanisms. But the inversion is certainly part of the reason why pro-dommes' discussions of risk tend to focus on potential harm to the clients, rather than themselves.

The effect of this dramatized power reversal on pro-dommes' well-being becomes particularly apparent when we look at pro-dommes' descriptions of potentially dangerous situations in which they preserved their safety by turning fantasy frameworks to their advantage. While most women told me that they had never feared for their safety because of their work as pro-dommes, I heard a handful of stories about women who had worked within their roles as dominant to extricate themselves from potentially threatening scenarios. A Bay Area woman, for example, recalled using such a tactic in a threatening situation with a client at one of the city's larger dungeons:

> I was straddling his body, and I was getting towards the end of the scene, and I loosened up his right hand so he could masturbate—because most clients do want to have an orgasm at the end of the scene, so they get to do "self-release." And after I let his hand go, he immediately, like, grabbed my throat. And I just pushed his hand away and was like, "What the fuck was that?" You know, "Just, like, jerk off and get the fuck out of here!" And he did [*laughs*]. But that was the only time I ever felt like I was in any danger, and I think if I had not been in a very dominant mode—if I had reacted with fear—it would have gone farther.

The way that these women "do" their femininity—as powerful and controlling, in accordance with the fantasy of inversion that sustains their exchange—is crucial here. Within pro-dommes' discourses about gender and power, it is not the woman alone with the stranger who is potentially in jeopardy but rather the male client who must be protected. They suggest that risk works differently here, not only than it does in other forms of sex work but also than it does in everyday life.

In fact, one of the main concerns that arose when I proposed this project was a concern for my safety, as a researcher. While I think the presupposition that those who engage in non-normative forms of sexuality are "dangerous" is inherently a faulty and offensive one, as a (female) researcher going into unfamiliar locations I did take measures to minimize my personal risk. At first, I conducted each interview in a public place, unless I had met the interviewee before or she had been referred to me by someone I trusted, but as my fieldwork progressed, this was not always the case. When I was meeting an unfamiliar informant at a private location, such as a personal dungeon, I sent the address via text message to a friend I trusted; he deleted it after the interview had been completed. Ultimately, I believe I subjected myself to the same level of risk that any researcher encounters when interviewing strangers, if not less risk, since many pro-dommes participated in this study because they were trying to change the negative public perception of BDSM. Any fear I may have experienced derived not from the interview subjects themselves but from navigating unfamiliar and potentially unsafe neighborhoods. I also received several prank phone calls about this project, none of which I regarded as threatening.

Sessions with Women

One potential counter to the argument that pro-dommes invert the standard gender/power arrangement is that, by actively purchasing an erotic experience, clients reinforce the notion of men as sexual aggressors. Professional erotic dominance is, in fact, an industry that is overwhelmingly female on the supply side. There are few male commercial dominants, and rarely do they have female paying clients. When I asked them about women clients, most pro-dommes in this study indicated that they "would love to" see women. Most, however, told me that all of their clients had been male.

Bay Area pro-dommes were more likely than New York pro-dommes to report having seen female clients, but women on both coasts indicated that most often these clients were part of heterosexual couples who had come in to do sessions together. One dominatrix from New York, for instance, recalled that, during fifteen years in the industry, "I've had one or two [women] by themselves and probably about four or five couples." Interactions with couples can take the form of "teaching" sessions, in which the domme instructs the clients in various aspects of D/S, so that the couple can use that knowledge in their private sex life.

The assertion that "women don't have to pay" for sadomasochistic exchanges in particular, and for erotic experiences in general, was common on both coasts. "I love women!" one Bay Area woman exclaimed. "I would love to dom[inate] a lot of women, but women don't pay. Women don't *have* to pay, you know?" A Manhattan-based domme who had been in the industry for six years concurred that women are "the rarity" and that she has never had one as a client: "Women generally don't have to pay for anything. Whether you're a submissive or a dominant there's guaranteed some other guy or some other woman who wants to do it for free." This idea that "women don't have to pay for anything" plays into the cultural notion of the male as sexually insatiable, always ready, and always willing, and the female as sexually passive, or resistant to, the erotic exchange.

While sessions involving female clients constitute a small percentage of all dungeon interactions, it is instructive to look at them because they represent commercial BDSM stripped of a power dynamic between interacting male and female bodies. Pro-dommes who had done sessions with female subs described these interactions as fundamentally different from those with male clients, in the sense that they were more oriented toward accommodating the clients' particular requests. "It's a lot harder [dominating women] in some ways," one informant told me. "I think maybe I just feel more pressure to do a good session." Other pro-dommes described their interactions with women as being particularly geared toward fulfilling the sub's particular fantasies. One indie discussed her past experiences with female clients:

> I found it was harder for me to be just as sadistic as I would be with men. With men, I would take more freedom. I would just, like, know what they needed and then play with it. Not give them everything they need but knew what they really needed and played with it and then fuck around with what *I* felt was creative to bring into the scene. With the women, I would really ask them what they want. Like, "Do you just want a flogging so you can cry your heart out? Do you want a flogging and do you want fisting?"—which, with guys I wouldn't do, but with women I would do. And be really clear about what they wanted, and just give it to them as a service. So, [I was] more service-oriented with women.

Interestingly, this was the same woman who said that she did not tolerate topping from the bottom from her male clients, because professional dominants are not a "pizza ordering service." The struggle to get over does not appear to be a fundamental element of female sessions; in these scenarios, pro-dommes, by their own accounts, are much more likely to behave as service tops.

Other interviewees echoed this domme's comment that she found it difficult to be "as sadistic" with women as she was with her male clients. One woman, for instance, told me, "I have a very erotic style. It's almost a rape," adding that, when a female client comes into the dungeon, "It's a much more toned-down session from my point of view."

If the cultural figure of the dominatrix "works" because, as Mackinnon theorizes, it mimics or parodies or negates or reverses the "standard arrangement" of gender and power, then there must be something else happening in interactions with female clients. Informants' descriptions of their sessions with women hint at the idea that these encounters are structured differently from encounters with men, in part, because female submissives do not carry patriarchal privilege with them into the dungeon. That is, there is nothing to reverse. Finally, larger society's proscriptions against physically harming women may also play into the "toned down" nature of some of these sessions. One informant, for instance, related an experience with a female client who wanted to be anally penetrated with a dildo in a painful manner. As she described the details of the interaction, she kept telling me, "I really felt bad about it"—a sentiment she did not use to characterize her emotions about any of her other sessions.

Reliance on Conventional Gender Scripts

On a chilly evening in late November, I'm attending a "body image forum" sponsored by TES at a rehearsal space in midtown Manhattan. Down the hall, young Asian girls in red leotards are practicing ballet to piano music. Every once in a while our room rumbles with the sound of the group next door doing primal screams. I'm recalling how one of my interviewees had described TES as "the PTA of the New York Scene," by which she meant that people at TES meetings tend to be "frumpier" than the average lifestyle players, as well as more interested in the intellectual aspects of BDSM and more "old school." The crowd here, to be sure, is more mature than at other Scene events I have attended. Many people in the audience are middle-aged or older; a line of silver-haired men adorns the front row.

Tonight's discussion, which is being moderated by a young black man in a sweater vest, focuses on how mainstream expectations about the body have pervaded the BDSM community. Panelists recall how they have been judged by other people in the Scene for a variety of reasons ranging from weight and physical proportions to disability status and age. A woman in her thirties describes having been turned down by a fifty-something man on a BDSM-related dating site because she was "too old." "Although we're kinky people, we're not really that kinky in the way we think about the body," one lifestyle dominatrix told me afterward.

These mainstream body aesthetics infiltrate the commercial end of BDSM as well, and pro-dommes strive to duplicate conventional models of feminine beauty through a variety of different mechanisms. First, they often wear fitted corsets that exaggerate their feminine curves, cinching their waists and pushing up their breasts. Other traditional markers of the female body, such as long, flowing hair, are also highly valued within this industry. One Bay Area pro-domme described an ongoing internal conflict she'd experienced over the length of her hair:

> I had my hair like this [very short] when I started this. And it grew as soon as I started this work. The Head Mistress was all about long hair. Long, goddess hair, right? I never cut it. I had it grow even down to here, and everyone said, "Oh, your beautiful mane!" And one of the things I've talked about with my partner is how I really want to get out of this. And he's like, "Will you please

cut your hair for me? For us? You look so great with short hair." And I'm like, "Well, yeah, the subs—I know they like long hair."

She ultimately got a haircut—an act, she said, that "freed" her—but her story was typical of pro-dommes who were conscious of changing their looks to fit a more stereotypically feminine mold. As one woman put it, "You find yourself leaning more and more towards trying to look mainstream. 'Cause as kinky as [professional erotic dominance] is, most of the clients are quite vanilla in terms of what they think is attractive." One former dungeon manager confirmed that, when women submitted photos or came in for interviews, "We'd try and go as conventionally attractive as possible."

Conformity to the structure of contemporary male desire, even within this "alternative" industry, is supported and perpetuated by the various websites on which clients "grade" dommes via message boards with threads such as "Who has the best hair?" and "Who has the sexiest feet and toes in NY???" Some women expressed anxiety about being able to meet these standards and frustration with the message boards, though several mentioned that they had altered their appearances after reading negative reviews. The same dominatrix who had grown out her "goddess hair" to fulfill her clients' fantasies explained that the reviews had made her hypervigilant about male perceptions of her attractiveness, not only in sessions but in everyday life:

> When I started [in the industry], I always wore glasses in my scenes, and then I would read these reviews, and I felt like they didn't convey—okay, I had a big ego coming into this, because I was from the club scene and the swinger scene, and I'd been going around, and everyone would say to my partner, "You're so lucky! She's so hot!" and I would always be validated. Then you come into sex work and it's like, you're in an even bigger theater. And there's even more of the harshness and the throwing of tomatoes. I actually was really surprised to be judged so harshly. People would write, like, "Good body, but her face is okay," and stuff like that!

Later in the interview, she added:

> There's a whole review system that really rubs me the wrong way—people coming into session with me and behind my back, without even asking me, writing every detail of the scene, and rating my face and my body on a scale of 1 to 10. It's made me want to quit many times. I swear to God, when I look at these guys, I'm like, "Are you running my face on a scale from 1 to 10?" I know I need to excise that, to liberate myself from that paradigm. But it's definitely something that has stayed with me that has limited my ability to interact with men.

The fact that the dungeon, while a subversive world, is subject to normative ideas about what beauty should be tells us something important about the influence that societal expectations have on sexuality more broadly. In short, it is evidence that what arouses us is fundamentally social. In making this point, I draw upon one of Chancer's arguments (1998, 83): that beauty expectations are "social facts" in the true Durkheimian sense. Distinguishing social causes from psychological manifestations, Durkheim describes social facts as those phenomena that exist "outside the consciousness of the individual." He goes on to explain, "Not only are these types of behaviour and thinking external to the individual, but they are endued with a compelling and coercive power by virtue of which, whether he wishes it or not, they impose themselves upon him" (1982, 51). While the world of commercial BDSM creates room for resistance, it is not immune from the particular coercive processes by which the gendered body gets judged; expectations from everyday life percolate its fantasy environment.

Informants maintained complex and varied relationships to the standards of female attractiveness that filter from daily life into the industry. One indie spoke disdainfully of women she called "Disney dommes"—"Blonde, fake boobs, plastic"—while others consciously molded their appearances to fit such archetypes or discursively legitimated themselves within the industry by employing rhetoric about their own conventional attractiveness. Describing a House where she had formerly worked, for instance, one woman explained, "I've got big tits, I'm pretty, I've got good legs, I've got a good body. I'm not like those fat bitches who are there now."

At the same time that it feeds into mainstream conceptions about the body that pervade the world of professional erotic dominance, this dominatrix's comment about "those fat bitches" also sheds light on the internal complexity of this industry when it comes to gender display. Despite the pressure to conform to conventional standards of feminine beauty, women who are overweight or otherwise do not fit the "Disney domme" mold can still become successful pro-dommes. Because pro-dommes' interactional scripts often rely upon the clients' perceptions of dominatrices' expertise and maturity, the ageism and pressure to physically conform that exist within other forms of erotic labor—stripping, for instance—are less pronounced here. Age can function as a proxy for competence and authority. Further, because sessions are often role based, physical appearance can become less important to a sub, as long as his dominatrix is able to convincingly play a particular part.[10] One woman who regularly takes on the role of an "aunt" or governess in "domestic discipline" scenes told me, "Because of the niche I've created for myself, it doesn't matter if I'm a thousand pounds and I'm using a walker. I'll still be able to work." Even as this industry, to some extent, relies upon the conventionally drawn image of the female body—a young, hourglass-shaped blonde—there is still room for deviation from that paradigm.

However, one of the reasons that dommes are able to deviate from the norms of feminine beauty is because they are playing into other female archetypes. A "domestic disciplinarian," for instance, may invoke classic images of femininity—the mother, the babysitter, the school marm, the cruel governess—in her "punishment" scenes. Thus, a woman who is not a young vixen with a "perfect" body in gleaming latex sometimes engages in a trade-off, fitting into one classical model of femininity in lieu of conforming to another. Additionally, as discussed, in playing the roles of nurses, mommies, and babysitters, pro-dommes often produce a nurturing femininity, even as they maintain their dominance.

Pro-dommes further do gender in a way that plays into conventional ideas about femininity by maintaining their erotic value through withholding sexual extras. This power dynamic plays into the cultural stereotypes of the male as the aggressor and the female as the resister when it comes to heterosexual eroticism. Bailey, for instance, discusses the institutionalized and de facto systems of "sex control" underlying dating on college campuses in the 1950s: "While the regulatory systems attempted to control sex by controlling women, this ideological system made women, themselves, the controllers of sex. By its logic, women, according to their nature and in their own self-interest, must enforce sexual limits." Moreover, Bailey adds, "if men refused to allow the women the power to control their mutual sexual experience, this system of sexual control could not function" (1989, 87, 88).

This imperative to enforce sexual limits in order to increase one's value to men was not only a convention of the 1950s but is also a concept that pervades contemporary popular culture. In the 1995 best seller *The Rules* and its 1997 sequel, *The Rules II*, self-help authors Ellen Fein and Sherrie Schneider advise women to wait to have sex in order to hold on to the men they are dating. In a chapter entitled "*Rule #15*: Don't Rush into Sex and Other *Rules* for Intimacy," they explain, "You will just have to exercise a bit of self-restraint and character building here and trust that if you hold off for a few weeks or months, you won't be sorry. Why risk having him call you easy (and think of you that way) when he's talking to his buddies in the locker room the next day? Better that he be angry and strategizing ways of seducing you on the next date than moving on to the next girl" (2007, 79). This idea about the economic value of "holding off" also emerges in American vernacular—for instance, the expression that women who have too much sex, or casual sex, or sex too early in a relationship, are "cheap."

In the dungeon, pro-dommes play upon this trope of the resistant female in order to preserve their dominance. One woman, who had been in the industry for six years at the time of our interview, indicated that, at the beginning of her career, she had provided sexual extras to clients. Ultimately, however, she found that extras disrupted the underlying power dynamic of the interaction. "The more sexual you get," she explained, "the harder it is to maintain dominance." Refraining from particular forms of sexual contact also emerges as a theme in some pro-dommes' "humiliation scenes," in which they tempt clients with offers of sexual favors but ultimately deny them these experiences. "It's a dance," one informant explained. "I make them think I'm gonna have sex with them. Then [I say], 'Are you kidding me? I'm a beautiful, glorious domme. Why would I have sex with a little troll like you?' . . . It's all part of the dance."

Clients, however, are typically keyed into the terms of these exchanges. They know that they will never receive the sex that is offered. Such scenes would not work if they did receive it. One man wrote on his client profile: "Do not be offended by my request/plea for contact—I know it cannot happen and should be ridiculed for the suggestion." Such interactions mirror the aforementioned model of heterosexual economy, as pro-dommes preserve their erotic value by withholding various forms of physical affection. Those dommes who do cross the line, as the woman above suggests, run the risk of forfeiting part of their control over the encounter.

A third way that pro-dommes mobilize traditional gender scripts in their dungeon interactions is by requiring manners from their clients that draw upon conventional ideas about "ladylike" and "gentlemanly" conduct. Some women, like the aspiring pro-domme discussed at the beginning of this chapter, refer to themselves as "high ladies," and it is not uncommon for their industry names to include the title "Lady." Some of these women indicated that they prefer this honorific to be used even outside of the dungeon setting. At the beginning of one interview, I wrote down the informant's Scene name, minus the "Lady," in my field notebook. "Well, I have to stop you right there," she interjected, pointing at the page. "That's Lady ——." Women who went by "Lady," as opposed to "Mistress" or "Domina," tended to be among the dommes who were more "protocol oriented." They were more likely to tell me that, in session, they insisted upon certain stylized modes of behavior involving gender-specific etiquette. However, such protocols were not particular to pro-dommes who called themselves "Lady." One thirty-eight-year-old woman, who did not identify with the term, for instance, described her negotiation processes with clients prior to sessions:

When he shows up, I'm going to go out and meet him in the welcome room. There are two little curtained cubicles. I'm gonna sit down and talk to him. I'm gonna very carefully—although I go out of my way to not have him be in-scene with me to begin with, I *do* make sure that they treat me as a lady from the get-go. When I walk in—and I get a little bit of mileage out of the fact that I'm a little older—when I walk in, if they don't stand up—You know, they're sitting in these sort of comfortable, squashy chairs—If they don't stand up, I'm standing in the doorway of the cubicle and I tease them about it. "Your mother taught you better than that. What do you do when a lady enters the room?' And some of them have *no* clue. Some of them, their mothers did *not* teach them [*laughs*].

Here is a clear example in which a pro-domme indicates that she sustains her dominance by and through the use of a gendered trope. She employs this etiquette rule as a kind of verbal riding crop, playfully flicking her client with it. Requiring clients to stand when they entered the room, to not interrupt them when they were speaking, and to call them "Lady" or "Ma'am," were common protocols pro-dommes employed in their sessions.

Oftentimes, these protocols hearkened back to courtly eras when male and female roles were even more clearly defined than they are today. It is no social accident that the BDSM community intersects with the Renaissance Faire circuit: another community involved in the production of courtly, ro-mantic fantasy. Several informants described incidents in which they had done gender atavistically within the theater of the dungeon. One excellent example of such courtly role-playing came from the woman whose client "went right into *mode*—calling me, 'My Lady.'" In that instance, by not be-having like a proper Renaissance or medieval lady, she created a rip in the fabric of fantasy woven by the client. Underlying these types of encounters is a conception of gallantry that sustains the woman's dominance, as she is put on a pedestal, and gender is produced in accordance with anachronistic behavioral standards.

"*I* Have the Dick Now": The Recontextualization of Gender

Another gendered archetype that emerges, both in related fantasy-sustained environments such as Renaissance festivals and in the dominatrix's dungeon, is the "damsel in distress." In the world of commercial BDSM, this archetype can be seen most often in cross-dressing sessions, in which the client is femi-nized and treated like a helpless woman.[11] The sample of 305 client profiles from the New York House provides an indication of the prevalence of cross-dressing sessions; of 249 clients who checked "like," "love," or "dislike" for the item "cross-dressing," 106 indicated that they were favorably disposed to this activity. In the industry, these encounters are often referred to as "forced feminization" or "forced femme" scenes,[12] although some pro-dommes also use these terms to refer to sessions in which they penetrate clients anally with dildos, even if there is no cross-dressing involved.

Cross-dressing and bondage are commonly merged in dungeon scenarios—a combination that attests to the popularity of the "damsel in distress" role play. One man, now in his late twenties, explained the genesis of this fetish in his own life:

> The women's clothing thing was actually a precursor to the bondage. That came first. Because that was the escape. That was the first escape when I was, like, thirteen [or] twelve years old. Something like that. I don't even know how, but somehow I ended up in a pair of pantyhose. And I was like, "That feels kind of interesting." And then it turned into, like, how would this look? How would *this* look? I don't even know why, but then it turned into, shortly thereafter or maybe around the same time as the bondage—I remember looking at a site, and it was damsels in distress, basically. So then what I started to do was dress up, and by "dress up" I mean usually just pantyhose. You know? And then I would take, like, shoelaces, clothesline—anything I could find. Tape, chains, you name it. Take 'em into the bathroom with me, like, "Oh, I'm takin' a bath!" And then I'd tie myself up on the tile floor of the bathroom. Struggle around. And then actually shower and try to hide all the marks on my wrists and ankles when I got out. It started out as an escape. It wasn't me anymore. It was some damsel in distress that was struggling.

Here, he does gender in a way that feeds into the cultural image of the passive female. When he goes to see a pro-domme to experiment with this fetish, her dominance is upheld by their reliance upon this particular trope.

Thus, while the production of femininity is not bound to the female body—the pun, while not deliberate, is unavoidable—femininity is still produced in accordance with the idea of womanly weakness that underlies traditional behavioral scripts. Here it is useful to draw upon the work of psychoanalyst Jessica Benjamin, who makes the point that the fantasies of submission and "rational control" underlying SM are always linked to the differentiation between male and female roles, although these roles are not always played by individuals of their corresponding sexes (1985, 43). Cross-dressing sessions represent a particularly salient example of a BDSM encounter in which the gendered relationship is distinct from, and takes precedence over, the sexed relationship. The differentiation of clients as female becomes the crux of the role play and of the power exchange between domme and sub.

Butlerian theory can also be used as a tool for considering these interactions, as Butler's characterization of drag is particularly relevant to "forced femme" scenarios in the dungeon. Recall that, for Butler (1999), drag denaturalizes gender by caricaturing it. While it is important to note that cross-dressing is distinct from drag—cross-dressing employed for humorous or fantastical effect—their particular effect is the same in the dungeon. Putting a client in women's clothing produces an exaggerated form of femininity that plays upon "hegemonic, misogynist" meanings. At the same time, when she dresses the sub in women's clothing and outfits herself with a strap-on or arms herself with a dildo, the dominatrix exaggerates gender/power dynamics and divorces gender from the body, denaturalizing its trappings.

The "parodic recontextualization" of femininity in a cross-dressing session, like the domme's production of her own gender, often relies upon highly stylized representations of femininity, such as the aforementioned "damsel in distress." "Sissy maid," similarly, is a trope in which the client dresses in a maid's outfit and the dominatrix orders him to perform chores, such as dusting, which have traditionally been tasks performed by women. Another common variant of feminization scene is "slut training," in which the client is teased or reprimanded for "her" overt sexuality. Such sessions, in which clients put on "slutty" women's clothing and then get chided for their sexual libertinism, invoke the archetypal image of the "cheap" woman described earlier in this chapter.

At the same time that feminization scenes draw upon various gendered meanings central to a hegemonic culture, the other part of Butler's characterization also applies: pro-dommes denaturalize femininity through this recontextualization, exposing gender as a performance. This ability to challenge the false naturalness of masculinity and femininity emerged as a theme in many pro-dommes' descriptions of their work. When asked "What do you like most about being a pro-domme?" one San Francisco-based woman spoke directly to the issue of gender roles:

> It's the idea that I don't just accept the dominant paradigm of how men and women should interact with each other on a sexual basis or on a power basis. . . . It's that you screw up gender in general, in terms of who can be penetrated and who can be the penetrator, who can top and who can bottom. There can be a fluidity there. There doesn't have to be such a rigidity to our labels and our distinctions.

A New York-based woman asserted, similarly, that she likes to "play with gender." She went on to explain:

> So, [the client] doesn't have a dick. He has a pussy stick. He doesn't have an asshole; he has a slut-hole. I might tell him, "I'm gonna rent your ass out on

the street." That's part of humiliation. "You're not even a real man. You're not good enough to be a woman, either." . . . Or I make them suck my cock. Once again, that's a submissive thing to do. The person getting their cock sucked is the dominant. When you take something inside of you, you're the submissive. Or, at least, in our society. . . . I'll put a strap-on on and make them suck it until their jaws hurt. "You ever make your wife do that? Yeah? Okay, guess what? You're a bitch; you're my slut." . . . I want them to think about it. What does this mean? How powerless do they feel right now? *I* have the dick now.

Here, she makes a Butlerian assessment of the gender play involved in her cross-dressing and dildo scenes. Although she relies upon patriarchal elements in these scenes, asserting that her "dick" gives her power and exploiting misogynist epithets ("bitch," "slut"), by drawing upon these elements she exposes the false essentialism of gender-based power.

Pro-Dommes' Narrative Connections to Feminism

Later in the interview, the New York domme told me she hopes that, as a result of their experiences with her, her clients will begin to question gendered norms for erotic behavior. She noted, for instance, that she often forces her clients to taste their own semen, "And then they realize how icky that is. And I hope when they go home they don't ask their wives or assume their wives are gonna swallow anymore. I hope I do a service for humanity. It's also for me, to impart empathy, because this is a male-dominated society. . . . I try to, you know, change the world positively." The women I interviewed commonly expressed this kind of desire to change the way the people think about masculinity and femininity as they relate to dominance and submission.

Several informants expressed ambivalence about the fact that some clients had significant others who were unaware of their visits to the dungeon. At the same time that pro-dommes indicated that they experienced guilt over being the "other women," however, many asserted that their activities in the dungeon ultimately benefited the clients' romantic relationships. "The fact that I often end up being complicit in deceiving other women is the hardest—the one really hard thing about this job for me," one informant told me, " 'cause I'm too much of a feminist to be very comfortable with that." She added, however, "Don't come to me and bad-mouth your wife, because she puts up with your hairy ass. I am extremely pro-woman and pro-wife and pro-girlfriend, which is a shame because, most of these women, if they ever found out, would hate me. They have no idea that I'm they're biggest supporter." She, like the woman quoted above, argued that her interactions with clients were positively influencing male/female dynamics outside the dungeon's walls.

Some pro-dommes told me that they even counseled their clients to "come out" as kinky to their romantic partners, for the clients' own benefit. A Bay Area woman, for instance, talking about a client who was "into a little bit of cross-dressing" recounted:

> He really, really, really wanted to share it with his wife, but he wasn't . . . sure how she'd be about it. And we did a lot of talking about it, and at first he was like, "I'm gonna tell her. I'm gonna leave the panties where she can find them." I'm like, "Honey, she's not gonna assume you're wearing them. That is such an unfair way to have somebody find out. That's not really gonna be useful. . . . She isn't gonna think they're yours. She's gonna think you're having an affair. She's gonna be really hurt. That is not an okay way to do this." We talked about, you know, "Here are some books that you can read." It was right after *When Someone You Love Is Kinky* had come out, so I was like, "Go buy a copy of that. You should read it. Read it first. I think you should tell her verbally. You're welcome to give her *my* e-mail address. If you're willing to have me tell her that I've seen you, I'm happy to tell her that." I've had several people have their partners e-mail me, and I've had one person come in with his partner. Just, "I want you to teach her how to spank me." [I said,] "Okay. That's great! I'd be happy to." But this particular client, we did some rehearsing. We did a session that wasn't play at all. It was, "These are some ways to rehearse doing this." And he doesn't see me anymore. He hasn't come back in years. He calls me about once a year. Last time he called me he was like, "Guess where I am? I'm calling you from the riding lawnmower. My wife made me put on panties and a buttplug and go out and mow the lawn!" He was really happy. He was deeply relieved to—She was perfectly happy to do what made him happy and be a part of it. . . . It worked out beautifully and it meant that I lost a client, but I'm completely fine with that. He's *so* much happier.

Talking about the clients they had persuaded to come out to their significant others was just one way in which pro-dommes deployed the pro-woman discourse. Effectively, they made the argument that many of their sessions do what a lot of feminist sociology does, questioning normative gender expectations and exposing the social artifice of gender display. At the same time, these scenes reinforce conventional gendered meanings through the appropriation of the penis as a symbol of power and by relying upon female archetypes.

These highly conventionalized displays of masculinity and femininity in the dungeon are all the more striking when one considers pro-dommes' rhetorical emphasis on the fluidity of gender and sexuality. It is revealing that a majority of informants, forty-four women (67 percent), self-identified as

"bisexual."[13] This finding is more or less in line with the results of prior studies of BDSM communities. Levitt, Moser, and Jamison noted, for instance,
that a "substantial minority" of their respondents were bisexual (1994, 472),[14]
and Scott found that, of the dominatrices she encountered during her early
1980s fieldwork, "most were exploring bisexuality, though they considered
themselves primarily either heterosexual or gay" (1997, 219). Ernulf and Innala similarly call attention to this erotic fluidity among lifestylers: "It seems
socially desirable in the S&M community to be able to shift roles, and adver-
tisers in S&M contact publications often make a point of their 'flexibility,'
'versatility,' and 'bisexuality'" (1995, 635; drawing on T. Weinberg 1983).

One reason for the prevalence of pro-dommes who self-identify as bisexual is likely a selection effect. It seems probable that individuals who engage
in some forms of non-normative eroticism (BDSM, erotic labor) are more
likely than the average person to be engaging in other ones (queerness, rejecting the gay/straight binary). Additionally, the fact that I was asking about
their sexual orientation in the context of an interview about their experiences
with BDSM is important. Some informants emphasized that "play sexuality"
is a different animal from "sex sexuality" and tends to be a lot more fluid.
"I'll play with pretty much anyone," one man in the Scene, who identifies as
straight, told me, adding that he was far more selective about his sexual partners. Another lifestyler similarly explained that, though he considers himself
straight, he regularly visits a male dom because "men are better at [rope]
tying."

Another interesting aspect of sexual fluidity within the BDSM world is the
prevalence of anal penetration requests among male clients—almost all of
whom identify as "straight," according to my interviewees. "I love to worship
a beautiful mistress," one client wrote in a session request, "Ass & legs. I like
to prove my love by getting dildoes [sic]. I want to surrender to a beautiful
mistress, by taking her dildo then masturbating as my final surrender. I don't
like to suck a dildo. I am only heterosexual." Anal penetration of a male,
widely interpreted within contemporary American society as a marker of homosexuality, is reappropriated as the ultimate proof of straight devotion, in
this man's fantasy. He conceptualizes the performance of oral sex, even on a
latex penis, however, as nonheterosexual. When discussing "dildo service"
scenarios, informants emphasized this incompatibility with mainstream in-
terpretations of anal sex. "The fact that straight men like to be fucked in the
ass is, like, America's best-kept secret," one pro-domme told me, laughing.

Despite BDSM participants' emphasis on sexual versatility, however, as
I have argued in this chapter, there is often inflexibility in the gender roles
dominants and submissives play in the dungeon. In role-playing scenes, pro-

dommes do gender in the form of various feminine archetypes—the teacher, the nurse, the damsel in distress, the slut, the Renaissance lady. At the same time, there is no question that the work these women do challenges the "standard arrangement" of gender. They destabilize the established gender/power hierarchy by assuming the role of the dominant female in the erotic dyad and by "playing" with gender, challengeng the primacy of the body in gender displays through cross-dressing and dildo sessions.

My informants' discussions about the production of gender in the dungeon thus offer us further insight into how BDSM practices can paradoxically offer freedom through constraint. Pro-dommes point out that they transcend the gendered categories that are available in everyday life, while their own narratives indicate that they do so through engagement with these very paradigms.[15] Looking at the (re)production of gender in the dominatrix's dungeon also reveals something interesting about how conventional archetypes can be mobilized to subversive effect in erotically charged, fantasy-sustained social contexts. Connections can be drawn to other areas of social life in which normative gendered paradigms sustain the production of alternative sexualities—for example, gay and lesbian relationships. Maureen Sullivan (1996, 747), for instance, finds that some lesbian coparents adopt a "Rozzie and Harriet" approach to family life, in which one partner is the primary breadwinner and one is the primary caretaker, and that this division of labor "mimics modern heterosexual expectations." Dungeon interactions also shed light on the production of gender within other fantasy-based organizations, such as the Renaissance Faire community, in which, even in the alternative, imaginative world of the community, gender is often done according to normative cultural standards.

Professional dominatrices demonstrate what the transgressive production of gender hierarchy can look like, while, at the same time, illuminating the robustness of normative categories and roles. Not every session involves the dominatrix role-playing as a female archetype or another type of gender play, such as forced femme. However, many do, and, in these scenes, the pro-domme's transgressive sexuality is produced and sustained via the use of these conventional tropes. It is revealing that one trans-female pro-domme, who had undergone her sex change in her late forties, indicated that this work has given her the chance to "be a woman" in erotic situations. "That may have been my primary motivation for [becoming a pro-domme]," she explained. "It's kinda making up for missing out."

Conclusion: The Emperor's New Leather Thong

In the pages that follow, I review the series of arguments I have made in this book about the importance of professional erotic dominance as a window into "normal" life. This erotic subculture is interesting, but not for the reasons that one might expect, given the history of my discipline. Two intertwined traditions within sociology have been an effort to make the invisible visible and to look at how people in marginalized and stigmatized communities negotiate the "secret deviation" of their practices (e.g., Rubington 1973, Humphreys 1975, H. Becker, 1963). Here, I explore how pro-dommes navigate the dual worlds of stigma and normalcy. Ultimately, however, I conclude that the answer to the puzzle "What can pro-dommes teach us about the larger social world?" is not "They can teach us about marginality" but, rather, "They can teach us about many of the underlying qualities of our daily lives, which become highlighted in this unexpected social space."

"The Emperor's New Clothes" is an apt metaphor for considering this topic, for a few reasons. First, as discussed, there is a classed dimension to these practices, in that they tend to attract the relatively privileged. Second, commercial BDSM is a thriving industry that involves men in relative positions of power, and yet there is a kind of denial of its existence, including within the social scientific community. Finally, in the same way that the story of the emperor works as a parable to illuminate a larger social truth, the ways that dominatrices speak about their interactions with clients shed light on various aspects of the world outside the dungeon—ranging from the power dynamics of service-industry exchanges, to the structure of art worlds, to adult play, to the relationship between gender and therapy. Ultimately, the importance of the dungeon lies not in the fact that it shows us the ways in which professional dominatrices are "normal people" but in the fact that our knowledge of "normal" everyday processes is informed by their activities in the dungeon.

Professional Erotic Dominance as "Secret Deviation"

One day in the spring of 2008, I meet up with a lifestyler in his late twenties—a well-groomed man wearing khakis and a polo shirt, his hair gelled back impeccably. He has been e-mailing me about the interview from his office, and when I ask if he had any reservations about sending these e-mails from his work address, he shrugs: "The way I think of it is, if they know, they know."

He has not always been so cavalier about potential disclosure of his erotic practices. Another time I speak with him, he describes the "deep remorse" he felt in the past about his sadomasochistic activities, resulting in several suicide attempts, and the extreme measures he took to hide his predilections from family members. "I can't tell you how many times, when I was younger, when I did this stuff, I took all my toys and all the stuff and, after finishing, I destroyed it or threw it out," he tells me, his tone matter-of-fact. "I felt tremendous guilt. Because it's not, you know, standard. It's not what you're supposed to be doing. It's everything that you've been taught not to do, not to look at, and not to participate in."

His narrative about his attempts to suppress his participation in these "not standard" activities—both physically and psychologically, by purging his paraphernalia—feeds into a longstanding sociological literature about the management of stigma. While professional erotic dominance may not be the subject of much prior sociological research, for nearly half a decade social scientists have been concerning themselves with individuals who covertly engage in socially prohibited activities. Howard Becker (1963, 21) uses SM as a specific example of this "secret deviance,"[1] while at the same time attesting to the widespread nature of the practice. Erving Goffman, more generally, discussing what he calls "the normal deviant," observes that various types of individuals must manage potentially damaging information about themselves while, at the same time, "passing" as normal. "Taken through time," Goffman explains, "the individual is able to play both parts in the normal-deviant drama. But one must see that even boxed within a brief social moment, the individual may be able to perform both shows, exhibiting not only a general capacity to sustain both roles, but also the detailed learning and command necessary for currently executing the required role behavior" (1965, 133). In light of Goffman's argument, perhaps it should come as no surprise that pro-dommes and their clients are just "regular" members of society. Goffman asserts that we are trained to take on the role of the other and we do it all the time. Additionally, we are all socialized into the same society, so we are generally aware of the rules for normalcy, even if we do not always adhere to all of them. Becker and Goffman and other scholars of deviance provide evidence that BDSM practitioners are in the company of numerous other individuals who must negotiate the tension between their socially stigmatized behavior and their public lives, with varying degrees of success.

This tension is humorously encapsulated in a May 1998 *New Yorker* cartoon. In the image, a dominatrix sits in the middle of her dungeon, writing a note, while a desk blotter and pens rest at her feet. The caption reads: "Dear Mom and Dad: Just a quick note to thank you for the very lovely desk set" (Cheney 1998, 68). The key to the humor here lies in the disjuncture between the ordinary gift from the woman's parents—who, we infer, are clueless about her occupation—and the sadomasochistic paraphernalia scattered around her dungeon.

In actuality, pro-dommes are much more likely than their clients are to discuss their interest in SM with their romantic partners, friends, and families. The fact that pro-dommes are more likely to disclose their involvement in BDSM to their own intimate partners suggests that "secret deviation" gets negotiated differently when the socially proscribed act is one's occupation rather than a leisure activity—that is, when the individual is earning income from it and maintaining a public professional persona (for instance, by advertising with photographs on the web). In addition, it is socially acceptable to ask what one does for work, rather than in the bedroom, and thus our jobs define us to the public in ways that our sexual activities do not.[2] As one indie explained, about why she had come out to her parents about being a dominatrix the year she turned thirty, "I mean, this is what I *do*."

Pro-dommes indicated that their families had varying reactions to their disclosure, ranging from complete acceptance to denial to disowning. The following statements from four of my informants, taken together, paint a picture of the diverse ways in which the family members of pro-dommes have processed their involvement in the industry:

> I was just defending my "lifestyle choice" to my sister the other night. She was like, "What good does it do? What's the purpose? Why is this not just frivolous? Why should I respect this?" I'm like, "You don't have to respect it. *I* don't necessarily respect it. But it *amuses* the hell out of me." . . . But the family knows. They hate it. They consider it prostitution. My *sister* says—she's a liberal-type person—"I have no problem with it, but it's frivolous." I'm like, "Damn right it's frivolous. It makes me money, and it's fun."

My mom loves my two subs. I bring them everywhere. Family outings. Every-where. My mom has them running around at parties. "Go do that. Get that. Make the potato salad." My mom loves that—a little power trip. My sister just shakes her head.

When I decided to advertise as a dominatrix on the Internet, I was like, "Okay, I have to talk to you all, because I don't want my nephews or somebody find-ing me and then you find out that way, so I'd rather tell you myself." And ev-erybody was amazingly cool about it, but for some reason when they thought I was gay, *that* was like the big tipping point for my sister.

My in-laws think I'm a whore. Now, they found out by accident; they over-heard a phone conversation. . . . They just assumed that it was sex. Because why would anybody pay this much money *not* to have sex, or nudity for that matter. And that I must be cheating on my husband. And I tried to explain to them—I'm like, "Hey, go to my website, go to my videos, or come to a session. I could send a submissive to clean your house for you. I could have a submissive pick you up. What do you need?" [They were like], "Lalalalala! I can't hear you!" So they'd rather think that I'm a hooker that takes money for sex than to actually know what I really do, which is kinda fucked up.

There were ripples of these varied reactions to pro-dommes' disclosure in the reactions—of family, of friends, of other academics, and of strangers—to my own disclosure about this project. Because being an academic is what *I* do, and studying dominatrices was the salient feature of my job for two years, that fact came to define me in many types of social situations. What inter-ested me most about my moments of disclosure were the people who asked many follow-up questions and those who abruptly stopped the conversation after I had said what I was working on—and the fact that the individuals who fell into these two groups were not always the individuals I would have expected. A liberal feminist acquaintance, for instance, angrily accused me of "normalizing domestic violence" and refused to discuss the issue further. On the other hand, my mother, a conservative schoolteacher from suburban Long Island, not only asked me multiple questions about the topic but pro-ceeded to discuss it with her neighbors, friends, and colleagues and report back to me with *their* questions: "[My friend] from down the street wants to know how much these women get paid." These moments, in which I became implicated in pro-dommes' "secret deviation" by virtue of my research, are evidence that the slippage between "good woman" and "bad woman" that Chancer observes in the response to female sex researchers is a process rather than an event. My "contamination" by my subject matter was not a one-time occurrence that happened when I interviewed my first dominatrix but rather was systemically reaffirmed every time I disclosed my object of study to a new person.

While, as Becker observes, in practice BDSM activities are more widespread than one might imagine, the reactions both to my research and to pro-dommes themselves provide evidence that BDSM acts continue to be conceptualized by some as a deviant. The stigmatization of the practice both facilitated and hindered my ethnographic process. While gaining entry into the BDSM world was difficult because potential informants feared negative representation by academics, once they were convinced that my intent was descriptive rather than moralistic, many people expressed a desire to speak to me because of the pervasive negative image. "The bad guy in the movie is always wearing a leather hood and has a dungeon," one of my informants explained, "so people either take the fetish out of context or assume that we're all sociopaths." Another informant told me, similarly, "You know, the portrayal of dommes and the portrayal of BDSM in general is [as a] very sociopathic kinda thing. A very mean thing. [But] it's not mean. It's a *decadent* thing. It's really self-indulgence." And a dom, with sadness in his voice, explained, "You read in the papers about this one girl who got chained to a bed for days and died, and that gives us a bad name. But we're good people. We're good people."

His assertion that individuals who inhabit this social world are "good people" is part of a discursive thread that frequently weaved its way into interview responses: not only do pro-dommes think of themselves as well-adjusted individuals, but they emphasize that there is a kind of moral economy to what they do. The BDSM dungeon as a moral universe is a theme that has been touched upon throughout this text but never fully unpacked. I have noted, for instance, that some pro-dommes are deeply ambivalent about engaging in types of sessions that conflict with their principles—for instance, Nazi scenes, race play, and switch sessions that appear to normalize spousal abuse. Further evidence for the moral dimensions of erotic dominance may be found in some informants' statements that they will not participate in race play with people they do not like or hit clients out of anger; that they take health and safety precautions, both for their own sake and their clients' sake; that they want their scenes to be psychologically beneficial for clients; and the fact that behavior in BDSM clubs and at parties is organized around rules of etiquette functioning to preserve participants' level of comfort and well-being.

A woman at a play party told me, for instance, that her friends who were curious about the Scene were unwilling to attend such events. "They're afraid people are just gonna start spanking them!" she told me, laughing. Their fear was absurd to her because, in many ways, the Scene is a rationally ordered social world. It is unlikely that anyone at a public party would initiate any kind of physical contact with a newcomer who had not first consented to play. There are protocols within the moral economy of the Scene, and there are sanctions for those who break the rules. Individuals who behave inappropriately at the BDSM club, for instance, are banned from the premises.

I should note that I am not the first to bring to light the moral rhetoric employed by those who participate in erotic labor (see, for instance, Prasad 1999). Furthermore, the conclusion that the producers and consumers of erotic labor exist within their own form of moral economy is perhaps a predictable one. Here, it is useful to draw a parallel between the claim I make about pro-dommes and their clients and Duneier's embattled contention that his booksellers exist in a "moral world." Wacquant (2002, 1472) has notably found Duneier's claim to be "unexceptional," as "who does not?" However, while Duneier's intent in *Sidewalk* (1999) was "to understand the ways in which 'moral' behavior and 'decency' are and are not constructed within settings seemingly unfavorable to such behavior" (Duneier 2002, 1551), here I am concerned with a setting that is conceived of by some as amoral and even, as the one informant asserts, "sociopathic." The salient fact is not that professional erotic dominance is a moral universe but that, in interviews, pro-dommes so often spoke about their actions in terms of right and wrong, despite the fact that they were not asked any questions about morality. They articulated their actions as principled within the rule structure of this particular social context—a reverse discourse that, like the therapeutic discourse, could be interpreted as a reaction to social stigmatization.

Although many informants consented to be interviewed because of the stigmatization they had faced, it should be noted that I also ran across individuals—primarily lifestyle players in the New York Scene—who had no interest in "proving" their normalness and were, oppositely, invested in preserving the social marginality of BDSM and resisting its commercialization.

Many of the pro-dommes who sat for interviews, however, not only spoke about the safety and sanity of their activities in the dungeon but also emphasized how "average" and "normal" they are, as people. "Part of the reason why I'm talking to you today is because I want to be an example," one informant told me, "And I think it's important for people—you know, like my neighbors know what I do, and I talk to them, and I make a point to be very friendly. Because it's the unknown and the unfamiliar that you fear. And, you know, if somebody's like, 'Hi, I have some extra muffins!' [*laughs*], then you're more likely to have a favorable response."

"If I Wasn't a Dominatrix, I'd Be So Boring": The Discourse of Normalcy

Not only did the pro-dommes in my sample emphasize the pervasiveness of BDSM practices—in a sense, exposing the emperor—but they regularly engaged in rhetoric highlighting their own "normalcy." The word "normal" emerged frequently in interviewee's self-descriptions, although most informants also pointed out that there are other women in the industry—specifically, lifestylers who "live it 24/7"—to whom they would not apply that term. "All the women that I know [who are pro-dommes], and I know like attracts like, but they're all really well-adjusted people," one indie in her late thirties explained. "They have a normal life. They have solid relationships. This is their job." She added the caveat, however, that some women in the industry are "more on the fringe of society." Another informant observed that it is difficult for people to grasp the concept that she is "normal" and "even boring": "I think that there's this preconceived notion that I'm going to be crazy, or that I'm going to steal their wallet or something." We had the following exchange over coffee in New York's financial district:

Outside of this, I'm pretty conservative . . . I consider myself a P. J. O'Rourke Republican. You know, less government; stay out of it. You know, "conservative." Like, I'm monogamous. Straight. Workaholic but generally "pretty normal," quote-unquote. Outside of being in the adult industry, I'm very straight-laced. Like I was thinking about it the other day, like, "Goddamnit, if I wasn't a dominatrix, I'd be so boring." . . . [When I try to date] it's hard to find someone who's straight-laced like me but is okay with, "Oh, you stick things in men's butts for a living."

By "straight-laced," what do you mean?

I don't download songs for free. I don't pirate software. I pay my taxes. I clean up my dog's poop. I don't cheat on my boyfriends. I don't drink, I don't smoke, I don't do drugs. I drink a lot of coffee, and that's about it. I'm very—I separate my recyclables. I do a lot for the environment. I'm trying to get on NYC Rescue Mission so I can work in the soup kitchens. I vote in primaries! I think jury duty is, like, an honor [*laughs*]. What's wrong with me? . . . There's a cognitive dissonance of—like, I was on the subway and someone threw this wrapper on the ground. I picked it up. Like, "You dropped something." Then I was like, "Why are you judging them? You're a dominatrix."

Like this woman, other pro-dommes also mentioned that they are not promiscuous and that they are invested in various social causes. Informants also regularly emphasized the commonplace quality of pro-dommes' everyday appearances—an assertion supported by my inability to pick interviewees out of a crowd. One indie in her early thirties, for instance, explained that some of her best friends are also professional dominatrices: "If you'd see us walking down the street together, you would *never* think."[3]

Pro-dommes' characterizations of themselves as ordinary suggest that the boundary between "normal" and "deviant" is not as clear-cut as the characterization of the dungeon as an exotic little corner of social life would suggest. In a moment from a November 2009 episode of the American television show *The Office*, the character Michael Scott, the boss, speaks to the potential instability of this distinction. Discussing the prospect of being punched by one of his female colleagues, he muses, "Am I scared of getting hit in the face? No. Every day, weirdos pay dominatrices hundreds of dollars for that privilege." Then he pauses and adds, "I'm scared I'm gonna love it." Here, he mobilizes the social concern that there is something "weird" about these men,who are not subscribing to our norms. At the same time, he hints that human beings invest energy in maintaining the line between normalcy and deviance precisely because this boundary is so unstable. He acknowledges that he might enjoy pain like those men, given the chance.

However, whether or not pro-dommes and their clients are "normal people" was not the question at the heart of this project. Nor was whether professional dominatrices are "adjusted" or "successful" or "rational" or "respectable" or whether or not they lead "ordinary" lives outside the walls of the dungeon—all of which seemed to be true of most of the women I interviewed. The central concern of this book has been the narratives pro-dommes tell about the interactions in which they participate inside the dungeon and the everyday social processes that these narratives illuminate. Professional erotic dominance may, from the outside, look like an inconsequential area of social life, interesting only to those fascinated by its prurience, or who see it as silly or amusing, or who are invested in whether or not BDSM is conceptualized as "wrong" or "bad." As I have contended throughout this explication, however, observing this corner of social life helps us to better understand what is happening in other social contexts.

What Can We Learn from Pro-Dommes?

At the beginning of this text, I introduced the following question: What can pro-dommes teach us about the categories, processes, and tensions that organize our daily lives? The answer is that we can learn a great deal by looking at the activities of these women, who work in places seemingly on the fringe of society. The dynamics of social relations that we take for granted in daily life, they highlight. These include hidden qualities of gender, power, eroticism, and hierarchy. At the same time, categories, roles, and expectations from the larger social world work themselves into, and become visible within, their world. In short, from pro-dommes, we can learn more about both what we *are not* and what we *are.*

The narratives pro-dommes tell about the sphere of commercial BDSM show us what we are not when they describe how that sphere's underlying organization is based upon a skewing of the normative structure of gender. In the theater of the dungeon, my informants assert, a female professional undermines the complicit masculinity of her client, typically, a white man in a position of relative power in his daily life. She flips gendered expectations for eroticism and hierarchy by functioning as the sexual aggressor and inflicting physical pain upon the client. The fact that this social world is rooted in an inversion of the gender/power hierarchy is evidenced by the way risk "works" within its walls. Pro-dommes' dialogue about safety focuses on their clients' well-being: a fact that distinguishes the gendered interactions within this social realm from those within other forms of erotic labor as well as within the larger social world.

At the same time that it shows us what an inversion of the gender/power hierarchy can look like, the dungeon also reflects and magnifies the larger social world. I have, using distinct but interlocking frames, presented three ways that pro-domme/client encounters can shed light on the nuances of control within everyday professional interactions. First, sessions are the result of "scripting" processes. These processes bring into focus the nuanced negotiations that happen within commercial exchanges. Dominatrices also reveal a fundamental tension that underlies these exchanges: the tension between the service provider making a claim to professionalism and the customer whose money and demand have created the interaction in the first place. Third, the way that pro-dommes talk about these exchanges highlights some of the basic tensions that lie at the intersection of commerce and art. The authenticity to which pro-dommes, both as professionals and as artistic purists, lay claim is a key to understanding the disjuncture between customers' demands and professionals' stake in such exchanges.

These professional tensions are magnified in the dungeon because, there, it is particularly jarring that the client exerts control over the encounter. After all, "submissive" is his explicit role in the theater of the exchange. Further, pro-dommes, as women who behave dominantly for a living, are likely to highlight such tensions by asserting their dominance, pushing back against their clients' topping from the bottom. For a similar reason, they also highlight a particular tension of the researcher/informant relationship; the moments in which they "dommed" me, as an ethnographer, were revealing of the struggle to get over that can characterize social research. Even the informants who, by their own accounts, do not push back against their clients, are acutely aware of the paradox involved in being a service top.

Pro-dommes also lay bare the relationships of gendered hierarchy that structure interactions in everyday life, both within and outside of the professional sphere. On one hand, pro-dommes indicate that the dungeon provides a space in which men and women can play with atypical expressions of gender. The aspect of "playing" is central to the fantasy space of the dungeon, and clients can engage in a variety of roles, ranging from animals to hospital patients to naughty little boys. Pro-dommes also suggest that clients can participate in feminized displays of vulnerability that are typically incompatible with the compulsory expressions of masculinity required by their particular stations in life. On the other hand, while pro-dommes assert that they are vigilant about maintaining the boundary between the edge of the dungeon and the beginning of "real life," roles and expectations from everyday life still filter into this realm. For instance, dominatrices often perform a kind of nurturing emotional labor that has historically been connected with women.

In talking about themselves as "therapists," my informants underscore the way in which commercial BDSM can draw out the repressed facets of postmodern masculinity, while at the same time illuminating both their own roles as nurturers and the gendered dynamics of therapy more generally. Paradoxically, pro-dommes actually perpetuate the destabilizing of gender by and through the use of normative gender scripts, mobilizing various motifs of femininity in order to sustain their dominance.

So What? Exposing the Emperor

Pro-dommes' descriptions of their work have something to teach us about various facets of social life, from the structure of postmodern masculinity to the way we interact with our hairdressers. In short, they are people we should care about. They are people social scientists should care about because their seemingly peripheral world uniquely taps into such hefty sociological concerns as gender, power, and hierarchy—categories that structure society on a fundamental level. They are people whom individuals who are interested in sexuality should care about because of their unique, yet in some ways typical, brand of commercial eroticism. And they are people whom human beings should care about, because they reveal some of the underlying dynamics of the connections we make with other people every day.

Rarely in real life do we give voice to the power relations governing our face-to-face interactions, explicitly stating, "I am in control. You're not. You obey me." There are exceptions, such as dealings with children or interactions within military units, but more often power exchange is more subtle. In some ways, pro-dommes and their clients are just playing out in the dungeon what many of us do in our professional and personal interactions every day; the difference is that they lay bare the microdynamics of these power exchanges. Even in dungeon interactions, in which power dynamics are made explicit, however, the fact that there is still a nuanced struggle for control tells us something important about the fundamental nature of interpersonal exchange. Even in a type of relationship in which power is presented as unidirectional, there is a complex jockeying for control between the participants in the interaction. Even self-identified submissives want to be dominated the way they *want* to be dominated. As we have seen, few clients say "Do anything to me" and mean it. Dominatrices assert that seldom are clients aroused by just the loss of control. They want to have control over the way they lose control. They want to script their pain.

The work performed in the dungeon thus has broader implications for scholarship about gender, sexuality, and control, in that it attests to the durability of the relationships of power that structure our social world. It suggests that they can hold up, even in an erotic space in which they continually suffer the slings and arrows of nonconformity. In some ways, pro-dommes kick the gender/power hierarchy on its head with their shiny black boots. In other ways, it is not the case that relationships of gender, eroticism, and power are radically transformed in the dungeon. In making this argument, I hope I have opened the curtain and shined a spotlight on this corner of social life, and that I have identified how pro-dommes' interactions with their clients are both like and revealing of the relationships in which we engage on a daily basis. In essence, I have not only argued that the emperor is naked but that, in some fundamental ways, the emperor is *you*.

This book is about professional dominatrices and about the world of commercial BDSM, but it is also about a series of tensions that have a role in structuring postmodern life—between professional and client, dominator and dominated, artist and customer, purist and commercialist, man and woman, complicit masculinity and marginalized masculinity, and traditional femininity and nonconformity. Like someone wiping a hand across a foggy window, the professional dominatrix brings the world into focus, while at the same time giving us a glimpse into a world where things could work differently.

Appendix A: Methods

The Sample

The pro-dommes represented within these pages were most often college-educated, white, single, bisexual women in their thirties. They ranged in age from twenty to fifty-eight, with a median age of thirty-seven (mean = 37.3). Of the sixty-six pro-dommes interviewed, forty-one (62 percent) self-identified as white, four (6 percent) as black, four (6 percent) as Latina, four (6 percent) as Asian, and one (2 percent) as Native American. The remaining twelve women (18 percent) identified as biracial. All of the biracial women were either Asian/white or black/white, except for one, who is Native American/white. When asked about marital status, thirty-six women in the sample (55 percent) indicated that they were single, twenty-one (32 percent) were married or in domestic partnerships, eight (12 percent) were divorced, and one (2 percent) was widowed. Twelve (18 percent) indicated that they had children. All of the women I interviewed had at least a high school degree, and only one informant's highest level of education was high school. Of the sixty-one interviewees who answered the question about education, sixteen (26 percent) indicated that their highest level of education was some college (this included women who were still in college at the time of interview), twenty (33 percent) received college degrees and stopped there, and twenty-four (39 percent) received some sort of graduate training. The majority of informants—forty-four women (67 percent)—identified as bisexual. Ten (15 percent) identified as straight, four (6 percent) identified as lesbian, and the remainder either did not indicate an orientation or identified with other labels (for instance, "queer," "bi-dyke," or "polymorphously perverse"). The median length of time that they had been working as professional dominants at the time of interview was about seven years, but this figure varied widely.

I spoke to a woman who had just started working in her first House weeks before our interview and another who had been in the industry for twenty-seven years.

While I made efforts to keep the sample as representative as possible, it is not a simple random sample of all pro-dommes working in New York City and San Francisco between 2007 and 2008. It is skewed toward pro-dommes who worked independently, rather than so-called dungeon dommes, as well as toward older dommes. Of the sixty-six female professional domiants in the sample, only eleven worked in Houses; the rest were indies. Like any cross-sectional study of individuals working in an industry, it underrepresents those individuals with shorter career tenures. The women who responded to my requests for interviews also disproportionately tended to be "in the life-style." This is likely because these are the women who have the most at stake in legitimating BDSM in the eyes of the general public. A woman who has been practicing BDSM personally and professionally for ten years has more invested in the public perception of erotic dominance than does a woman who is working at a dungeon for a month to help with her college tuition. I took steps to correct this skew by using my personal connections specifically to seek out younger dommes and dommes who worked in the larger dungeons. I also had informal conversations with dungeon dommes at BDSM events and did interviews with clients who had gone to both larger Houses and independent dommes. Further, about half of the indies I interviewed had at some point worked in larger Houses, so they were able to shed light on their experiences there.

Participants in the study used a diversity of self-referents in discussing their professional personas and preferred that their clients refer to them by varied terms as well. The following explanations of their professional identifiers from three of the informants, all from the San Francisco Bay Area, illustrate this variance in preferred terminology:

> I will answer to "Mistress ——" but *not* "mistress" alone. I answer to "ma'am" as a term of address, but I don't want people to call me "mistress" as a term of address.

> In session, I prefer to be called "mistress." When I'm feeling like I'm a little bit kinky and I'm out in the community, I use "dominatrix" because it still has a little shock value. And in e-mails and letters and discussions about the work, I use "pro-domme," which is the most common term nowadays, I think.

> My Scene name is Madame ——. Generally, I don't allow [clients] to call me "mistress" unless they're willing to make a commitment, because "mistress"

designates worship. So I prefer "ma'am." In general, I prefer "professional dominant," because I think it's more PC. Not so dated. Although my personal favorite is "fantasy engineer."

As the responses above attest, many participants self-identified not as "dominatrices" but as "professional dominants," "mistresses," "ladies," "high ladies," "femdoms," "goddesses," "madams," or in one case, "recreational violence specialist." However, every woman in this study advertised in an online pro-domme directory and/or self-identified as a "dominatrix," "dominant," or "domina." While many of the women in this study are also "lifestyle"— that is, they engage in noncompensatory D/S within their personal relationships—all of them have received money to engage in erotic dominance. Where I have used the word "professional" in this text, in regard to dominance, I mean it to refer to sessions in which money changes hands, as opposed to uncompensated encounters.

I made initial contact with potential informants via an e-mail (appendix E) introducing myself and the study and requesting an interview. Those who consented to be interviewed were not compensated for their time, although in many cases I did buy them coffee or a small meal as a gesture of appreciation. Interview location was left to the discretion of the interviewee and for this reason was extremely varied. Perhaps unsurprisingly, informants generally provided clear, excellent directions to our meeting spots. I conducted interviews at pro-dommes' homes and dungeons, in restaurants and bars, and at so many Starbucks coffee shops I memorized the menu. I interviewed one domme at her sister's apartment in Midtown Manhattan. As we did the interview, she alternately poured me champagne and fed carrots to her asthmatic little dog. Her sister napped sporadically on an adjoining couch and snow swirled outside. Another time I conducted an interview at a diner near New York's Penn Station; my interviewee and I snacked on burgers and fries next to a table of about ten police officers. On a chilly spring day, an interviewee and I chatted at a trendy coffee shop in San Francisco, as the couple at the next table eavesdropped obviously and unabashedly. On a drizzly autumn day, I sloshed through leaves to interview a dominant who worked out of his house in Queens. When the interview was finished, he showed me his session room and toys—which included, memorably, a cow speculum. Another interviewee, a graduate student, invited me to her university office. When her office mate walked in partway through the interview, and I reached over to stop the recorder, my informant assured me, with a casual wave of her hand, "Oh, you can keep going. She's heard it all before."

Interviews ranged from about forty minutes to two and a half hours, with the typical interview lasting a little over an hour. I, alone, conducted every interview and did all of the transcribing and analysis. Appendices F and G contain, respectively, the original and final interview schedules for this project. Over the course of my fieldwork, I changed the organization of the questions, added new questions as common themes emerged in interviews, and made semantic changes as I became more familiar with the terminology of the trade and to modify potentially offensive phrasing. For example, "Can you give me a list of the services you provide?" was changed to "Can you give me a list of the things you do in sessions?" after it elicited negative reactions from informants who believed "services" had sex-work implications when they did not self-identify as sex workers.

I acknowledge that this text suffers from a problem that plagues many studies of erotic labor: that, although the erotic exchange is fundamentally a relational practice, the research primarily focuses on the (usually, female) producers of the labor. However, from the beginning of this project, I was most interested in the women who inhabit this social world, how they think about their labor, and in what ways they produce and/or reproduce models of femininity. Further, there were methodological hurdles involved in locating male clients to interview. Many of these men are closeted about their BDSM practices and wary of speaking to an outsider, and pro-dommes are generally unwilling to "sell out" clients to a researcher. However, I did conduct ten in-depth interviews with male clients—men who had paid for erotic dominance at least once—whom I found through personal connections. They are not representative of the clients of professional dominants, in that they are all relatively young; all except for one were in their twenties or thirties. Further, eight of them are "in the Scene" and openly attend public BDSM events in New York City.[1]

I supplemented these interviews with the sample of 305 client profiles from the New York dungeon. These were forms the clients had filled out before sessions, listing some general personal information, such as their ages and health limitations, and their specific session interests.[2] Some of the forms also had notes about particular clients scrawled on the back by the dommes: "Grouchy at the beginning of a session." "Would like a switch session." "Likes to be worked up slowly not just hard spanking." "Brings ugly lingeries." "Crazy loser: just wants a hooker. Not submissive. Very difficult." "Tries to touch & hug you." "Big fat guy! Ewwwww." The 282 clients who indicated their ages on these forms ranged from twenty-two to sixty-eight years old, with a median age of thirty-nine (mean = 40.16).

The Specificity of the Locations

I chose New York City and San Francisco as the sites for this study because I had connections within both of their Scenes, the two cities share a relative social closeness, and they have, respectively, the highest and second highest number of pro-dommes who advertise on the Internet of any cities in the United States.

Could I have done this study in the suburbs? Probably not. Although there are dominatrices with dungeons in suburban America, they are geographically dispersed and would be difficult to cull into an interview sample. Further, there is something fundamentally urban about the industry of professional erotic dominance, its dependence upon the spatial clustering of males in relative positions of power, and the potential for anonymity of the exchange. Although I visited dungeons in, for instance, suburban Long Island and suburban Oakland, these were areas with proximity and transportation pipelines to the major cities in which I was doing my research. The abundance of powerful men in New York as a financial center and San Francisco as a technological center, as well as their social liberalism relative to the country at large, further make these cities magnets for the industry.

Could I have done this study in Detroit or St. Louis? Probably, but I readily admit that it may not have been the same study. New York and San Francisco are what Bernstein (2007) calls postindustrial cities where, she has argued, transformations in the private sphere have made the erotics of contemporary sex work profitable. Other cities have different kinds of underground economies and different moral economies. This is not to say that there are not dominatrices in Middle America—just that their local industries are likely organized in different ways. Returning for a moment to my professor's comment that I will never get an academic job in Omaha if I pursue this topic, a recent Google search produced at least a dozen listings for dominatrices in Nebraska. Further, although the underlying organizations of these industries might differ across cities, many of the terms and concepts that shape these practices likely remain the same, as my parallels to prior studies of BDSM practices throughout time and space have suggested.

Gaining Access to Informants

The primary barrier to gaining access to interviewees was that I was not a part of the BDSM Scene. The most common responses I received to my initial e-mail, aside from the request for further information about my project, were

"Are you in the Scene?" and "What are your own experiences with BDSM?" Several of the women I contacted had spoken to reporters in the past and felt they had been misrepresented, and so they were wary about going through the interview process again. During interviews, many informants wanted to know if I, personally, had inclinations toward D/S. Throughout the process, I felt my own sexuality was on trial. As one female submissive in the Scene told me during one of my first interviews for the project, "With people who aren't in the Scene, you worry that it's like, 'Oh, look at the monkeys in the cage.'" Mentioning that I have friends in the Scene as well as distinguishing myself from reporters and psychologists—asserting that, as a sociologist, I was interested in describing the social world of professional BDSM, not examining the psychological forces underlying it—also seemed to help me gain access to informants. I am sure that I was further aided by the fact that the majority of what pro-dommes do is legal, at least in New York City. (See appendix B for more on legal issues surrounding commercial BDSM.)

Throughout the early stages of research, several informants became skeptical of me during interviews when I lacked specific insider knowledge. In one of my first interviews with a pro-domme, for instance, when I was unfamiliar with the term "sounds,"[3] the informant cautioned me about future interviewees, "Oh, honey, you need to know this stuff or they'll eat you alive." Even when I reached a point at which I felt relatively secure in my understanding of BDSM practices, occasionally I encountered participants who questioned my level of expertise. During my second-to-last interview, for instance, the informant, a pro-domme and teacher of a D/S workshop, positioned my personal knowledge at the center of the discussion when I asked a routine follow-up question:

You mentioned that in your course you go over the difference between the fantasy of D/S and the reality of D/S? What is the difference?
Well, first I want to ask you a question: How cued in are you to the lifestyle?
How cued in am I?
Because that's such a basic question. Nobody would ask me that question except somebody who's not cued in.
Well, I'm asking what you think the difference is. Which I guess is a different question than "What is the difference?" You know what I mean?
That's true. So how cued are you anyway?
I mean, I can think of some answers to that question. But I'm interested in knowing how you would answer it.

The informant went on to answer the question. Reading books and attending Scene events to familiarize myself with the practices and lingo of BDSM helped increase my legitimacy in the eyes of my informants, but as the interview segment above illustrates, throughout the process there were still times when I got "quizzed" during interviews. "You know what TES stands for, right?" one of my informants asked, for instance, as we drank tea at a Chinese restaurant in Midtown Manhattan. "The Eulenspiegel Society," I replied. "Good girl!" she told me, tapping her spoon against her water glass. The crowning moment in my resolution of the inside/outside problem came when I received an e-mail from a woman in the Scene who had heard about my project and wanted "tips on becoming a prodom [*sic*]."

Though I was an outsider in relation to this social world, I was not an "other" in the sense that, oftentimes, there was very little social distance between myself and the women in the study. Interviewing was facilitated by our demographic similarities. As Bourdieu observes (1999, 609), the interview process "combines a total availability to the person being questioned, submission to the singularity of a particular life history—which can lead, by a kind of more or less controlled imitation, to adopting the interviewee's language, views, feelings, and thoughts—with methodical construction, founded on the knowledge of the objective conditions common to an entire social category." In my case, controlled imitation was less important—with the exception of my appropriating the language of BDSM—because I already inhabited the same objective social categories as many of the women in this study. I was, like the majority of my informants, a college-educated Caucasian female. "I wouldn't have done the interview if you were a man," one informant told me, over chai in a trendy San Francisco café. She thought for a moment and added, "Well, maybe—okay, I would do it. But I would charge them my session fee." Additionally, some pro-dommes were current or former graduate students and expressed empathy about the challenges of locating willing research subjects.

Once I got past the initial barriers, informants for the most part were incredibly open about sharing this aspect of their lives with me. They invited me into their dungeons. They sent me e-mails with lists of books to read, websites to visit, and films to watch. They took me with them to discussion panels, workshops, and parties. In sum, because of my own positionality, getting enough interviews and facilitating candid responses were not my greatest difficulties, as data problems go. Culling a *representative* sample, as noted, was the true challenge.

Appendix B: Getting Collared: Pro-Dommes and the Law

Although terminology remained relatively consistent across locations, there were a few salient dissimilarities between pro-dommes in New York City and those in San Francisco that can be attributed to context. Perhaps most salient is the differing relationship between pro-dommes, sex work, and state law.

The dominatrix/client interaction is an erotic encounter. Even if a woman in leather being paid to flog a naked man does not pass the "I know it when I see it" test for what constitutes a commercial sexual exchange,[1] there is a more tangible reason to consider it sexual: a common feature of the interaction is male ejaculation. At the same time, my research found that the pro-domme/client interaction does not regularly involve oral sex or intercourse. Informants told me that avoiding such acts was the "industry standard" in the United States,[2] although ten women in this study indicated that they had performed those acts on at least one client. Some of these women indicated that they do sexual extras only for certain clients, some of whom then become personal subs. One told me that she regularly has intercourse with her clients, but she added that she is "way more extreme than most people." There also exist "dominant escorts" and "domme courtesans"—women who work for call-girl outlets and combine dominance with sex—who were outside the purview of this study.

The stereotype was that extras like hand jobs, oral sex, "full body worship," and even intercourse were happening more often in the Houses than among indies, who rarely perform these acts, and in a few Houses this was true. There certainly exist "full-service" Houses, and word gets around the Scene about which places these are. An indie who had formerly worked at one such House told me, "There was a *lot* of pressure from the management to do extras, and they would sort of, like, get you do to hand jobs. And then they'd be like, 'Well you're *already* doing hand jobs, so it doesn't really matter if you start doing blow jobs.'" However, informants who currently or had formerly worked in most of the larger dungeons told me that they had never been pressured to perform these acts. In fact, in some cases, the reverse was true. One dungeon had cameras in the rooms, not for the women's safety, according to one woman who worked there, but to make sure no nudity or extras were taking place. Informants emphasized that it was in a House's financial interest to prohibit these sexual acts; Houses where extras were happening were much more likely to experience police sweeps and be forced to close.

Even if they are not doing extras, however, some of what pro-dommes in New York State do and much of what pro-dommes in California do violate the letter of the law. In New York, "a person is guilty of prostitution when such person engages or agrees or offers to engage in sexual conduct with another person in return for a fee."[3] Because "anal sexual conduct" qualifies as "sexual conduct," when a professional dominatrix inserts a dildo into a client's rectum and gets paid for it, she is technically in violation of the law. She can also receive a health code violation for doing golden or brown showers. In California, on the other hand, prostitution is defined in section 647(b) of the penal code as "any lewd act between persons for money or other consideration." Case law in the state clarifies that "for a 'lewd' or 'dissolute' act to constitute 'prostitution,' the genitals, buttocks, or female breast, of either the prostitute or the customer must come in contact with some part of the body of the other for the purpose of sexual arousal or gratification of the customer or of the prostitute."[4] Under this definition, common dungeon activities such as spanking a nude client with a bare hand are technically illegal.

This legal discrepancy between the two states goes hand in hand with regional differences in the ways pro-dommes perceive their labor. Few of the women I interviewed in New York referred to themselves as "sex workers," whereas in San Francisco, all but one of the interviewees self-identified that way. Dominatrices in San Francisco were not having fundamentally different interactions with their clients than those in New York. Bay Area pro-dommes, however, embraced their legal status and used it to mobilize with other sex workers. While, arguably, a major reason for this discrepancy is that San Francisco is a more sex-positive city in the sense that there are more resources available for sex workers, interviewees from both cities repeatedly contextualized their descriptions of their work as "sex work" or "not sex work" in terms of the law. As one woman pointed out, in a statement I commonly heard while conducting interviews in San Francisco, "All of us, under the letter of California law, can get popped for prostitution, so why not just fess up to the fact that it's sex work?"

Additionally, professional BDSM and other kinds of erotic labor historically have been intertwined in San Francisco. The city was the birthplace of
the "Eros Guide," an Internet directory started by a House in the Bay Area;
it expanded to include other types of sex workers, such as escorts, in various major cities throughout the United States, Canada, and the United Kingdom. There are also social benefits to joining forces with sex workers in San
Francisco, where they are relatively highly organized, where there exists the
St. James Infirmary—a city-run free clinic that provides healthcare and support for sex workers, including BDSM professionals—and where attorneys
offer free lessons to sex workers on how to deal with law enforcement.[5]

In New York City, on the other hand, where sex workers are not as highly
organized, and where most of what pro-dommes do is legal, pro-dommes
were more likely to draw a hard line between themselves and people who
have sex for money. Correspondingly, there existed a much more palpable
rift between those pro-dommes who were willing to do extras and those who
were not. One Manhattan domme in her early thirties complained, about
pro-dommes who give hand jobs and blow jobs, "How dare you say you're a
domina when you're gonna do shit like this and make the rest of us look bad?"
A Queens-based informant told me, similarly, "I do have a problem with one
of the dungeons, where they do naked face-sitting, and I'm like, I'm sorry,
that's not part of BDSM! Naked face-sitting? I'm sorry, that's sexual contact. I
do have [a] problem with women who call themselves 'dominas' when they,
in fact, are whores." Contrast this with a statement from a Bay Area pro-
domme, who noted that she identifies as a sex worker, adding, "What's the
difference between touching a hard genital and pinching it, knowing that the
person enjoys the pinch, and giving a hand job?" An informant based in Oakland took a similar tack, telling me laughingly, "I'll playfully refer to myself
as a whore because that's probably the worst insult somebody could sling at
me and it's just like, 'Yeah' [*laughs*]. 'Go ahead! Call me a ho! Bring it! I don't
care! I *am* a big ho.'"

Although activities such as anal penetration of clients in New York and
spanking of clients in California are technically illegal, it is rare for pro-
dommes to come under the scrutiny of law enforcement for these acts alone.
Indies, in particular, rarely had issues with the law; police raids were much
more common in the larger dungeons. As one indie explained, "I'm the nice
little girl who doesn't bug my neighbors and who pays my taxes and my rent.
It's a much bigger collar to get a big House." None of the women I interviewed had ever had any kind of legal troubles because of their work as pro-
dommes, although some knew other pro-dommes who had. In all of these
instances, however, the court cases were ultimately thrown out, except for

one case in which the woman was charged with massage without a license. The general consensus was that police raids were much more likely to happen if a House was known for including extras or if there were drugs on the premises. One informant told me that, while some of the things they did at her former House were technically illegal, they never had legal problems during her time there: "It was always the dungeons that were giving hand jobs or blow jobs that were busted—*obviously*, you know."

Police also tended to get involved when injury occurred on the premises. In February of 2008, for instance, the women at one Manhattan dungeon called 911 when a client turned blue after being suspended by his arms (Wilner, Celona, and Alpert 2008).[6] He was rushed to the hospital where, according to news reports, he lingered in a three-day coma before regaining consciousness (Goldman 2008). Although no charges were filed against the dominatrix involved in that incident, in the wake of the event the police raided other New York City dungeons, and at least one was forced to close temporarily when a domme there offered an undercover cop a "prostate massage" (Del Signore 2008).

While, in this instance, the client's medical emergency brought media attention to the industry and led to a citywide dungeon sweep, pro-dommes seldom got arrested for BDSM. One indie in San Francisco told me, during a discussion about raids on Houses, "The thing is, in this town I think they try to stay away from that sort of thing." She added, "Vice wants to pick on the most vulnerable people, which is the street whores. That's who vice wants to bust, 'cause it's easy. They just have to drive by and pick them up."[7] Many pro-dommes have included detailed lists of their session activities on the Internet with impunity. That the law tends to look the other way when it comes to dominatrices would seem indicative of the way the public tends to treat BDSM "with a casual shrug" (Gosselin and Wilson 1980, 11), compared to other socially stigmatized erotic practices. In a way, even masturbation is more closely regulated in this country than sadomasochism. As I have noted previously (Lindemann 2006), the sale of sex toys such as vibrators has been criminalized in some places in the United States. The sale of handcuffs, whips, and bondage gear, however, remains perfectly legal; it does not fall under these antiobscenity statutes, which are reserved for devices "designed or marketed as useful primarily for the stimulation of human genital organs."[8] Even Gayle Rubin (1992, 288), who, as indicated, identifies sadomasochism as one of the "most detested erotic behaviors," acknowledges that it has not come under the scrutiny of the law in the same sense that, for instance, homosexuality has.

The women I interviewed also said that they took specific measures to avoid

attracting police attention. First, they relied upon word of mouth within the
BDSM community about ongoing sweeps. One Manhattan dungeon domme
explained, "You'll usually get a heads-up that there's a vice cop coming, and if
you don't do anything illegal—if you just do what you're supposed to do—
then they can't do anything about it. . . . Usually if we hear other places get
busted, we'll be more cautious." When it came to the technically illegal act of
anal penetration, she added, "Usually a trick that we use [to identify a cop] is
to ask them to stick something up their own ass first, to see if they're willing
to do it. . . . With [golden] showers, most cops don't wanna do that. So we
don't worry about that, but usually strap-on and anal play we're really careful about." And most pro-dommes told me that they require their clients to
strip naked or to their underwear prior to the session, some explicitly stating
that this was to confirm they were not police officers. Finally, although arrests
were not common, many pro-dommes maintained the attitude, as one informant put it, "If they want to get you, they can get you for *something*."[9]

Appendix C: Historical Context

The professional dominatrix is such an appropriate figure for illuminating the fundamental tensions of postmodern life because the professional dominatrix, as she exists today, is a fundamentally postmodern social invention. While sex work has been around since at least the days of ancient Rome, and a statutory definition of the term "prostitution" dates back to the early twentieth century (Bernstein 2007, 24), the commercial dominatrix does not have a presence on the social landscape until the 1960s.

However, she does have her precursors. Medieval scholar Marilynn Desmond (2006, 13–27) observes that sadomasochistic themes in art stem back to the medieval adaptations of Ovid's *Ars Amatoria*. She describes, for instance, a drawing that began to proliferate as graffiti in the thirteenth century: the image of the "mounted Aristotle," in which a woman sits atop the old philosopher, her upstretched hand clutching a whip. Such dominant females also populate the works of the French and British libertines of the eighteenth and nineteenth centuries, including the eponymous Sade and Sacher-Masoch. Historian Edward Shorter (2005, 209) characterizes the figure of Juliette, who inhabits Sade's 1791 book *Justine* and his later work "The Story of Juliette" as the bookend to the victimized Justine, as "history's first dominatrix." Sacher-Masoch's 1870 work *Venus in Furs* is similarly notable for involving a sadomasochistic relationship in which power and control emanate from a woman.

There is no question that these characters are, like the women who were interviewed for this book, people who engage in scenarios of erotic dominance. But the professional dominatrix who works out of a dungeon, and whom men pay to engage in D/S, is a far more recent historical development. The *Oxford English Dictionary* traces the word "dominatrix"—a word

derived from the Latin for "mistress" (the feminized form of "master")—
back to an English translation of a Spanish navigation manual from 1561:
"Rome . . . dominatrix of nations" (Cortés de Alvacar, I.xix.20b). After that,
however, it disappears for over four centuries. It reappears, now in its contemporary meaning, in 1967, within the pages of a pulp text about aberrant
sexual practices: "Professionally, she is an expert dominatrix, a girl whom
men pay to have her humiliate and torment them in ways that satisfy their
sex-guilt neuroses" (Rogers 1967, 37). In contrast, the *OED* locates the first
printed usage of "prostitute" back in 1607.

Similarly to "dominatrix," the word "dungeon," in the sense of "a room
or building used for sado-masochistic sexual activity," traces back to only
1974. The *OED* locates its first printed usage in a classified ad from 1974: "See
an actual dominant session in our medieval dungeon upon a male subject by
two primier dominatrix [*sic*]" (*Los Angeles Free Press*, L2). Although references to professional erotic dominance begin to appear around this time, for
decades commercial BDSM was not nearly as pervasive as it is today. One of
my interviewees, who had been working as a pro-domme in San Francisco
since the early 1980s, described herself as one of the first pros in that city.
Other pro-dommes who had been in the Scene for decades also remarked
upon the extent to which the industry exploded in the 1990s—a development in which the accessibility of the Internet no doubt played a role.

Why did the commercial dungeon, as it is described on the pages of this
book, come into being when it did? The argument could be made that this
was due to a confluence of factors, including the dual threads of women's lib-
eration and free love, and the influence of the Warren Court on ending an era
when "vice" was so tightly controlled. It could also have been catalyzed by the
appearance of the gay male SM scene, including the biker communities and
leather organizations that had already begun to spring up in postwar America
(Hennen 2008, 136). Some of my informants told me that in the 1970s and
1980s, in the absence of a widespread heterosexual Scene, they used to play
with gay leathermen, picking up tricks of the trade. These are all compelling
potential explanations. However, any argument that could be mobilized to
explain the origins of the dominatrix as a cultural figure would be a post hoc
explanation based on extremely limited historical data. What *is* significant
about pro-dommes is that they emerge so late within the larger history of
erotic labor in particular and sexuality more generally. The fact of their late
appearance corresponds with this text's argument: that their relationships are
a reaction to, and expression of, social dynamics as they exist within contemporary life.

BDSM: Initialism for "bondage, discipline, sadism, masochism."

Bondage: "Physical materials applied to a submissive to restrain their ability to move and/or to otherwise restrict them. Also, the act of placing the submissive in such materials" (Wiseman 1996, 368).

Bottom: The participant who is the recipient of the action in a scene.

CBT: Initialism for "cock-and-ball torture," a term sometimes used interchangeably with "ball bondage" (tying-up of the testes) and sometimes applied as a general term for inflicting genital pain.

Clients: People, predominantly men, who pay for the services of pro-dommes. Sometimes used interchangeably with "submissives," "bottoms," and "slaves."

Corporal: An activity in which the client is struck (e.g., whipping, flogging, spanking, or paddling). Often used in "disciplinary" scenes.

Co-topping: An activity during which two or more mistresses dominate a client together.

Dungeon: Term for a wide variety of BDSM "play" spaces, including the space in which professional dominance occurs. I use "larger dungeon" to indicate a place in which several dominatrices (dungeon dommes) work out of one location (also called a "House") and are hired directly by the owner, who takes a cut of the money they earn. However, independent dommes also call their play spaces "dungeons."

D/S: Initialism for "dominance and submission."

Edgeplay: An activity (such bloodletting or fire play) that is potentially more dangerous than the typical scene.

Fetish: Sexual gratification from a particular object, body part, activity, smell, or other sensation that is not normatively considered erotic.

Financial domination: A D/S practice in which the exchange of money it-self constitutes the act of dominance. Sometimes known as "financial blackmail."

Full-body worship: A client's performance of cunnilingus on a pro-domme. Also called "pussy worship."

Full-service domme: A professional dominatrix who performs sexual extras, such as intercourse, oral sex, or hand jobs.

House of Domination, House: See **Dungeon**.

Lifestyle domme: A dominatrix who engages in BDSM in her personal rela-tionships and/or attends the parties and events that constitute the BDSM "Scene."

Mistress: See **Pro-domme**.

Pervertible: An object from everyday life that is reappropriated as kinky within the context of a scene. One domme in San Francisco, for instance, touts the Williams Sonoma spoontula as an excellent corporal tool.

Play: Participation in BDSM or fetish activities. For instance, "We were play-ing in the dungeon" or "We were doing a puppy-play scene."

Pro-domme: A professional dominatrix, also known as a "mistress" or "professional dominant." Dominatrices are women who physically and verbally dominate "submissives" through spanking, verbal humiliation, bondage, forced cross-dressing, and other tactics. "Professional" domi-nation is operationalized here as the receipt of money for serving as the dominant partner in these practices.

Professional dominant: See **Pro-domme**.

Sadomasochism: The giving and receiving of physical and/or psychological pain for erotic pleasure.

Saint Andrew's cross: An X-shaped cross used in BDSM activities, usually with cuffs at the edges for the restraint of a submissive's hands and feet. It is sometimes attached to a wall.

Scene: Lowercased, the term describes a BDSM interaction between two or more participants: "We were doing a scene at the club." Capitalized, the term identifies the social realm of BDSM. People "in the Scene" attend public events and parties and/or go to BDSM clubs. Many, but not all, lifestyle dommes are "in the Scene." More rarely, participants refer to the entirety of the BDSM world—including those people who engage in it solely for money—as "the Scene."

Service top: A participant in a BDSM exchange who is performing the action but is fully catering to the demands/fantasies of the bottom. The bottom is the de facto dominant partner in the exchange.

Session: A paid interaction between a dominant and a client. Also called a "scene" and sometimes "playing," although both of these latter terms are also used for unpaid D/S encounters.

Shibari: A type of bondage viewed as artistic; from the Japanese term for "the art of tying boxes with string."

Slave: In a lifestyle context, a person who gives up control over certain daily decisions to a "master" or "mistress" and performs acts of service for him or her. Pro-dommes sometimes use the term interchangeably with "submissive" or "client" and will call a client "slave" in the context of a session.

Sounds: Metal rods (originally medical in nature) that are inserted into the urethra for sexual pleasure.

Submissive (sub): The person in a BDSM interaction who is dominated and surrenders control. Its nuance is slightly different from "bottom," which identifies the party receiving the action and does not necessarily denote a loss of control.

TES: An acronym, pronounced "tess," referring to the Eulenspiegel Society, a New York City–based BDSM education and support organization formed in 1971.

Top's syndrome: A situation in which one becomes so identified with the dominant role that one begins to take on an attitude of superiority. Also called "top disease."

Topping from the bottom: "Attempting to control the session while ostensibly in the submissive (non-controlling) role. A type of behavior generally frowned upon" (Wiseman 1996, 375). Also known as "topping from below."

Tribute: A session fee.

Vanilla: A person or activity that is not kinky—for instance, "a vanilla profession," "He's completely vanilla," or "We played vanilla games, like Scrabble."

Appendix E: Initial Contact E-mail

Dear ——

My name is Danielle Lindemann and I'm a graduate student in the sociology department at Columbia University. I'm writing my PhD dissertation on professional dominatrices in New York City, and I would really love to be able to interview you for my project. It would take about an hour of your time, and it would entail answering some questions about your experiences as a pro-domme. I could come interview you at your dungeon, a coffee-shop, or wherever you'd like. All responses are kept completely anonymous.

If you have a free hour when I could come interview you, I would be so grateful. Unfortunately, I can't compensate you for your time, but I can buy you a cup of coffee, if you'd like. You can reply to this e-mail or call me [on my cell phone].

I hope to be able to meet with you.

All the best,
Danielle

Appendix F: Original Interview Schedule

You will be participating in a project about professional dominatrices in New York City and San Francisco. I have already requested your written consent for me to tape this interview, but I would also like your verbal consent. Do I have your consent to tape this interview?

I. Demographics

First, I'd like to get some information about you.

How old are you?

What's your marital status?

Do you have any children?

IF YES: How old?

II. Being a Dominatrix

Do you call yourself a "dominatrix" or a "mistress"? Is there a difference between the two?

How did you find out about being a dominatrix?

I'm interested, specifically, in your interactions with your male clients. How long have you been dominating male clients for money?

How old were you the first time you received money to dominate a man?

Tell me about the first person you dominated for money.

How did you know what to do?

Have you ever taken a class or workshop on how to dominate someone?

IF YES: Taught by whom? Where? What did you learn?

Have you ever *taught* a class or workshop on how to dominate someone?
>   IF YES: What did you teach? What kinds of people did you teach? (Other dominatrices? Couples?)

What do you call the people you dominate?

How do the people you dominate get in touch with you?

Do you advertise?
>   IF YES: Where?

Have you ever refused to take a particular man on as a client?
>   IF YES: Why?

Where do you hold your sessions with clients?
>   Do you see clients in one place or several places?
>   IF YES: Is there a difference in the *types* of clients you see at different places?

What would you say is the average age of your male clients?
>   Race?
>   Do you know what they do for work? How do you know?

How did you get your job in the place(s) you work now?

How long does a session with a client generally last?

How many hours a week would you say you spend dominating people for money?

How many clients do you have right now?

III. Types of Services

Can you give me a list of the services you provide?
>   Do you ever dress up your clients in women's clothes or accessories?
>   IF YES: Can you tell me about the last session in which you did this? Whose idea was it?

Have you ever been asked to recite specific dialogue in a session?
>   IF YES: What was it? Did you do it? How often do you do that?

Do you ever dominate women?
>   IF YES: How many of your clients are women?

Is that different from dominating men?
>   IF YES: How?

Have you ever dominated more than one person at the same time?
>   IF YES: How often do you do this?
>   Can you tell me about the last time you did this?

Is there anything you *won't* do?
>   IF YES: What? Why?

Many dominatrices have a procedure for the client to stop the interaction if he wants to—What's yours?

Can you tell me about the last time this happened?

IV. Getting Requests / Starting a Scene

When a new client comes to you for the first time, what do you do to him in your session?

After they answer: Do you usually do the *same* thing to first-timers, or do you mix it up?

Let's talk about the last man you had a session with. Can you describe what took place?

How did you know what he wanted you to do to him?

Did you communicate with him beforehand?

Had you had a session with him before?

IF YES: Was this different from sessions you've had with him in the past? How so?

[*Can you be more specific?*]

How many clients have you seen in the past 7 days— since last [insert day]?

Is that about the number you usually see in a week?

Can you tell me about the men who came in yesterday?

Key info baseline:

How did you know what he wanted you go do to him?

Did you communicate with him beforehand?

Had you had a session with him before?

IF YES: Was this different from sessions you've had with him in the past? How so?

[*Repeat for past week.* E.g., Can you tell me about the men who came in Sunday . . . Saturday . . . Friday . . . etc. Use calendar.]

If your clients request beforehand that you do something particular during the session, do you add your own touches during the sessions themselves?

IF YES: Like what?

Can you tell me about the last time this happened?

How did the client react?

Have you ever done something completely different from what had been agreed upon beforehand?

IF YES: Can you tell me about the last time this happened?

Why did you decide not to follow the script?

Once a client is in a room with you, can he tell you he wants a particular thing done to him?

IF YES: Can you tell me about the last time this happened?

V. Repeat Clients / Changing the Scene

Let's talk for a moment about the last person you saw who was a "repeat" client—a man who has come to you more than once.

How many times have you had a session with this person?

Have you continued to do the same thing with him in sessions over time?

IF NO: Why did you change? Does this scenario happen often with repeat clients? [*Example*]

IF YES: Is it typical that there's no change?

IF NOT TYPICAL: Can you give me an example of a repeat client whose scene changed over time?

VI. Money

How much do you charge for the average session?

What's the least you've charged for a session?

What's the most?

How do clients pay [cash, credit]?

Do they pay before or after the session?

Do you ever dominate clients for something other than money, like gifts or services?

IF YES: Can you tell me about the last time you did this?

Do clients ever give you money, goods, or services over and above what you're charging?

IF YES: Can you tell me about the last three "tips" or "tributes" you've gotten?

What has been your favorite?

Do you give anyone else a cut of the money you earn?

IF YES: Who? How much?

Do you charge more or less for doing certain types of things?

IF YES: Can you give me an example? Why do you charge more/less for that?

How much money would you say you make in a week, as a dominatrix?

In a year?

Do you currently have any other sources of income?

IF YES: What?

What is your primary source of income?

VII. Personal

What is your sexual orientation?

What is your race?

What's your highest level of education?

Do you ever get aroused when you're dominating someone?

Do you engage in sadomasochism within your own romantic relationships?

IF YES: Are you the dominant partner?

Are you a part of the fetish "scene"?

IF YES: How so?

To you, what's the difference between a "pro-domme" and a "lifestyle" domme?

What do you like about being a dominatrix?

What do you dislike about being a dominatrix?

Has this job ever made you fear for your safety?

IF YES: Can you give an example?

VIII. Potentially "Threatening" Questions

Do you consider what you do with your clients a "sex act"?

Why?

Have you ever masturbated one of your submissives?

IF YES: How often do you do that?

Have you ever had sex (intercourse, oral, or anal sex) with one of your submissives?

IF YES: How often do you do that?

Have you ever in your life had sex for money?

IF YES: Why?

Do you still do that?

How do you handle cleanup between sessions?

Do you sterilize your equipment between sessions?

Do you require that your clients have HIV tests?

Do you provide your own test results to your clients?

Have you ever been asked to provide them?

Have you ever come under the scrutiny of the law for doing dominatrix work?

IF YES: What happened?

Can you tell me about the last person who came in for a session and never returned?

Is there anything else you think I should know about your experience of being a dominatrix?

Appendix G: Final Interview Schedule

You will be participating in a project about pro-dommes in New York City and San Francisco. I have already requested your written consent for me to tape this interview, but I would also like your verbal consent.

Do I have your consent to tape this interview?

I. Demographics

First, I'd like to get some information about you.

How old are you?

What's your marital status?

Do you have any kids?

IF YES: How old?

What is your sexual orientation?

What is your race?

What's your highest level of education?

Would you say you are a "lifestyle" domme?

To you, what's the difference between a "pro-domme" and a "lifestyle" domme?

Are you a part of the fetish "Scene"?

IF YES: How so?

II. Being a Dominatrix

Do you call yourself a "dominatrix" or a "mistress," or neither?

IF NOT "DOMINATRIX": Is there a difference between [that] and a dominatrix?

How did you find out about being a pro-domme?

How old were you the first time you received money to dominate a man?

Can you tell me about the first person you dominated for money?

How did you know what to do?

Have you ever taken a class or workshop on how to dominate someone?

IF YES: Taught by whom? Where? What did you learn?

Have you ever *taught* a class or workshop on how to dominate someone?

IF YES: What did you teach? What kinds of people did you teach? (Other dominatrices? Couples?)

How do your clients get in touch with you?

Do you advertise?

IF YES: Where?

Have you ever refused to take a particular man on as a client?

IF YES: Why?

Where do you hold your sessions with clients?

IF APPROPRIATE: Do you own or rent? What is your financial arrangement with the house?

What would you say is the average age of your male clients?

Race?

Do you know what they do for work? How do you know?

How did you get your job in the place(s) you work now?

How long does a session with a client generally last?

How many hours a week would you say you spend doing this professionally?

How many clients do you have right now?

III. Types of Services

Can you give me a list of the things you do in sessions?

Do you ever do feminization scenes?

IF YES: Can you tell me about the last session in which you did this?

Have you ever been asked to recite specific dialogue in a session?

IF YES: What was it? Did you do it? How often do you do that?

Do you ever dominate women?

IF YES: How many of your clients are women?

Is that different from dominating men? [IF YES: How?]

Have you ever dominated more than one person at the same time?

IF YES: How often do you do this?

Can you tell me about the last time you did this?

Is there anything you *won't* do?

IF YES: What?

Do you use safe words?

IV. Getting Requests / Starting a Scene

When a new client comes to you for the first time, what do you do to him in your session?

> *After they answer.* Do you usually do the *same* thing to first-timers, or do you mix it up?

Let's talk about the last man you had a session with. Can you describe what took place?

> How did you know what he wanted you to do to him?
>
> Did you communicate with him beforehand?
>
> Had you had a session with him before?
>
> IF YES: Was this different from sessions you've had with him in the past? How so?

[*Can you be more specific?*]

How many clients have you seen in the past 7 days— since last [insert day]?

Is that about the number you usually see in a week?

Have you ever done something completely different in session from what had been agreed upon beforehand?

> IF YES: Can you tell me about the last time this happened?

Do you ever get clients who try to "top from the bottom" and take control of the scene?

> IF YES: How often does this happen?
>
> Can you give me an example?

V. Repeat Clients / Changing the Scene

Let's talk for a moment about the last person you saw who was a "repeat" client—a man who has come to you more than once.

> How many times have you had a session with this person?

Have you continued to do the same thing with him in sessions over time?

> IF NO: Why did you change? Does this scenario happen often with repeat clients? [*Example*]
>
> IF YES: Is it typical that there's no change?
>
> IF NOT TYPICAL: Can you give me an example of a repeat client whose scene changed over time?

VI. Money

How much do you charge for a session?

How do clients pay [cash, credit]?

Do they pay before or after the session?

Do you ever let clients barter for sessions?

IF YES: Can you tell me about the last time you did this?

Do you ever get tips?

IF YES: How often? How much are they, on average? What's the most you've gotten? What's the least you've gotten?

Do you charge more or less for doing certain types of things in session?

IF YES: Can you give me an example? Why do you charge more/less for that?

How much money would you say you make in a week, as a pro-domme? In a year?

Do you currently have any other sources of income?

IF YES: What?

Is this your primary source of income?

VII. Miscellaneous and Potentially "Threatening" Questions

Other pro-dommes have told me that they think of this kind of work as "theater" or a "performance." Do you agree with this?

Why / Why not?

Do you consider what you do with your clients a "sex act"?

Why? / Why not?

Other people I've interviewed have told me that they see this work as a form of therapy, or as therapeutic. Do you agree with this?

Why / Why not?

Have you ever masturbated one of your submissives?

IF YES: How often do you do that?

Have you ever had sex (intercourse, oral, or anal sex) with one of your submissives?

IF YES: How often do you do that?

How do you handle cleanup between sessions?

Do you sterilize your equipment between sessions?

Do you require that your clients have HIV tests?

Have you ever come under the scrutiny of the law for doing dominatrix work?

IF YES: What happened?

IF NO: Do you know anyone who has?

Has this job ever made you fear for your safety?

IF YES: Can you give an example?

Have you ever had a medical issue with a client?

IF YES: Can you tell me about it?

What do you like most about being a pro-domme?

What do you dislike most about being a pro-domme?

Is there anything else you think I should know about your experience of being a dominatrix?

Notes

Introduction

1. "Pro-dommes" is a term used by the women themselves, and by other participants in the BDSM subculture. Throughout this book, all of the technical BDSM terms I use are those employed by the participants themselves. See appendix D for relevant terminology and definitions.

2. In defining "complicit masculinity" throughout this text, I borrow from R. W. Connell, who identifies the term as "the configuration of gender practice which embodies the currently accepted answer to the problem of the legitimacy of the patriarchy, which guarantees (or is taken to guarantee) the dominant position of men and the subordination of women" (1995, 77).

3. A book in the BDSM literary canon, recommended to me by several informants, defines "bondage" thus: "Physical materials applied to a submissive to restrain their ability to move and/or to otherwise restrict them. Also, the act of placing the submissive in such materials" (Wiseman 1996, 368).

4. Mosley has since admitted to the sadomasochism but denied the Nazi overtones and successfully sued the tabloid.

5. Krafft-Ebing who, as noted, considered SM a mental disease, also recognized the origins of it in the horseplay and love bites of the average couple (1965, 53). Sigmund Freud, too, saw sadism as existing in "the normal individual" (1938, 569). In his 1929 study of two hundred spouses, G. V. Hamilton found that 51 percent of men and 32 percent of women had at some point in their lives derived "pleasant thrills from inflicting pain on either animals or human beings" (1986, 458). Alfred Kinsey and his colleagues' study of sexual behavior, furthermore, found that 55 percent of females and 50 percent of males had a "sado-masochistic response" to being bitten (1953, 677–78). Although the Kinsey study has been criticized for its heavy reliance on convenience sampling (e.g., Michael et al. 1994, 18), it nevertheless provides some evidence of the pervasiveness of supposedly "deviant" sadomasochistic practices.

6. While the word "deviant" has a history of being mobilized for pathologizing and moralistic effect, that is not my intent in this text. I mean it to refer to an individual who regularly participates in an activity that is perceived as deviating from a cultural norm, and who may feel the need to hide that participation.

7. Of course, there is also the population of people who engage in BDSM in their personal

relationships, without any organizational ties to the BDSM community. This will always be the most difficult group to study.

8. Tellingly, an article entitled "Sociology of Sex Work" in the 2009 *Annual Review of Sociology* gives a detailed summary of work that has been done on strip clubs and prostitution, for instance, and pays attention to the paucity of research on, for instance, telephone sex agencies and transgender workers. However, it fails to discuss professional erotic dominance, either as a prior or potential avenue of study (Weitzer 2009).

9. When I argue that narrative itself can be used as a basis for methodologically rigorous empirical work, I am not alone (Maynes, Pierce, and Laslett 2008, 148). Donald Spence (1982, 296), for instance, usefully distinguishes between "historical truth" and "narrative truth"—the latter of which is valuable in and of itself, he argues, because it allows us to understand how people construct meaning in their worlds.

10. Chapkis's text is one salient example of such a study. The researcher explains that she engaged in "minimal participation" in erotic labor. She became a licensed massage practitioner, and she explored her subject personally if briefly in two other situations: "On one occasion, I arranged to pay for sexual services in the form of hands-on sexual instruction from two professional sex workers. And, finally, I also arranged to work one afternoon selling sex to women clients in Amsterdam" (1997, 6). Katherine Frank (2002) is also notable for doing an ethnographic analysis of strip clubs while working as a stripper.

11. From this perspective, one interesting counterexample that may prove the rule about "going native" in sexuality studies is an ethnography by a gay man, Peter Hennen (2008), who positions himself from the beginning of the text as a somewhat active participant in a gay male SM ("Leatherman") community. In the early pages of his book, for instance, he describes his participation in a flogging scenario (5). Although it is a carefully crafted ethnography, throughout which he meticulously elaborates his subject-position, whether or not to participate in these practices is not a question he addresses on the pages of his book. I want to suggest that the intersectionality of his identity as a gay man and those of his gay male informants are salient factors here. A straight male ethnographer who flogged women during his research, for instance, would surely face his own set of critiques.

12. Some dommes also use "full service" to denote a wider range of sexual activities, including hand jobs and oral sex.

13. Also called "pussy worship."

14. Independent dommes also refer to their spaces as "dungeons," but in this instance it is used to distinguish between indies and women who work in the larger Houses of domination ("dungeon dommes").

15. Sometimes, the entirety of the BDSM world—including paid encounters—is referred to as "the Scene."

16. I did this in spite of the fact that some informants requested that I use their Scene names. "There goes my free publicity," one chuckled.

Chapter One

1. Thomas Weinberg (1983) is not the only scholar who has used a dramaturgical frame to consider sadomasochism; in fact, the element of theatricality is central to many accounts of the BDSM subculture (Gebhard 1969, Gosselin and Wilson 1980, Lee 1983). Within the recent psychological literature about BDSM, authors have pursued this dramaturgical analysis in the form of "script theory," suggesting, for example, that "the order in which people engage in dif-

ferent sadomasochistic behaviors is not random and . . . specific, less intense behaviors generally precede more intense behaviors" (Santtila et al. 2002, 185).

2. About half of the women I interviewed told me that they and their clients always have an agreed-upon safe word, while the rest only use safe words in certain types of sessions or do not use them at all. Those pro-dommes who did not work with safe words generally did not believe their practices were extreme enough to warrant their use. Others felt they had the expertise to know when their subs were in distress. One West Coast domme, who indicated that she sets up safe words in some sessions but not in others, told me, "A lot of the stuff we do, it's like: You're going to get fucked in the ass. I'm going to fuck you. Do we *really* need a safe word? Come on."

3. In some ways, forms of labor, such as pro-dominance, that combine eroticism and conceptions of artistry may have more in common with other theatrical pursuits than they do with prostitution. I was recently struck to find, during a visit to the Barnard College library, that the books about strippers were sandwiched between texts relating to pantomime and vaudeville, while the texts about prostitutes inhabited a different aisle.

4. This is distinguishable from the "sadistic" session, which may involve physical or psychological pain.

5. "Service top": a participant in a BDSM exchange who is performing the action but is fully catering to the demands/fantasies of the bottom. The bottom is thus the de facto dominant partner in the exchange.

6. Some women refused to do "competitive" wrestling sessions, in which the client aggressively fights back, but would engage in "fantasy" wrestling sessions, in which the woman always comes out the victor.

7. The vast majority of independent dommes I spoke with expressed a dislike for talking to clients on the phone. Dungeon dommes usually do not schedule appointments; these go through a receptionist or House manager. For this reason, much initial negotiation takes place via e-mail, although the majority of dommes in this study also preferred to talk to new clients on the phone at least once before the first session.

8. No dungeon dommes with whom I spoke, but some independents, have swapped sessions for goods or services. A thirty-three-year-old indie explained, "One of the things I love the most is trade, or barter. [If] you're going to make me some equipment, you get a session. My dentist has done dental services for a session. My lawyer. So many things. Make my equipment, fix my teeth, perhaps send me to Florida or send me to Vegas." Another indie will do sessions in exchange for computer programs: "My panty-boy . . . gets me editing and Final Cut Pro. Adobe After Effects. And these are worth hundreds of dollars."

9. Women who had taken clients up on these offers complained that the clients who came in to clean their houses were poor at cleaning, and were less interested in cleaning than in being punished for not cleaning.

10. The "Tuskegee Study of Untreated Syphilis in the Negro Male": Between 1932 and 1972 the US Public Health Service analyzed the progression of syphilis in a group of poor, black men. Many of these men were not aware that they had syphilis (the researchers referred to it as "bad blood"), and they were not treated for the disease, even when a treatment became available.

Chapter Two

1. Used as an adjective, "vanilla" refers to a person or activity which is not kinky—for instance, "a vanilla job," "He's completely vanilla," or "We played vanilla games, like Scrabble."

2. "Houses" do not include session-wrestling companies.

3. Those who had been in the industry longer tended to do longer sessions, on average, which many informants attributed to their expertise and ability to create more involved scenes. A House session is typically an hour long (half an hour for wrestling sessions), while most of the more experienced independents set a minimum session time of an hour and a half to two hours.

4. There were several similar widely circulated stories of high-profile lifestyle players in the New York Scene. While celebrity status may render a man more likely to choose the anonymity of a commercial dungeon in which to enact his fantasies, some still chance exposure by playing more publicly. Additionally, the unwillingness of high-profile men to play publicly may have something to do with the relative social visibility of the New York Scene. An acquaintance who has had experience with the Scene in both New York and Washington, DC, told me that the New York community was far more "public." Events were more likely to be invitation-only, and less likely to allow photography, in America's political hub.

5. Interestingly, many indies in this study made the claim that they charge more than anyone else in town.

6. Pedal pumping is a specific foot fetish—arousal from watching women push car pedals. It seems that often the appeal is that these cars are stalled and the pedal pushing is fruitless. There are websites devoted to this practice.

7. Many people in the BDSM community draw a distinction between "submission" and "bottoming." They use the term "submissive" to refer to the person in a BDSM interaction who is dominated and surrenders control, while a "bottom" is a general term for a participant, including a submissive, who is the recipient of an action.

8. Prior research on BDSM communities has indicated that the practice of starting out as a bottom is common for dominants outside the commercial realm. Kurt Ernulf and Sune Innala, for instance, found that dominants "may explain this themselves with a need for training as submissive-recipients to become good and empathetic dominant-initiators" (1995, 635).

9. Some session wrestlers only engage in wrestling sessions and some combine wrestling with other aspects of erotic dominance. One woman who worked for a session-wrestling company, for instance, described a scene in which she wrestled a client and won, and her "prize" was putting him in bondage.

10. One exception is "Whore College," a program in conjunction with the San Francisco *Sex Worker Film and Arts Festival.* While technique is discussed, however, it does not appear to be the focus of these seminars. The program's website describes it as a place where "sex workers, adult entertainers, and erotic service providers come together for private education relating to their health, safety, prosperity, and pleasure in the business" (www.whorecollege.org/).

11. I continue to refer to the practice as "*professional* erotic dominance," however, to distinguish it from unpaid D/S.

12. Those who do genital piercing, however, must be certified by the local health department.

13. Wilensky (1964) indicated that the professions were characterized by the following attributes: (1) creation of a full-time occupation, (2) the establishment of a training school, (3) the formation of a professional association, and (4) the formation of a code of ethics.

14. It should be noted that I am not the first author to explore the professional claim within the context of an occupation that does not fall under the rubric of a "true" profession. Peter Bearman argues that for New York City doormen "the claim to professional status is central to their sense of self" (2005, 5). The social distance between pro-dommes and their clients, how-

ever, is not as vast as the one between doormen and their tenants. As noted, pro-dommes, in large part, are well-educated white women. Professional erotic dominance is thus distinct from the practice of being a doorman in the sense that it falls under the rubric of the "close professions," as described by Bearman. These are occupations—for instance, psychiatry, medicine, or the law—in which practitioners with relatively the same or higher social status as their clients learn intimate details of their clients' lives in the course of doing their jobs (8).

Chapter Three

1. Shibaricon, http://www.shibaricon.com/index2.html. "Shibari" derives from the Japanese for "the art of tying boxes with string."

2. While these authors have made empirical comparisons to Bourdieusian theory in particular, other texts have more generally examined creative domains to which purity regimes are crucial. Vanina Leschziner (2007), for instance, observes that commercial high cuisine is structured around the issue of purity, and Loïc Wacquant has found that notions of authenticity are also crucial to sports. One of the signs, for instance, of an "authentic boxer" is "the capacity not to bow under pressure, to 'suck it up' and keep on fighting, no matter what the physical toll" (Wacquant 1995, 496).

3. "Full service" refers to sexual "extras."

4. "Habitus," in Bourdieusian terms, refers to the sensibilities, beliefs, tastes, and dispositions into which a person is socialized based upon his or her position in the social structure.

5. Further, from the perspective of economic utility theory, one would have the same expectation: that a lifestyler would charge less, since she gets subjective utility in addition to economic capital from doing sessions.

6. One informant encapsulated this mentality when she told me, "I charge more than a lot of those girls, but also I'm a real dominant."

7. Thus, after being arrested for hiring prostitutes, the actor Charlie Sheen reportedly told a judge, "I don't pay them for sex. I pay them to leave." Interestingly, and a point of contrast, as discussed elsewhere in this text, pro-dommes do receive gifts from clients.

8. TES is a New York City–based BDSM education and support organization. Formed in 1971, it is the oldest such organization in the city.

9. The concept of the topping-from-the-bottom client also appears in various other cultural artifacts surrounding the industry. On December 2, 2008, for instance, a man wrote in to advice columnist Dan Savage, objecting to a column in which Savage had advised a pro-domme's client that he was wrong for asking to make sure the domme's dildo was cleaned for their session. "Let's not forget who the employee is here," the reader, who identified himself as a submissive man, cautioned Savage. By casting the domme as the employee in this scenario, this sub bolsters pro-dommes' assertions about many of their less than ideal clients.

10. Professional D/S is similar to folk art in this respect (H. Becker 1978).

11. Ironically, I wrote the first draft of this book while in bed recovering from a martial arts injury.

12. All of these elements of the dommes' "anti"-economic discourse were not necessarily true in practice. Although in the rhetoric employed by lifestylers, "girls in the dungeons" became conflated with "fakes" and "prostitutes," in reality some "purist" dommes did work in the larger dungeons, and some independent mistresses indicated that they performed "extras" or were not in the lifestyle. What this analysis lacks, for the reasons discussed in appendix A,

are interviews with a sample of non-lifestyle pro-dommes significant enough to assess whether their logic is in line with that of the commercial artists in Bourdieu's model, just as the logic of the lifestylers fits that of the autonomous artists.

Chapter Four

1. Mead sees the "play period" also as specific to "more primitive people" (1967, 153).

2. The element of sexual arousal, in and of itself, is another distinction between dungeon scenarios and most childhood play, assuming that children play asexually. An exploration of whether or not children's play involves an erotic component is beyond the province of this text, which focuses on adult activities.

3. Interestingly, Juizinga concludes that sex is not play. Although he points to multiple examples of Germanic languages in which the words for "copulation" and "play" are linguistically linked, he concludes, "Caresses as such do not bear the character of play, though they may do on occasion; but it would be erroneous to incorporate the sexual act itself, as love-play, in the play category" (1955, 43). One wonders where SM, with its stylized scene enactments, would fall within his rubric—perhaps as one of the "occasional" exceptions.

4. Another place we see the term "play" used in reference to adult life is in the case of word play—for instance, rap battles on urban street corners (Lee 2009) and verbal dueling in Balinese life (Sherzer 1993). However, these "battles" and "duels" are like games, in a Meadian sense, in that they are fundamentally contests; there are winners and losers within these interactions.

5. To lock a client in chastity means putting his genitals in a chastity device.

6. This corresponds with some previous work on erotic labor and arousal. In one study, for instance, Martin Weinberg, Frances Shaver, and Colin Williams (1999, 517) found that few female prostitutes in the San Francisco Tenderloin found their work sexually enjoyable, and even then, typically only "sometimes" or "rarely."

Chapter Five

1. The most recent revision of the American Psychiatric Association's *Diagnostic and Statistical Manual of Mental Disorders* (*DSM-IV-TR*), a text revision of the fourth edition, was published in 2000. A fifth edition is due to be published in 2013.

2. In unpacking this particular discourse, this chapter intersects with a literature about the increasing importance of notions of "the therapeutic" within spheres of social life outside of the healthcare industry. Much has been made of our "culture of self-help" (Illouz 2008) and the increasing importance of this form of rhetoric within modern life, both on and off the therapist's couch. Dana Cloud (1998), for instance, discusses the ways in which dialogue about "consolation" has infused modern sociopolitical movements, and Dana Becker (2005, 1) discusses the repercussions for women of this "repackaging of the psychological as power."

3. Her description resonates with the characterization of therapy more generally. Verna Rensvold and colleagues, for instance, have described recreation therapy as bringing "personal refreshment of the spirit" (1957, 87).

4. This folk narrative about the reaffirmation of the self through shame can be contextualized within the sociology of emotions literature. In *The Cultural Politics of Emotion*, for instance, Sara Ahmed argues that shame and pride are similarly structured emotions. Drawing upon Braithwaite (1989), Ahmed explains that, both at the individual and national levels,

"Shame can reintegrate subjects . . . in their moment of failure to live up to a social ideal. Such an argument suggests that the failure to live up to an ideal is a way of taking up that ideal and confirming its necessity" (2004, 106). She goes on to assert that shame "may be restorative *only when the shamed other can 'show' that its failure to measure up to a social ideal is temporary*" (107; emphasis in original), adding that shame can be transformed into pride (110).

5. Evidence for the recuperative properties of verbal aggression can also be found in the sociology of emotions literature, specifically cross-culturally. Jean L. Briggs, discussing the "benevolently aggressive model" of Inuit parenting, for instance, indicates that in some Inuit societies, parents bond with their children by alternately expressing aggression and affection. "One form of teasing which may be used with a child as young as a year (or even younger)," Briggs explains, "is to frighten him by making horrid faces at him or by speaking to him very loudly, or in a throaty voice associated with scolding until he cries, whereupon the audience and the tormenter will laugh and either the latter or the child's mother will comfort him by offering food" (1978, 67). Just as in the pro-dommes' discourse, Inuit families interpret as psychologically healthful the combination of teasing with soothing words and gestures. Mothers in these societies bond with their young children by, like dominatrices with their clients, tearing them down only to build them up again.

6. This was true in San Francisco more than in New York City. See appendix B for further discussion of the distinctions between the pro-dommes in these two cities.

7. In addition to those who have written about SM as a transformative practice and gateway to self-awareness, other scholars have explicitly touched upon the notion of BDSM as a kind of psychological healing. Meg Barker, Camelia Gupta, and Alessandra Iantaffi (2007), for instance, explore the "healing narratives" surrounding such practices on BDSM websites, in BDSM literature, and in media representations outside of the BDSM community. And Katharine-Lee H. Weille (2002, 157–58), looking at a case from a qualitative research study exploring consensual sadomasochistic and dominant-submissive sexual play, concludes that "when certain kinds of conditions (loving, playful, symbolizing, paradoxical, 'homeopathic,' etc.) are present, there is a potential for using these psychodramatic sexual scenarios in the service of both relational and intrapsychic growth."

8. "In all the history of human thought there exists no other example of two categories of things so profoundly differentiated or so radically opposed to one another" (Durkheim, 1968, 53).

9. Women in this study reported having seen clients as young as teenagers: "I once saw a kid who was sixteen. He told me he was nineteen. Had a great body. I was enjoying him very much, until his bus pass fell out, and I was like, '[*gasp*] How old are you?!'" And at the other extreme, they entertain senior citizens: "It's cracking me up—I've had two recently who were over eighty. Two! In the course of a week I've had two." However, men under the age of thirty or over sixty were relatively infrequent customers. Clients at the Houses tended to be slightly younger than those who saw indies, probably because House rates are lower, and dommes in specialized practices sometimes had a slightly older clientele. A self-identified "Enema Madam," for instance, indicated that she generally saw men in their fifties or sixties, because they had been brought up during a time in the history of American childhood when enemas were used as punishment.

10. Interestingly, while many of the women in this study indicated that they regularly ask their clients what they do for work, and that they believe what they hear, they also overwhelmingly suspected their clients of giving false names. A line I heard repeatedly about clients was "They're all 'John' and 'Bob.'" The client profiles from the defunct New York dungeon also

show the exceptional repetition of a few generic male names. John/Jon was the second most commonly used name, and variants of Robert (Robert/Bob/Bobby/Rob) were the fourth. The name that clients most often gave was Michael or Mike.

11. Sam Janus, Barbara Bess, and Carol Saltus (1977, 50) discovered that powerful men frequently request SM scenarios from prostitutes and call girls. Raymond Eve and Donald Renslow (1980, 103), analyzing questionnaire data from students at a southern public university, found that the higher the students' socioeconomic status, "the greater the probability that they had either fantasized about (or actually engaged in) bondage-type behaviors." Similarly, Gini Graham Scott (1997, 6), a sociologist who became an active participant in the San Francisco Scene for two years in the early 1980s, found that "D&Sers tend to be better educated and from higher income and occupational brackets than the average American."

12. Some New York dommes reported having seen a number of Hasidic Jews, as well. Hasidic communities tend to be relatively socially closed environments organized around the differentiation of male and female spheres and within which masculine dominance is a salient social fact. Thus, the fact that these men go to see pro-dommes would support the idea that men go to the dungeon to express submissive, vulnerable forms of masculinity that are subordinated to compulsory expressions of hegemony in daily life.

13. One study of 680 soldiers who had served in combat support units in Iraq, for instance, found that being perceived as "weak" was one of the concerns associated with visiting a mental health professional (Wright et al. 2009, 112; see also Vogel, Wade, and Haake 2006).

14. Scott has also observed that some commercial dominatrices view themselves as therapists (1997, 213).

15. In making this argument, I recall my mother's words from my childhood, as she applied stinging ointment to my repeatedly scraped knees: "If it hurts, that just means it's getting better."

16. Ronald W. Maris also argues that seemingly self-destructive forms of behavior—often interpreted as manifestations of the death instinct—can, in fact, be psychologically productive. Drawing on Kai Erikson, Emile Durkheim, and R. K. Merton, Maris (1971, 113) contends that deviant behaviors among women—in the form of sexual deviance, drug abuse, and suicide attempts—may be viewed as "coping mechanisms operating to preserve rather than cripple or end life."

Chapter Five

1. Hennen's analysis (2008) of the production of masculinity within "leatherman" communities is one notable counterexample.

2. When I discuss how pro-dommes and their clients "do" gender, like Salzinger I describe the ways in which gender gets produced and maintained in a specific context. I conceptualize gender in terms of its "conventionalized expressions," not as a constant, routinized performance.

3. Bernstein (1999) and Chancer (2000a) provide excellent summaries of these debates.

4. Though I have thought a great deal about the relationship of this study to feminism, I deliberately do not locate myself on either side of that debate in this book. At the end of the day, this is a book about professional dominatrices, the interactions that take place in their dungeons, and what these interactions can teach us about processes and conventions within larger social life. Its project is not to condemn or condone these interactions from a feminist perspective.

5. In terms of actual erotic tastes, the structure of male desire does not necessarily uphold the dominant gender paradigm. John Levi Martin, for instance, indicates that both men and women find certain elements of power "sexy" in the other gender. Looking at network data—a national sample of sixty naturally occurring communities—he finds that "it is . . . women whose high status increases their sexiness (to men), while it is the interpersonal power of men that makes them sexy, both to men and women" (Martin 2005, 408). However, in the case of commercial D/S, it is the woman's dominant role in the specific interpersonal exchange that renders her appealing to her client; thus, based on this evidence, it could be argued that gendered desire works differently in the dungeon than in everyday life.

6. However, the extent to which pro-dommes took safety precautions varied widely. For instance, the majority of women in this sample told me that they asked their clients some questions about preexisting medical conditions before their sessions, but these ranged from general queries ("Is there anything I need to know before we start?") to more detailed checklists of potential maladies.

7. Poppers are drugs (amyl nitrite or butyl nitrite) taken by inhaling to enhance sexual stimulation.

8. There is also a competing, but not wholly incompatible, philosophy in the Scene—RACK (risk-aware, consensual kink)—which acknowledges that there are risks involved in BDSM play and focuses on self-aware, consensual encounters between adults, rather than the safety of specific practices.

9. Informants told me that they minimized safety risks through various mechanisms. A few independent dommes had their personal subs wait outside the door while they were doing sessions. One woman told me that when she started working out of her apartment, she began pretending her husband was home, even when he was not. The larger dungeons tended to keep "86 lists" of clients who had broken the House rules and were not welcome back, and they also had the built-in security feature of other pro-dommes on the premises.

10. Sensuous Sadie (2003, 40), a BDSM columnist who wrote a book about her experiences in the Scene, has made a similar observation about lifestyle players: "I don't have any research basis for this, but there does seem to be more plus-sized women in the scene. Perhaps they are attracted in greater numbers because their size is less of an issue than what they have to offer through their submission or their domination."

11. Prior evidence suggests that such cross-dressing scenarios are a common feature of BDSM more generally. For example, Martin Weinberg, Colin Williams, and Charles Moser (1984, 382) found that at New York and San Francisco SM clubs in the late 1970s and early 1980s, "female dominants 'demeaned' their male partners by forcing them to wear female clothing (a prevalent theme in SM fantasies and literature), or by giving them tasks (e.g. as a 'maid') which raised the possibility of 'misbehavior' and 'punishment.'"

12. These encounters are "forced" within the theatrical context of the scene. They, like other types of sessions, are negotiated beforehand by domme and sub.

13. Ten (15 percent) identified as straight, four (6 percent) identified as lesbian, and the remainder either did not indicate an orientation or identified with other labels, such as "polymorphously perverse."

14. Levitt and colleagues used the seven-point Kinsey scale to assess orientation, whereas I asked individuals to self-define.

15. At the same time that they engage with set roles and boundaries, however, based upon how dommes and subs shake up established gender and power roles, one might argue that it is precisely the flexibility in regard to which participant inhabits each role that renders the

encounter sexually exciting. The potential undecidability of, for instance, "Who *really* has control?" or "Who *really* is the woman?" may be the very element of the exchange that charges it with an erotic energy. Such an interpretation would posit these activities as deeply subversive of gender binaries, undercutting "radical" feminist claims about SM.

Conclusion

1. Howard Becker uses the term "deviance" while Dale Patrias (1978) uses "deviation." Here, I use the two interchangeably.

2. Sexual orientation is one possible counterexample.

3. Informants' emphasis on their own "normalcy" is unsurprising, in the sense that it echoes the findings of researchers who have tackled the subject of BDSM. R. J. Stoller (1991, 21), for instance, observed that conducting research on bondage participants changed his preconception that they are maladjusted individuals. A study of 164 men in two sadomasochistically oriented clubs indicated that "participants were socially well-adjusted and that sadomasochistic behavior was merely a facilitative aspect of their sexual lives" (Sandnabba, Santtila, and Nordling 1999, 273). It has also been argued that the element of make-believe involved in BDSM might work precisely because participants are well-adjusted, that "at the core of the D&S community are mostly sensible, rational, respectable, otherwise quite ordinary people, for whom D&S is a way of playing with unique, bizarre, unusual, and often taboo forms of fantasy and erotic expression, as a release from the everyday world" (Scott 1997, 289). And there is evidence that SM participants are socially high-functioning, even in a clinical sample; Lynn Cowan observed that her masochistic therapy patients were "successful by social standards: professionally, sexually, emotionally, culturally, in marriage or out" (1982, 31).

Appendix A

1. At the time of interview, however, at least one of these eight had a long-term primary partner who did not know about this aspect of his life.

2. These forms were completely anonymous. I at no point had access to the clients' last names. Although the forms included a "mailing address" line, no clients filled it in.

3. Sounds are metal rods (originally medical in nature) that are inserted into the urethra. Dommes sometimes use these on clients in session.

Appendix B

1. Judge Potter Stewart: "hard-core pornography" is hard to pin down, but "I know it when I see it" (*Jacobellis v. Ohio*, 378 US 184, 1964).

2. This finding is consistent with prior research (Weinberg, Williams, and Moser 1984) and journalistic accounts of professional erotic dominance (e.g., Smith and Cox 1983). Several dommes who had worked in Europe, and one who had worked in Australia, indicated that the "industry standard" was different there; professional dominance regularly included oral sex and hand jobs.

3. New York Penal Code § 230.00 ("Prostitution").

4. 46 Cal.3d at 424, 758 P.2d at 1130, quoting *People v. Hill*, 103 Cal.App.3d 525, 534–535, 163 Cal.Rptr. 99, 105 (1980).

5. Many of the women I interviewed in California were highly knowledgeable about the law, rattling off the statute to me practically verbatim.

6. Wilner, Celona, and Alpert (2008) incorrectly identify the locale as a "bondage club," not a dungeon.

7. Bernstein (2007), too, argues that street prostitution is more heavily policed than sex work within "indoor" contexts.

8. Ala. Code § 13A-12–200.2 (2005). See also La. Rev. Stat. Ann. § 14:106.1 (2005) and *State v. Hughes*, 792 P.2d 1023 (Kan. 1990).

9. In addition to the difference in how New York and San Francisco dommes perceived their labor in relation to prostitution, in California there was also a stronger hippie under-current within the BDSM Scene. This came across vividly in Bay Area informants' rhetoric about their work; they tended to use variations on the word "spiritual" and talk about "energy" when describing what they do. One San Francisco–based domme indicated that the women at a House where she had worked would get together and do "inner work," like "vision quests" and "meditation retreats." Another told me, "My two main goals are to bring beauty to BDSM and to use it as a path for spiritual growth." A few Bay Area informants even commented on what I must be thinking of this kind of rhetoric, as a researcher accustomed to speaking with New York dommes. One San Francisco–based woman, explaining the process by which she negotiates with clients, told me, "Normally, when he calls, ideally the person who is on the phone has asked good questions and has gotten good feedback, and he sounds not just like he wants to *do* stuff I would enjoy but that his *energy* is something I would enjoy." She stopped herself, chuckling, and added, "I know that sounds *so* Californian. I'm sure nobody in New York uses that term!" While there were a few New York dommes whose interviews were peppered with terms like "spiritual-ity" and "energy," this rhetoric was nowhere near as pervasive as it was on the West Coast.

References

Agar, Michael. 1996. *The Professional Stranger: An Informal Introduction to Ethnography.* San Diego: Academic Press.

Ahmed, Sara. 2004. "Shame before Others." In *The Cultural Politics of Emotion,* 101–21. New York: Routledge.

Allen, Louisa. 2003. "Girls Want Sex, Boys Want Love: Resisting Dominant Discourses of (Hetero)Sexuality." *Sexualities* 6, 2: 215–36.

Avery, Nicholas C. 1977. "Sadomasochism: A Defense against Object Loss." *Psychoanalytic Review* 64, 1: 101–9.

Bailey, Beth L. 1989. *From Front Porch to Back Seat: Courtship in Twentieth-Century America.* Baltimore, MD: Johns Hopkins University Press.

Barker, Meg, Camelia Gupta, and Alessandra Iantaffi. 2007. "The Power of Play: The Potentials and Pitfalls in Healing Narratives of BDSM." In *Safe, Sane, and Consensual: Contemporary Perspectives on Sadomasochism,* edited by Darren Langdridge and Meg Barker, 197–216. Houndmills, Basingstoke, Hampshire: Palgrave Macmillan.

Barry, Kathleen. 1995. *The Prostitution of Sexuality: The Global Exploitation of Women.* New York: New York University Press.

Barton, Bernadette. 2006. *Stripped: Inside the Lives of Exotic Dancers.* New York: New York University Press.

Baumeister, Roy F. 1988. "Masochism as Escape from Self." *Journal of Sex Research* 25, 1: 28–59.

Bayma, Todd. 1995. "Art World Culture and Institutional Choices: The Case of Experimental Film." *Sociological Quarterly* 36, 1: 79–95.

Bearman, Peter. 2005. *Doormen.* Chicago: University of Chicago Press.

Bearman, Peter, and Katherine Stovel. 2000. "Becoming a Nazi: A Model for Narrative Networks." *Poetics* 27, 2: 69–90.

Becker, Dana. 2005. *The Myth of Empowerment: Women and the Therapeutic Culture in America.* New York: New York University Press.

Becker, Howard S. 1963. *Outsiders: Studies in the Sociology of Deviance.* New York: Free Press.

———. 1978. "Arts and Crafts." *American Journal of Sociology* 83, 4: 862–89.

———. 1982. *Art Worlds.* Berkeley: University of California Press.

Beckmann, Andrea. 2001. "Deconstructing Myths: The Social Construction of 'Sadomasochism'

Versus 'Subjugated Knowledges' of Practitioners of Consensual 'SM.'" *Journal of Criminal Justice and Popular Culture* 8, 2: 66–95.

———. 2009. *The Social Construction of Sexuality and Perversion.* Houndmills, Basingstoke, Hampshire: Palgrave Macmillan.

Benjamin, Jessica. 1985. "The Bonds of Love: Rational Violence and Erotic Domination." In *The Future of Difference*, edited by Hester Eisenstein and Alice Jardine, 41–70. New Brunswick, NJ: Rutgers University Press.

Bernstein, Elizabeth. 1999. "What's Wrong with Prostitution? What's Right with Sex-Work? Comparing Markets in Female Sexual Labor." *Hastings Women's Law Journal* 10, 1: 91–119.

———. 2007. *Temporarily Yours: Intimacy, Authenticity, and the Commerce of Sex.* Chicago: University of Chicago Press.

Bourdieu, Pierre. 1969. "Intellectual Field and Creative Project." *Social Science Information* 8, 2: 89–119.

———.1993. *The Field of Cultural Production.* New York: Columbia University Press.

———. 1996. *The Rules of Art: Genesis and Structure of the Literary Field.* Translated by S. Emanuel. Stanford, CA: Stanford University Press. First published 1992.

———. 1999. "Understanding." In *The Weight of the World*, translated by Priscilla Parkhurst Ferguson, 607–26. Stanford, CA: Stanford University Press.

Blumer, Herbert. 1969. *Symbolic Interactionism: Perspective and Method.* Englewood Cliffs, NJ, Prentice-Hall.

Braithwaite, John. 1989. *Crime, Shame and Reintegration.* Cambridge: Cambridge University Press.

Briggs, Jean L. 1978. "The Origins of Nonviolence: Inuit Management of Aggression (Canadian Arctic)." In *Learning Non-Aggression*, edited by Ashley Montagu, 54–93. New York: Oxford.

Bruner, Jerome. 1986. *Actual Minds, Possible Worlds.* Cambridge, MA: Harvard University Press.

Bullough, Vern L. 1983. Foreword to *S and M: Studies in Sadomasochism*, edited by Thomas Weinberg and G. W. Levi Kamel, 9–11. Buffalo, NY: Prometheus Books.

Butler, Judith. 1999. *Gender Trouble: Feminism and the Subversion of Identity.* New York: Routledge.

Califia, Pat. 1988. *Public Sex: The Culture of Radical Sex.* San Francisco: Cleiss Press.

Cancian, Francesca M. 1986. "The Feminization of Love." *Signs* 11, 4: 692–709.

Cesario, AnneMarie, and Lynn Chancer. 2009. "Sex Work: A Review of Recent Literature." *Qualitative Sociology* 32, 1: 213–20.

Chancer, Lynn S. 1993. "Prostitution, Feminist Theory, and Ambivalence: Notes from the Sociological Underground." *Social Text* 37: 143–71.

———. 1998. "Prostitution and Feminist Theory: Notes from the Sociological Underground." In *Reconcilable Differences: Confronting Beauty, Pornography, and the Future of Feminism*, 173–98. Berkeley: University of California Press.

———. 2000a. "From Pornography to Sadomasochism: Reconciling Feminist Differences." *Annals of the American Academy of Political and Social Science* 571, 1: 77–88.

———. 2000b. *Sadomasochism in Everyday Life: The Dynamics of Power and Powerlessness.* New Brunswick, NJ: Rutgers University Press.

Chapkis, Wendy. 1997. *Live Sex Acts: Women Performing Erotic Labor.* New York: Routledge.

Cheney, Tom. 1998. "Dear Mom and Dad: Just a quick note to thank you for the very lovely desk set." Cartoon. *New Yorker*, May 11, 68.

Cloud, Dana. 1998. *Control and Consolation in American Culture and Politics: Rhetoric of Therapy.* Thousand Oaks, CA: Sage.

Comfort, Alex. 1978. "Sexual Idiosyncrasies: Deviation or Magic?" *Journal of Psychiatry* 9:11–16.

Connell, R. W. 1995. *Masculinities.* Berkeley: University of California Press.

Corsaro, William. 1979. "'We're Friends, Right?': Children's Use of Access Rituals in a Nursery School." *Language in Society* 8:315–36.

Cortés de Alvacar, Martín. 1561. *The Arte of Navigation.* Translated by Richard Eden.

Cowan, Lyn. 1982. *Masochism: A Jungian View.* Dallas, TX: Spring Publications.

Del Signore, John. 2008. "Vice Cops Shut Down TriBeCa Dungeon." *Gothamist*, September 18. http://gothamist.com/2008/09/18/vice_cops_shut_down_tribeca_dungeon.php.

Desmond, Marilynn. 2006. *Ovid's Art and the Wife of Bath: The Ethics of Erotic Violence.* Ithaca, NY: Cornell University Press.

Duffy, J. C. 1999. "Please listen carefully, as my menu options have changed." Cartoon. *New Yorker*, November 15, 66.

Duneier, Mitchell. 1999. *Sidewalk.* New York: Farrar, Straus and Giroux.

———. 2002. "What Kind of Combat Sport Is Sociology?" *American Journal of Sociology* 107, 6: 1551–76.

Durkheim, Emile. 1968. *The Elementary Forms of the Religious Life.* Translated by Joseph Ward Swain. New York: Free Press. First published 1915.

———. 1982. *The Rules of Sociological Method.* New York: Free Press.

Dworkin, Andrea. 1974. *Woman Hating.* New York: E. P. Dutton.

———. 1987. *Intercourse.* New York: Free Press.

Edlund, Lena, and Evelyn Korn. 2002. "A Theory of Prostitution." *Journal of Political Economy* 110, 1: 181–214.

Epstein, Steven. 1994. "A Queer Encounter: Sociology and the Study of Sexuality." *Sociological Theory* 12, 2: 188–202.

Ernulf, Kurt E., and Sune M. Innala. 1995. "Sexual Bondage: A Review and Unobtrusive Investigation." *Archives of Sexual Behavior* 24, 6: 631–54.

Eve, Raymond A., and Donald G. Renslow. 1980. "An Exploratory Analysis of Private Sexual Behaviors among College Students: Some Implications for a Theory of Class Differences in Sexual Behavior." *Social Behavior and Personality* 8:97–105.

Fein, Ellen, and Sherrie Schneider. 2007. *All the Rules: Time-Tested Secrets for Capturing the Heart of Mr. Right.* New York: Grand Central Publishing.

Ferguson, Priscilla P. 1998. "A Cultural Field in the Making: Gastronomy in 19th-Century France." *American Journal of Sociology* 104, 3: 597–641.

Fine, Gary Alan. 1992. "The Culture of Production: Aesthetic Choices and Constraints in Culinary Work." *American Journal of Sociology* 97, 5: 1268–94.

Flora, Cornelia Butler. 1971. "The Passive Female: Her Comparative Image by Class and Culture in Women's Magazine Fiction." *Journal of Marriage and the Family* 33, 3: 435–44.

Foote, Nelson. 1954. "Sex as Play." *Social Problems* 1, 4: 159–63.

Foucault, Michel. 1965. *Madness and Civilization: A History of Insanity in the Age of Reason.* Translated by Richard Howard. New York: Pantheon Books.

———. 1990. *The History of Sexuality.* Vol. 1, *An Introduction.* New York: Vintage Books. First published 1978.

———. 1997. "Sexual Choice, Sexual Act." In *The Essential Works of Foucault: 1954–1988*, vol. 1, *Ethics*, edited by Paul Rabinow. New York: New Press.

Frank, Katherine. 2002. *G-Strings and Sympathy: Strip Club Regulars and Male Desire*. Durham, NC: Duke University Press.

Freud, Sigmund. 1938. *The Basic Writings of Sigmund Freud*. Translated and edited by A. A. Brill. New York: Modern Library.

Gannon, Thomas M. 1971. "Priest/Minister: Profession or Non-Profession?" *Review of Religious Research* 12, 2: 66–79.

Garvey, Catherine. 1974. "Some Properties of Social Play." *Merrill-Palmer Quarterly* 20: 163–180.

Gebhard, Paul H. 1969. "Fetishism and Sadomasochism." In *Dynamics of Deviant Sexuality*, edited by Jules H. Masserman, 71–80. New York: Grune and Stratton.

Goffman, Erving. 1965. *Stigma: Notes on the Management of a Spoiled Identity*. Englewood Cliffs, NJ: Prentice-Hall.

———. 1974. *Frame Analysis*. Cambridge, MA: Harvard University Press.

———. 1976. "Gender Display." *Studies in the Anthropology of Visual Communication* 3:69–77.

Goldman, Russell. 2008. "Love Hurts: Sadomasochism's Dangers." ABC News online, February 14. http://abcnews.go.com/Health/story?id=4285958&page=1.

Gosselin, Chris, and Glenn Wilson. 1980. *Sexual Variations: Fetishism, Sadomasochism and Transvestism*. New York: Simon and Schuster.

Hall, Richard H. 1968. "Professionalization and Bureaucratization." *American Sociological Review* 33, 1: 92–103.

Hamilton, G. V. 1986. *A Research in Marriage*. New York: Garland.

Hansen, Helena, Maria Margarita Lopez-Iftikhar, and Margarita Alegria. 2002. "The Economy of Risk and Respect: Accounts by Puerto Rican Sex Workers of HIV Risk Taking." *Journal of Sex Research* 39, 4: 292–301.

Hennen, Peter. 2008. *Faeries, Bears, and Leathermen: Men in Community Queering the Masculine*. Chicago: University of Chicago Press.

Hochschild, Arlie Russell. 2003. *The Managed Heart: Commercialization of Human Feeling*. Berkeley: University of California Press.

Hughes, Everett C. 1963. "The Professions." *Daedalus* 92, 4: 655–68.

———. 1966. "Are the Clergy a Profession?" In *The Church and Its Manpower Management*, edited by Ross P. Scherer and Theodore O. Wedel. New York: National Council of the Churches of Christ.

———. 1971. *The Sociological Eye*. New York: Aldine-Atherton.

Humphreys, Laud. 1975. *Tearoom Trade: Impersonal Sex in Public Places*. Chicago: Aldine.

Illouz, Eva. 2008. *Saving the Modern Soul: Therapy, Emotions, and the Culture of Self-Help*. Berkeley: University of California Press.

Jameson, Frederic. 1990. *Signatures of the Visible*. New York: Routledge.

Janus, Sam, Barbara Bess, and Carol Saltus. 1977. *A Sexual Profile of Men in Power*. New York: Warner Books.

Juizinga, Johan. 1955. *Homo Ludens: A Study of the Play-Element in Culture*. Boston: Beacon Press.

Kamel, G. W. Levi, and Thomas S. Weinberg. 1983. "Diversity in Sadomasochism: Four S&M Careers." In *S and M: Studies in Sadomasochism*, edited by Thomas Weinberg and G. W. Levi Kamel, 113–128. Buffalo, NY: Prometheus Books.

Kinsey, Alfred C., Wardell B. Pomeroy, Clyde E. Martin, and Paul H. Gebhard. 1953. *Sexual Behavior in the Human Female*. Bloomington, IN: W. B. Saunders Co.

Krafft-Ebing, Richard Freiherr von. 1965. *Psychopathia Sexualis*. Translated by Franklin S. Klaf. New York: Stein and Day.

Largier, Niklaus. 2007. *In Praise of the Whip: A Cultural History of Arousal*. New York: Zone Books.

Lee, John Alan. 1979. "The Social Organization of Sexual Risk." *Journal of Family and Economic Issues* 2, 1: 69–100.

———. 1983. "The Social Organization of Sexual Risk." In *S and M: Studies in Sadomasochism*, edited by Thomas Weinberg and G. W. Levi Kamel, 175–93. Buffalo, NY: Prometheus Books.

Lee, Jooyoung. 2009. "Battlin' on the Corner: Techniques for Sustaining Play." *Social Problems* 56, 3: 578–98.

Leschziner, Vanina. 2007. "Kitchen Stories: Patterns of Recognition in Contemporary High Cuisine." *Sociological Forum* 22, 1: 77–101.

Lever, Janet. 1978. "Sex Differences in the Complexity of Children's Play and Games." *American Sociological Review* 43, 4: 471–83.

Lever, Janet, and Deanne Dolnick. 2000. "Clients and Call Girls: Seeking Sex and Intimacy." In *Sex for Sale: Prostitution, Pornography, and the Sex Industry*, edited by Ronald Weitzer, 85–100. New York: Routledge.

Levitt Eugene E., Charles Moser, and Karen V. Jamison. 1994. "The Prevalence and Some Attributes of Females in the Sadomasochistic Subculture: A Second Report." *Archives of Sexual Behavior* 23, 4: 465–73.

Lindemann, Danielle J. 2006. "Pathology Full Circle: A History of Anti-Vibrator Legislation in the U.S." *Columbia Journal of Gender and Law* 15, 1: 326–46.

Los Angeles Free Press. 1974. Classifieds. 14 June.

MacKinnon, Catharine. 1989. *Toward a Feminist Theory of the State*. Cambridge, MA: Harvard University Press.

———. 1994. "Sexuality." In *Theorizing Feminism*, edited by Anne C. Hermann and Abigail J. Stewart, 257–87. Boulder, CO: Westview Press.

Marcus, Steven. 1966. *The Other Victorians: A Study of Sexuality and Pornography in Mid-Nineteenth-Century England*. New York: Basic Books.

Marks, Stephen R. 1994. "Intimacy in the Public Realm: The Case of Co-Workers." *Social Forces* 72, 3: 843–58.

Martin, John Levi. 2005. "Is Power Sexy?" *American Journal of Sociology* 111, 2: 408–46.

Maris, Ronald W. 1971. "Deviance as Therapy: The Paradox of the Self-Destructive Female." *Journal of Health and Social Behavior* 12, 2: 113–24.

Maynes, Mary Jo, Jennifer L. Pierce, and Barbara Laslett. 2008. *Telling Stories: The Use of Personal Narratives in the Social Sciences and History*. Ithaca, NY: Cornell University Press.

McClintock, Anne. 1993. "Sex Workers and Sex Work: Introduction." *Social Text* 37 (Winter): 1–10.

Mead, George Herbert. 1967. *Mind, Self, and Society*. Chicago: University of Chicago Press. First published 1934.

Menkes, Suzy. 2007. "Dominatrix & Gabbana! Fendi Is Refined." *International Herald Tribune*, Feb 22. http://www.iht.com/articles/2007/02/22/news/Rmilan23.php.

Michael, Robert T., John H. Gagnon, Edward O. Laumann, and Gina Kolata. 1994. *Sex in America*. New York: Warner Books.

Miles, Lesley. 1993. "Women, AIDS, and Power in Heterosexual Sex: A Discourse Analysis." *Women's Studies International Forum* 16, 5: 497–511.

Moser, Charles. 1984. "Review of Dominant Women–Submissive Men: An Exploration in Erotic Dominance and Submission." *Journal of Sex Research* 20, 4: 417–19.

Moser, Charles, and Eugene E. Levitt. 1987. "An Exploratory-Descriptive Study of a Sadomasochistically Oriented Sample." *Journal of Sex Research* 23, 3: 322–37.

Norman, Stuart. 2004. "I Am the Leatherfaerie Shaman." In *Leatherfolk*, edited by Mark Thompson, 276–83. Los Angeles: Daedalus Books.

Paglia, Camille. 1992. *Sex, Art and American Culture*. New York: Vintage Books.

Pateman, Carole. 1988. *The Sexual Contract*. Stanford, CA: Stanford University Press.

Patrias, Dale. 1978. "The Sociology of Secret Deviance: The Case of Sexual Sado-Masochism." PhD diss., New York University, New York.

Pease, Allison. 2000. *Modernism, Mass Culture, and the Aesthetics of Obscenity*. Cambridge: Cambridge University Press.

Piaget, Jean. 1962. *Play, Dreams, and Imitation in Childhood*. Translated by C. Gattegno and F. M. Hodgson. New York: Norton.

"The Porno Plague." 1976. *Time*, April 5. http://www.time.com/time/magazine/article/0,9171, 913997–1,00.html.

Prasad, Monica. 1999. "The Morality of Market Exchange: Love, Money, Contractual Justice." *Sociological Perspective* 42, 2: 181–213.

Reik, Theodor. 1941. *Masochism in Modern Man*. Translated by Margaret H. Beigel and Gertrud M. Kurth. New York: Farrar and Rinehart.

Reinharz, Shulamit. 1991. *Feminist Methods in Social Research*. Bloomington: Indiana University Press.

Rensvold, Verna, Beatrice H. Hill, Elizabeth M. Boggs, and Martin W. Meyer. 1957. "Therapeutic Recreation." *Annals of the American Academy of Political and Social Science* 313, 1: 87–91.

Riviere, Joan. 1966. "Womanliness as a Masquerade." In *Psychoanalysis and Female Sexuality*, edited by Hendrik M. Ruitenbeek. New Haven, CT: Yale University Press.

Rogers, Bruce. 1967. *The Bizarre Lovemakers*. Buffalo, NY: Unique Classic.

Rubin, Gayle. 1992. "Thinking Sex: Notes for a Radical Theory of the Politics of Sexuality." In *Pleasure and Danger: Exploring Female Sexuality*, edited by Carol Vance, 267–319. London: Pandora Books.

Rubin, Gayle. 2004. "The Catacombs: A Temple of the Butthole." In *Leatherfolk*, edited by Mark Thompson, 119–41. Los Angeles: Daedalus Books.

Rubington, Earl. 1973. *Alcohol Problems and Social Control*. Columbus, OH: Merrill.

Sacher-Masoch, Leopold von. 2000. *Venus in Furs*. Translated by Joachim Neugroschel. New York: Penguin Books. First published 1870.

Salzinger, Leslie. 2003. *Genders in Production*. Berkeley: University of California Press.

Sanders, Teela. 2005. *Sex Work: A Risky Business*. Portland, OR: Willan Publishing.

Sandnabba, N. Kenneth, Pekka Santtila, and Niklas Nordling. 1999. "Sexual Behavior and Social Adaptation among Sadomasochistically-Oriented Males." *Journal of Sex Research* 36, 3: 273–82.

Santtila, Pekka, N. Kenneth Sandnabba, Laurence Alison, and Niklas Nordling. 2002. "Investigating the Underlying Structure in Sadomasochistically Oriented Behavior." *Archives of Sexual Behavior* 31, 2: 185–96.

Savage, Dan. 2008. "Is a Dude Who Screws Trees Gay or Straight?" *Village Voice*, December 3. http://www.villagevoice.com/2008–12-03/columns/is-a-dude-who-screws-trees-gay-or-straight.

Schram, Jamie, and Jennifer Fermino. 2008. "Lawyer's Deadly Secret: Slain by S&M Madman Obsessed with Victim's Whip-Mistress Girlfriend." *New York Post*, December 4. http://www.nypost.com/seven/12042008/news/regionalnews/lawyers_deadly_secret_142622.htm.

Schücking, Levin L. 1966. *The Sociology of Literary Taste*. Translated by B. Battershaw. London: Routledge.

Scott, Gini Graham. 1983. *Dominant Women–Submissive Men: An Exploration in Erotic Dominance and Submission*. New York: Praeger.

———. 1997. *Erotic Power: An Exploration of Dominance and Submission*. Secaucus, NJ: Citadel.

Sensuous Sadie. 2003. *It's Not about the Whip: Love, Sex, and Spirituality in the BDSM Scene*. Bitch Kitty Books.

Sherzer, Joel. 1993. "On Puns, Comebacks, Verbal Dueling, and Play Languages: Speech Play in Balinese Verbal Life." *Language in Society* 22, 2: 217–33.

Shorter, Edward. 2005. *Written in the Flesh: A History of Desire*. Toronto: University of Toronto Press.

Shrage, Laurie. 1994. *Moral Dilemmas of Feminism*. New York: Routledge.

Simmel, Georg. 1971. "Prostitution." In *On Individuality and Social Forms*, edited by Donald N. Levine, 121–26. Chicago: University of Chicago Press. First published 1907.

———. 1990. *The Philosophy of Money*. Translated by T. Bottomore and D. Frisby. New York: Routledge.

Smith, Howard, and Cathy Cox. 1983. "Dialogue with a Dominatrix." In *S and M: Studies in Sadomasochism*, edited by Thomas Weinberg and G. W. Levi Kamel, 80–86. Buffalo, NY: Prometheus Books. Reprinted from the *Village Voice*, January 29, 1979, 24:19–20.

Spence, Donald. 1982. *Narrative Truth and Historical Truth: Naming and Interpretation in Psychoanalysis*. New York: Norton.

Spengler, Andreas. 1977. "Manifest Sadomasochism of Males: Results of an Empirical Study." *Archives of Sexual Behavior* 6, 6: 441–56.

Stekel, Wilhelm. 1929. *Sadism and Masochism: The Psychology of Hatred and Cruelty*. Vol. 2. Authorized English version by Louise Brink. New York: Liveright.

Stoller, R. J. 1991. *Pain and Passion: A Psychoanalyst Explores the World of S&M*. New York: Plenum Press.

Sullivan, Maureen. 1996. "Rozzie and Harriet? Gender and Family Patterns of Lesbian Coparents." *Gender and Society* 10, 6: 747–67.

Venkatesh, Sudhir. 2002. "'Doin' the Hustle': Constructing the Ethnographer in the American Ghetto." *Ethnography* 3, 1: 91–111.

Vogel, David L., Nathaniel G. Wade, and Shawn Haake. 2006. "Measuring the Self-Stigma Associated with Seeking Psychological Help." *Journal of Counseling Psychology* 53, 3: 325–37.

Wacquant, Loïc. 1995. "The Pugilistic Point of View: How Boxers Think and Feel about Their Trade." *Theory and Society* 24, 4: 489–535.

———. 2002. "Scrutinizing the Street: Poverty, Morality, and the Pitfalls of Urban Ethnography." *American Journal of Sociology* 107, 6: 1468–1532.

Weille, Katharine-Lee H. 2002. "The Psychodynamics of Consensual Sadomasochistic and Dominant-Submissive Sexual Games." *Studies in Gender and Sexuality* 3, 2: 131–60.

Weinberg, Martin S., Frances M. Shaver, and Colin J. Williams. 1999. "Gendered Sex Work in the San Francisco Tenderloin." *Archives of Sexual Behavior* 28, 6: 503–21.

Weinberg, Martin S., Colin J. Williams, and Charles Moser. 1984. "The Social Constituents of Sadomasochism." *Social Problems* 31, 4: 379–89.

Weinberg, Thomas. 1983. "Sadism and Masochism: Sociological Perspectives." In *S and M: Studies in Sadomasochism*, edited by Thomas Weinberg and G. W. Levi Kamel, 99–112. Buffalo, NY: Prometheus Books.

Weinberg, Thomas, and G. W. Levi Kamel. 1983. "S&M: An Introduction to the Study of Sadomasochism." In *S and M: Studies in Sadomasochism*, edited by Thomas Weinberg and G. W. Levi Kamel, 17–24. Buffalo, NY: Prometheus Books.

Weiss, Robert. 1994. *Learning from Strangers: The Art and Method of Qualitative Interview Studies*. New York: Free Press.

Weitzer, Ronald. 2009. "Sociology of Sex Work." *Annual Review of Sociology* 35, 1: 213–34.

West, Candace, and Don H. Zimmerman. 1987. "Doing Gender." *Gender and Society* 1, 2: 125–51.

Whalen, Marilyn R. 1995. "Working toward Play: Complexity in Children's Fantasy Activities." *Language in Society* 24, 3: 315–48.

Wheeler, Britta B. 2003. "The Institutionalization of an American Avant-Garde: Performance Art as Democratic Culture, 1970–2000." *Sociological Perspectives* 46, 4: 491–512.

Wilensky, Harold L. 1964. "The Professionalization of Everyone?" *American Journal of Sociology* 70, 2: 137–58.

Wilner, Richard, Larry Celona, and Lukas I. Alpert. 2008. "Hangy Spanky: Kinky Clubgoer Is Choked Near Death." *New York Post* online, February 9. http://www.nypost.com/seven/02092008/news/regionalnews/hangy_spanky_414490.htm.

Wilson, Elizabeth. 1983. "The Context of 'Between Pleasure and Danger': The Barnard Conference on Sexuality." *Feminist Review* 13 (Spring): 35–41.

Wiseman, Jay. 1996. *SM101: A Realistic Introduction*. Eugene, OR: Greenery Press.

Wright, Kathleen M., Oscar A. Cabrera, Paul D. Bliese, Amy B. Adler, Charles W. Hoge, and Carl A. Castro. 2009. "Stigma and Barriers to Care in Soldiers Postcombat." *Psychological Services* 6, 2: 108–16.

Yun, Helen. 2007. "House Call: Dominatrix Dungeon." *Time Out New York*, October 4–10. http://newyork.timeout.com/shopping-style/apartments-home-design/17067/house-call-dominatrix-dungeon.

Zelizer, Viviana A. 2005. *The Purchase of Intimacy*. Princeton, NJ: Princeton University Press.

Index

www.ingramcontent.com/pod-product-compliance
Lightning Source LLC
Chambersburg PA
CBHW032130020426
42334CB00016B/1100